Alain Badiou

Key Concepts

Key Concepts

Published

Forthcoming

Alain Badiou

Key Concepts

Edited by A. J. Bartlett and Justin Clemens

ACUMEN

First published in 2010 by Acumen

Acumen Publishing Limited
4 Saddler Street
Durham
DH1 3NP
www.acumenpublishing.co.uk

ISBN: 978-1-84465-229-7 (hardcover)
ISBN: 978-1-84465-230-3 (paperback)

British Library Cataloguing-in-Publication Data
A catalogue record for this book is available
from the British Library.

This publication is supported by a grant from the Research and
Research Training Committee, Faculty of Arts, The University of
Melbourne.

Designed and typeset in Classical Garamond and Myriad.
Printed in the UK by the MPG Books Group.

pg. 32 !

Topology, 80.

Contents

Contributors

A. J. Bartlett teaches in the School of Culture and Communication at the University of Melbourne and in the School of Communication and Creative Arts at Deakin University. He co-edited *The Praxis of Alain Badiou* (2006) and is the author of "Plato, Badiou: An 'Education by Truths'" (forthcoming). He is currently extending the latter enquiry to the thought of Saint Paul, Marx and Lacan in order to establish the non-state foundations of contemporary state pedagogy.

Bruno Besana is fellow researcher at the ICI-Kulturlabor, Berlin, where he is in charge, together with Ozren Pupovac, of the Versus Laboratory Project. He has published (in French, English, Italian, German and Slovenian) several articles on the relation between philosophy and its aesthetic and political conditions, especially via the thought of Jacques Rancière, Gilles Deleuze and Alain Badiou. Together with Oliver Feltham he has edited the volume *Ecrits autour de la pensée d'Alain Badiou* (2007). He has also translated into Italian Jacques Rancière's *La fable cinématographique* and other philosophical texts.

Bruno Bosteels is Associate Professor of Romance Studies at Cornell University. He is the author most recently of *Alain Badiou, une trajectoire polémique* (2009). Two other books are forthcoming: *Badiou and Politics* and *Marx and Freud in Latin America*. He has published extensively on Latin American literature and politics, and on European philosophy and political theory. He is currently preparing *After Borges: Literature and Antiphilosophy* and a short book, *La Révolution de la honte*, on the twentieth-century uses of Marx's correspondence with

Arnold Ruge. He also currently serves as general editor of the journal *diacritics*.

Ray Brassier is Associate Professor of Philosophy at the American University of Beirut, Lebanon. He is the author of *Nihil Unbound* (2008) and is the translator of Badiou's *Saint Paul: The Foundation of Universalism* and, with Alberto Toscano, he has edited Alain Badiou's *Theoretical Writings* (2004).

Justin Clemens is the author of several books of poetry and fiction, including *Villain* (2009), *The Mundiad* (2004) and, with Helen Johnson, *Black River* (2007). He is also co-editor of *The Jacqueline Rose Reader* (2011) with Ben Naparstek, *The Work of Giorgio Agamben* (2008) with Nicholas Heron and Alexander Murray, and *The Praxis of Alain Badiou* (2006) with Paul Ashton and A. J. Bartlett. He teaches at the University of Melbourne.

Elie During is Associate Professor in Philosophy at the University of Paris Ouest – Nanterre. He studied at the École Normale Supérieure (ENS – Paris) and Princeton University. A member of the CIEPFC (Centre International d'Étude de la Philosophie Française Contemporaine, ENS), he also teaches "theory" at the École des Beaux-Arts de Paris. With Q. Meillassoux, P. Maniglier and D. Rabouin, he is series editor of "MétaphysiqueS" at the Presses Universitaires de France. His current research focuses on the interplay between metaphysics, art and science, with special interest in the contemporary constructions of spacetime. He is the author of *Matrix, machine philosophique*, with A. Badiou *et al.* (2003). More recently, he has produced a critical edition of Henri Bergson's *Durée et Simultanéité* (2009) and a study of the Bergson–Einstein debate: *Bergson et Einstein: la querelle de la relativité* (forthcoming). His publications on issues of aesthetics include *Faux Raccords: la coexistence des images* (2010), and a co-edited book, *In actu: de l'expérimental dans l'art* (with L. Jeanpierre, C. Kihm and D. Zabunyan, 2009). He has written several articles on Alain Badiou's philosophy, among them "How Much Truth Can Art Bear? On Badiou's 'Inaesthetics'" (2005) and "Alain Badiou" (2009).

Oliver Feltham is an associate professor in the Department of Comparative Literature and English at the American University of Paris, where he coordinates the Philosophy Program. His translation of Alain Badiou's *Being and Event* appeared in 2006. He has edited and contributed to two anthologies of essays on Badiou's work, *Ecrits autour de la pensée* *d'Alain Badiou* (2007), and *Autour de* Logiques des mondes *d'Alain Badiou* (2006). His monograph on Badiou, *Alain Badiou: Live Theory*, was published in 2008. He is currently working on a book on political action, playing seventeenth-century English radical politics against early modern philosophy in the conceptualization of action.

Z. L. Fraser is a doctoral student in philosophy at the University of Guelph, Canada. He has translated Badiou's 1969 book, *The Concept of Model*, and has written widely on Badiou's thought. Fraser's current research seeks to work out the philosophical significance of a recent metamorphosis in the science of logic.

Peter Hallward teaches at Kingston University, London, and is the author of *Damming the Flood: Haiti and the Politics of Containment* (2007), *Out of this World: Deleuze and the Philosophy of Creation* (2006), *Badiou: A Subject to Truth* (2003) and *Absolutely Postcolonial* (2001). He is currently working on a project entitled "The Will of the People".

Mark Hewson teaches in the School of Culture and Communication at the University of Melbourne. He has a study forthcoming, entitled *Blanchot and Literary Criticism*.

Sigi Jöttkandt is author of *First Love: A Phenomenology of the One* (2010) and *Acting Beautifully: Henry James and the Ethical Aesthetic* (2005). She teaches in the Writing and Publishing programme at NMIT, and is a co-founder of the Open Humanities Press.

Alex Ling teaches in the School of Culture and Communication at the University of Melbourne and is the author of *Badiou and Cinema* (forthcoming).

John Mullarkey was educated at University College Dublin, University College London, and the University of Warwick. He has taught philosophy for the past sixteen years at the University of Sunderland (1994–2004), and the University of Dundee (2004 to date). He has published *Bergson and Philosophy* (1999), *Post-Continental Philosophy: An Outline* (2006), *Refractions of Reality: Philosophy and the Moving Image* (2009), and edited, with Beth Lord, *The Continuum Companion to Continental Philosophy* (2009). His work seeks new ways of engaging with "non-philosophy", believing that philosophy is a subject that gains its identity through continual challenge from outsider-thought, such as in film, design and animality (the three non-philosophies with which he is most acquainted).

Nina Power is Senior Lecturer in Philosophy at Roehampton University and the author of *One-Dimensional Woman* (2009). With Alberto Toscano she edited Badiou's *On Beckett* (2003).

Jon Roffe is the founding convenor of the Melbourne School of Continental Philosophy, and the co-editor of *Understanding Derrida* (2004) and *Deleuze's Philosophical Lineage* (2009). He is currently completing a comparative study of Deleuze and Badiou.

Alberto Toscano is Senior Lecturer in Sociology at Goldsmiths, University of London. He is the author of *Fanaticism: On the Uses of an Idea* (2010) and *The Theatre of Production: Philosophy and Individuation Between Kant and Deleuze* (2006), as well as the translator of several works by Alain Badiou, most recently *Logics of Worlds*. He is an editor of the journal *Historical Materialism*.

Acknowledgements

The editors would like to express their gratitude to all the contributors and to thank the following for their support and encouragement: Angela Cullip, Haydie Gooder, Alex Ling and Jon Roffe.

Thanks and appreciation are especially due to Tristan Palmer at Acumen for his invaluable direction, advice and generosity. We would also like to thank Alain Badiou.

Abbreviations

Whatever is thought truly is immediately shared. ... whatever is understood is radically undivided. To know is to be absolutely and universally convinced.

(Alain Badiou, "Mathematics and Philosophy")

Introduction: Badiou's form

A. J. Bartlett and Justin Clemens

Alain Badiou is perhaps the world's most important living philosopher. Few, if any, contemporary philosophers display his breadth of argument and reference, or his power to intervene in debates critical to both analytic and continental philosophy. Badiou's influence upon contemporary philosophy, psychoanalysis, ontology, history and philosophy of science, film studies, art history, theatre studies, political philosophy and even geography has grown exponentially in the last few years alone. Badiou's work is now a constant reference for already-established figures such as Jacques Rancière, Giorgio Agamben and Slavoj Žižek, among others, and references to his work can be found in an enormous range of scholarly and non-scholarly texts. As a result, Badiou's work has begun to come under more intense scrutiny by those Academicians who understand their first duty to be to critique rather than to intelligibility and whose talent for negation sees them continue to conflate politics with philosophy, mathematics with authority, history with dialectic, and truth with knowledge – whether wilfully or "sophistically". If this current volume seeks to clarify and contextualize Badiou's work as respectfully as possible, it cannot avoid being at once a contribution to the explication, to the extension and to the academic institutionalization of Badiou's work.

Badiou's work emerges from what we might call a "post-poststructural moment". That is, his work both follows on from and confronts that of Jean-Paul Sartre, Jacques Lacan, Louis Althusser, Michel Foucault, Jacques Derrida, Gilles Deleuze, Jean-François Lyotard and others in a French context; but it also confronts some key elements of the predominantly anglophone analytic context as well, including the work of Ludwig Wittgenstein, W. V. Quine, Richard Rorty, Donald Davidson and others. From the so-called "continental" context, Badiou extracts what Heidegger calls "the questioning concerning Being"; from the analytic context, he extracts the questioning concerning the hard sciences, the fundamental emphasis the latter places on mathematics and logic. This allows him to subject the prejudices and aporias of each – most particularly in regard to the concept of the "subject" – to extensive investigation, while at the same time renewing a classical approach to philosophy, one that is professedly "Platonic", yet draws from a "neglected" mathematical tradition in contemporary French philosophy (Albert Lautman and Jean Cavaillès, for example).

In order to respond to the specificities of Badiou's project and to do so in a way consistent with properly philosophical enquiry, this collection proceeds in the following way: first, establishing Badiou's philosophical context; second, articulating and expanding upon his central and abiding concepts; third, elaborating his polemical relationships with his current and past contemporaries; and, finally, examining the way ahead for philosophy in the wake of Badiou's singular intervention. Precisely because of Badiou's peculiarly complex fusion of neo-classicism and radical novelty, this book is divided so that his key concepts – "truth", "being", "ontology", "the subject" – are at once given in their traditional signification *and* in their Badiouean extension, and both are given new impetus by the contributors themselves, who, as we note below, are uniquely placed to do so. As the editors of this volume, then, we attempt to present Badiou according to his own terms, as well as in the light of the problems that these terms present.

In a talk given in Vienna, an extended version of which introduces the collection *Polemics*, Alain Badiou defines a philosophical situation as that which presents an "impossible relation", an "encounter between essentially foreign terms". Philosophy, then, is organized by three tasks:

1. "Clarify the fundamental choices of thought" – a choice "in the last instance between that which is interested and that which is disinterested".
2. "Clarify the distance between thought and power, between the state and truths".
3. "Clarify the value of the exception, the event, of rupture". "Moreover, do so against" that which perseveres.

On this description, to forge the link between "a choice, a distance and an exception" is the philosophical programme par excellence, with the proviso that this is philosophy as that which "counts for something in life, for something other than an academic discipline" (P 8). Quite appropriately for a philosopher who conceives of his own project as the systematic articulation of a "Platonic gesture" or a "Platonism of the multiple", Badiou's contentious opposition between philosophy and the Academy here explicitly returns us to Plato's own foundational operations. However, there is a twist. It is worth articulating this twist because it is by no means tangential to the contemporary philosophical situation in which Badiou sees himself as intervening. It bears upon the fraught relationship between philosophy and the institutions necessary for its own transmission.

Following the *death* of Socrates, and in strict fidelity to his master's *life*, Plato formulates an "axiomatic question": "how are we to live?" This paradoxical determination directs the entire Platonic body of thought. In Plato's time the place of the *transmission* of this thought was the grove of the mythical hero Hecademus. This public park *outside* the Athenian city walls became the meeting point of Plato's "geometers" – more accurately, all those for whom the "doctrine of unfair shares" (see *Gorgias* 508a) was at once evident *and* unfounded, and consequently anathema. The goal of the gathering of the Hecademians was to subject this doctrine to unceasing review so as to break with its premises, and refound thought in the new distance thus opened up. Between the practice of the Hecademians and the thought that animates the Platonic corpus circulates an immanent dialectic of transmission and inscription, thought and practice, consequent on the exception named Socrates.

Plato's "Academy" – which despite widespread misapprehensions, was not a school in any straightforward sense of the word – knots together the philosophical trajectory Badiou outlines above. The singular concern of this knot is, precisely, "how are we to live?" In the *Phaedo*, on the day of his death, Socrates will talk of this with a few disciples – to live philosophically is to live *here and now* on the basis of the world to come. This is also to say that living philosophically is to make this Idea, whose intelligibility is thought through, manifest. Socrates tells his disciples that to live by this Idea, to decide for its existence, is to construct a present. In the *Republic*, Plato universalizes, and thus "subjectivizes", the principles elaborated in the *Phaedo*. To live "philosophically", in accord with the Idea, must be a matter *for all*. In Plato's corpus, then, there is no ultimate contradiction between philosophy as something that counts in life and philosophy as an academic discipline. The Academy, free and for all, is simply the place where such thought takes place.[1] The name of that which this thought *thinks*, Badiou notes, is *justice* and, without justice, freedom remains merely an aesthetic *flatus vocis*.

Where, then, is the fault line, the point at which philosophy and its meeting-place become opposed? How or why is the modern Academy the institution that, as Badiou suggests, confuses the distinction between interest and disinterest, truth and power, and disavows and denudes the existence of the exception in pretty much the same manner as the pious Ancients proscribed the existence of the irrational or the inexpressible on the pain of death? And thus, how is it that the modern Academy lays claim to the name *Academy*?

Undoubtedly these modern institutions still rely on the existence of the Platonic conditions of philosophical life: choice, distance and exception; or, address, transmission and inscription (Badiou 2007g). Yet the very existence of these institutions is conditional upon their representation of the Platonic conditions in such a way that they actively produce no active manifestation: choice is commodified, distance is administered, exception is hierarchized, and all too often wisdom is received. One is instructed, by and large, in how to "live *without* Idea". The ideological subterfuge at work today is the appropriation of the Platonic virtues – for that is what they are, and are, as such, recognized by all – as the means for their betrayal. Such is demanded by the perseverance of the state, understood as the principle of the actual organization of division, distribution, and other diverse inequities of goods. In Plato's time, the state considered the thought of the Academy – the *life* of philosophy – a real threat to its existence (as is well known, the revitalized Academy was ultimately shut down by the Emperor Justinian). Indeed, the *Republic* is Plato's intelligible dream of the overcoming of the state, an overcoming whose desire is also present in each and every dialogue. Today, lacking all such desire while still revelling in the name, the Academy, to the "Platonist", functions merely as an apparatus whose positivity as such reveals only a deleterious form of fetishism. However, as Plato said, we should not quibble over names: rather, it is crucial to insist on the fact *that* the name exists is enough to recall the "thing" itself. What insists, then, is *that* which it once named *does* in fact name even now despite the subterfuge; indeed, *can* only truly name.[2]

When Plato has Callicles – the arch-administrator of a calculating sophistry – declaim that if things were as Socrates said they were, the world would be turned upside down, we were not being given a warning but a task. If philosophy is to be something in life, to be a way of life, as its very foundation attests it does and must, then, *that it is* today other than an "academic quibble" (HI 15) must be reaffirmed and made manifest. The world must be turned upside down (or inside out), "existence changed", a present once again constituted. In this sense the contemporary world *houses* this desire in so far as it presents us with the impossibility of a relation between thought – that which "is nothing other than the desire to finish with the exorbitant excess of the state" (BE 282) – and the Academy. This, then, is an exemplary philosophical situation, and the impossible relation it forces upon us – precisely because it exists *as* nothing – demands the philosophical creation of its proper form. With full regard to what the situation presents, this means: "A certain number of parameters be abandoned, a certain number of novelties introduced."

It is with this foundational Platonic instance as both a warning and a task that this book seeks to re-present Badiou's key concepts to both students and specialists of contemporary philosophy, as well as to those working in related areas. Due in part to the difficulty any single author has in cogently reproducing Badiou's breadth and depth of reference in a manner that does justice to the constituent parts and to his innovative philosophical project, no other secondary material has yet properly followed Badiou in this articulation.[3] Paradoxically, the outstanding existing edited collections on Badiou's work achieve their success by *avoiding* the types of orientation and articulation this collection aims to embody.

This collection is therefore set up to explicate Badiou's key concepts in the clearest, most forceful possible way: it presents the outstanding scholars on Badiou's particular topics writing on their own specialism *vis-à-vis* Badiou. Each of these scholars has already produced extensive and well-respected critical work in their own fields, and has extended these researches into their appreciation and critique of Badiou's position. Not only are many of the contributors to this volume among the major commentators to date in the English-speaking world – and each has published on Badiou's new (and "old") work – we should note that the translators of Badiou's "major" works (in order of appearance: Oliver Feltham, Zachary Luke Fraser, Bruno Bosteels and Alberto Toscano), as well as the translators of Badiou's "shorter" works (Ray Brassier, *Saint Paul*; Peter Hallward, *Ethics*; Nina Power, *On Beckett*) – also contribute to this volume. Further, at least four of the contributors have completed major doctoral theses on Badiou, as well as contributing essays and translations of their own.

Nonetheless, in that this collection introduces Badiou's key concepts, it also augments and extends their appreciation, applicability and critique – thereby participating in the work of philosophy we outlined above. Each chapter focuses on the key points of one of Badiou's key foci – which are not always Badiou's "own" concepts so much as his revivification of the most traditional philosophical concepts – placing his contribution in its proper relation to the history of philosophy, and to the logic of his thought. At the same time, rather than simply painting Badiou's work "by the numbers", this book deals with Badiou's thought in Badiou's own terms – thereby giving a new and more adequate division of labour. This labour, if it may not always look quite like dealing with "concepts" at first glance, in fact places Badiou's project in its proper conceptual framework (in which, for example, "ontology" cannot be separated from "mathematics" or from "set theory").

Such a procedure has necessitated certain decisions on our part, which have consequences that go beyond the merely "editorial". For instance, *Logiques des Mondes* (*Logics of Worlds*, 2006) is simultaneously a major reassessment and, as a "sequel", a major reaffirmation of the concepts and categories of *L'être et l'événement* (*Being and Event*, 1988). Yet the relation of the latter to *Théorie du sujet* (*Theory of the Subject*, 1982) is of a different character. In *Théorie du sujet*, Badiou practises an "exhaustion of resources". Inasmuch as that work intimates a way forward for philosophy, it nevertheless constitutes a necessary aporia. The dialectic "suspends" itself at the point of its own lack. *Being and Event*, encompassing mathematics as ontology in all its formalism and rigour, implements thereby the return of philosophy itself. It is by aporia and the intervention it demands that philosophy will have recommenced. We suggest, perhaps contentiously, that it is still the case that *Being and Event* stands – despite the chronology – as the *foundational* work of Badiou's *œuvre*, one whose consequences have not fully been drawn, retrospectively or consequently. As such, it is this work that serves to orient the current collection. To invoke a motif central to Badiou – one that returns throughout his *œuvre* and is the driving force of his unique participatory "dialectics" – *Being and Event* serves as a *model*, which is to say, "the network traversed by the retroactions and anticipations that weave this history: whether it be designated in anticipation as a break (*coupure*) or in retrospect, as a remaking (*refonte*)" (CM 54–5). At the same time, if the key concepts here are ultimately derived from Badiou's work in *Being and Event*, the contributors make full use of the range of his *œuvre* to properly situate, expose and delineate his development as it relates to the concept, philosopher, or theme under review. Consequently, this book proposes to survey the broadest range of Badiou's "conditional" philosophy, extending the opportunities for those unfamiliar with his work to enter the fray, as it were, while not losing focus on the specificity of his thought. At every point, however, we ask the reader to bear in mind the problem of philosophy and its institution: that philosophy is always at risk of being betrayed by the Academies developed to transmit it, and that the most faithful exegesis itself cannot help but swerve from the concepts it claims to comprehend and convey.

In the end, then, we hope that *Alain Badiou: Key Concepts* may prove to be – in accordance with the fundamental *animus* of philosophy itself – a useful entrée to Badiou's own struggle with the question "What is it to live?" Philosophy must tie the concept to life, to the real lives of subjects – or it no longer deserves the name.

Notes

1. Debra Nails (1995: 214–15) suggests that some of the dialogues were in fact used wholly or partly as textbooks for the Academy and as "advertising" material for it. She recounts the story told by Aristotle of the farmer who, having read the *Gorgias*, gave up his trade and travelled to Athens to join the Academy. The point, Nails continues, is that whether they were or were not used that way, the dialogues could show to potential students that the dialectical trajectory recorded in the dialogues, which was subject entirely to the pursuit of truth, could also be pursued at the Academy.
2. See *Laws*, 644a–b. Cf. Agamben: "According to a Platonic tautology, which we are still far from understanding, the idea of a thing is the thing itself; *the name, insofar as it names a thing, is nothing but the thing insofar as it is named by the name*" (1993: 77).
3. We say this simply to note the distinct approach of this collection. This by no means reflects negatively on Peter Hallward's *Badiou: A Subject to Truth* (2003), Jason Barker's *Alain Badiou: A Critical Introduction* (2002) or Oliver Feltham's *Alain Badiou* (2008). These three texts are of immense importance to students of Badiou's philosophy in any language.

ONE

Biography and early works

Oliver Feltham

How can a life correspond to a proper name when that life is incomplete, its vicissitudes not exhausted, its past forever open before it? How does a mortal's life correspond to a proper name when the name itself marks the desire for immortality? And if a mortal life has intersected more than one *subject* – in the Badiouean sense of the term – and if each subject is properly infinite, then what possible correspondence can be written out between one name and a life? Only a correspondence of personae, of heteronyms.

First persona: the teacher, the master. A graduate student spends a year researching his doctorate in Paris, sits in on three notorious seminars. To distinguish the lecturers he disposes of three variables, each with two values: starts late or not, dresses up or down, audience rich or poor. One starts late, dresses up and the audience is rich; another starts late, dresses up, and the audience is rich; the other starts late, dresses down and the audience is poor – which one was Miller, which Derrida, and which Badiou? Badiou avows having encountered three masters in his youth: Sartre, Althusser and Lacan, but in each text he engages in a progressive multiplication of masters: Mao and Mallarmé, Hegel and Pascal, Canguilhem, Cavaillès and Lautman, Cantor and Cohen, not to mention the seven poets of the *Manifesto for Philosophy's* "Age of Poetry". What kind of filiation is possible amidst such a multiple matrix? How many voices? How many teachings? How many proper names to integrate? Is a philosophy solely systematic to the degree that it integrates its proper names or to the degree that it makes them resonate?

Second persona: the tragic voice. The preface to *Théorie du sujet* announces an "I" who stands alone in a philosophical desert. In his

Deleuze Badiou speaks of the reception of that very book; "Deleuze sent me a favourable note which was very touching given the public solitude in which I found myself ... the silence, the absolute disdain for what I was trying to do in philosophy" (D 9). In the introduction to *Being and Event* Badiou confesses "I groped around for several years among the impasses of logic – developing close exegeses of the theorems of Gödel, Tarski and Löwenheim-Skolem – without surpassing the frame of *Théorie du sujet* save in technical subtlety. Without noticing it I had been caught in the grips of a logicist thesis ... I had mistaken the route" (BE 5). So not only had Badiou been alone, deprived of recognition, but he had lost the way, perhaps more than once. What wilderness had he been through? And who had accompanied him – Lazarus, Mao, Gödel? Is this what led him to write: "the only definition of courage is exile without return, loss of name" (Badiou 1982: 185, my trans.)?

Third persona: the world-famous philosopher. Badiou is invited everywhere; almost as ubiquitous as Žižek, the floodgate of translations and commentary is finally opened. Rival bibliographies are published and disciples compete to publish their translations of the same article first. Badiou's disciples get jobs, teach his texts, his interlocutors are well placed and even the BBC interviews him on *Hardtalk*, hamfistedly trying to pin him down as an apologist for communism. *What is the meaning of Sarkozy?* is a bestseller in France and the UK, and his second magnum opus, *Logics of Worlds*, is translated into English only three years after its French appearance, whereas the first, *Being and Event*, took seventeen years to arrive. In one of the early English commentaries the authors say recognition of Badiou has been slow to come in the English-speaking world. What is it for a philosopher to come to fame, or recognition, late?

Fourth persona: the brilliant radical student, the *Normalien*. Badiou was also famous when he was young. Well placed in the École Normale Supérieure, member of a closed seminar of students around Althusser including Rancière, Balibar, Regnault and Macherey, he published three magisterial articles in the most avant-garde journal of the day, *Cahiers pour l'analyse*, completed television interviews with many of the major intellectuals of the day, Foucault, Aron, Hyppolite, Serres; wrote two novels before the age of twenty-eight; and his first book of philosophy, *The Concept of Model*, was a bestseller. What happened between that moment and his late fame? We know that May '68 was an event that signed a rupture with Althusser under the name of Mao, that years of activism and splintering groups followed: but for the philosopher who thinks life under the emblem of moments of intense and exceptional existence, what can this long period in between be called if its objective name is restoration? A calvary? A sustained period of self-critique – the Maoist activist's exercise par excellence? Or a fidelity, an exile without return?

Fifth persona: Scapin. Or rather, *Ahmed*, the 1984 Scapin. Badiou played Molière's Scapin in a high-school production, and sees his character, Ahmed, as Scapin's avatar. But Scapin is a troubleshooter, a fix-it man, a mischief-making middleman, a hatcher of farcical imbroglios whose harlequin habitat is the thick of things, an interrogator and ventriloquist of each and everybody. How could he be one of Badiou's heteronyms if the latter wrote "I practically boycott every instance of the department and the university, except my course"? (D3) What can you fix by boycotting? What milieu is Badiou in the middle of? One day, on the edge of a protest march for the *sans-papiers*, I see Badiou a block away negotiating with the police, on the fly, to guarantee right of passage for the thin winding ribbon of protestors, all too vulnerable to instant arrest and expulsion from the territory. And I hear the slogan echoing between the peeling façades of Rue Faubourg du Temple, "I am here. I am from here. I'm not moving!", and I think this slogan, in the end, is a mediating troubleshooting middleman's slogan, a slogan that creates its own milieu.

Teacher, solitary thinker, famous philosopher, student, middleman – in the end it is Scapin, the middleman, the fix-it man, who can make the most sense of the passage between these personae – Badiou is Scapin, that exemplary mortal, who creates as he finds his own milieu.

PART I

The foundations of Badiou's thought

TWO

Philosophy

Oliver Feltham

Badiou is a fellow traveller – not of communism, being a Maoist, but of poststructuralism. He sympathized with its critique of philosophy's ubiquitous presupposition of unity and identity; he sympathized with its attempt to think multiplicity. One can detect thousands of tiny post-structuralist influences in every one of his texts. For this reason it was all the more surprising – especially for the anglophone practitioners of theory and the permanent blurring of disciplinary boundaries – when Badiou suddenly called for a return to philosophy, for an end to the end of philosophy and its endless deconstruction, when he called for a restart. We were not ready. It sounded reactionary.

To understand Badiou's call it is not enough to realize that many poststructuralists, such as Jean-Luc Nancy, never gave up on the name. The very concept and position of philosophy must be investigated in each period of Badiou's *œuvre*. It is only in the third and apparently final period of his work, opened in 1985 by the text *Can Politics be Thought?*, that a full doctrine on the nature of philosophy is developed and promulgated, the doctrine of conditions. This chapter will briefly examine the place of philosophy in Badiou's early work and then his Maoist period before investigating the nature of philosophy under its conditions.

Althusserian epistemology

It is possible to distinguish a short period of Althusserian epistemo-logical enquiry before Badiou's Maoist commitment takes over in the

1970s. This period – the only one that really deserves the term "early work" – runs from 1965 to 1969, the year of publication of *The Concept of Model*, a text whose preface is Maoist but whose body is largely Althusserian. During this period Badiou practises a recognized form of French philosophy, epistemology in the tradition of Georges Canguilhem and Gaston Bachelard, albeit with a Lacanian twist and a rare focus on mathematics. Philosophy itself as the name of Badiou's discipline is not explicitly thematized. This is not to say that it was a tacit institutional background for Badiou: not only did he practise other disciplines, or rather the art of the novel, and mathematics; but the status of philosophy had become a serious problem in a seminar that he attended. The seminar was run by his early master, Louis Althusser, whose major teachings included a fundamental distinction between science and ideology. Althusser's students – Jacques Rancière, Etienne Balibar, Pierre Macherey, Badiou, François Regnault and others – were not happy about the status of philosophy with regard to this distinction.

Althusser argues that the field of theoretical practice is divided by a contradiction between science and ideology, defined in the following manner:

> Science is the productive practice of knowledges, whose means of production are concepts; whilst ideology is a system of representations, whose function is pratico-social, and which auto-designates itself in a set of notions. The proper effect of science – "effect of knowledge" – is obtained by the regulated production of an object essentially distinct from the given object. Ideology on the other hand articulates lived experience (*le vécu*); that is, not the real relation men have to their conditions of existence, but "the manner in which men live their relation to their conditions of existence".   (Althusser 2005b: 40; see also 239)

Philosophy is then defined as the theoretical practice that draws a line of demarcation between science and ideology. This line is not simply to be drawn between, say, the news on state television and Marxist science of history, but rather within scientific and theoretical texts themselves in so far as the latter spontaneously generate ideologies (see Althusser 1974). In his early review of Althusser's work, Badiou cites another definition of philosophy: it is the "theory of the history of production of knowledges" (1967: 448; see Althusser 1996: vol. I, 70). These two definitions are consistent thanks to Althusser's appropriation of Bachelard's notion of an epistemological break. For Bachelard a science constitutes its objects of knowledge by continually separating its results from the illusions of immediate knowledge and ideological representations of its field. This process of separation is called an epistemological break or cut. Unlike Kuhn's paradigm shift or even the shift between *epistemes* in the early Foucault, an epistemological cut is not chronologically situated between two stable structures of knowledge, but takes place continually as part of the very production of scientific knowledge. Indeed, Althusser appropriates it as a concept of both change and novelty. Philosophy's central task for Althusser is thus to trace an epistemological cut in a particular scientific field; in doing so it doubles the work of science itself, recalling the Platonic definition of philosophy as the thought of thought. This should already sound uncannily familiar to adepts of Badiou's doctrine of conditions, but the similarities do not stop here. For Althusser there is no proper object of philosophy, such as the limits of reason, or the epistemological foundations of science.[1] Kant's project, for instance, is problematic in so far as it situates philosophy as "the juridical guarantee of the rights of science, as well as its limits" (Althusser 1974: 92; see also LW 535–6). Rather, philosophy's task is to think what exactly emerges via an epistemological cut in a particular ideological field, such as Marx's science of history from humanist philosophy.

Badiou's early article "Subversion infinitésimale" and his book *The Concept of Model* both practise philosophy in this Althusserian acceptation, carefully delimiting ideological notions of infinity and mathematical models from their properly scientific concepts (CM 5–9). However, at one point in *The Concept of Model* Badiou ranges philosophy under the heading of ideology and later on he claims that philosophy must practise an "an impossible relation between science and ideology" (CM 9, 50). Evidently the Althusserian conception of philosophy is unstable: philosophy is supposed to trace the division between science and ideology, but the status of philosophy itself continually falls back into either side of that division: philosophy either pretends to be a science or to be an ideology. This is the first problem Badiou encounters in his work with regard to philosophy: the problem of the *status of philosophy*. Perhaps this instability, this oscillation between two stable types of discourse, is due to philosophy having been defined in a dynamic manner, as a process, or rather, as the double of a process. In any case, any suspicions about the stability of Althusser's initial conception of philosophy are immediately confirmed by the original 1969 preface to Badiou's work that denounces the text as a "theoreticist deviation"! This self-critique clearly marks the opening of Badiou's Maoist period. Note, however, that the charge of "theoreticism" also mirrors a turn in Althusser's own work. In the mid-1960s Althusser positions philosophy in the field of science, fights against the French Communist Party's silence on theoretical issues and critiques Marx's "practicism" in *Reading Capital* (1996: 47–8). In 1967–8 the auto-critique of "theoreticism" as another possible deviation emerges and Althusser redefines philosophy as "the class struggle in theory" (1967: postface; see also Althusser 1974: 115; CM 50; Badiou 1992b: 42).

Ironically, it is this very definition that Badiou adopts in his departure from Althusser. Nevertheless he manages to demarcate himself from his former master by offering a far stricter Maoist interpretation of such class struggle.

Maoist theory in the revolutionary dialectic

Badiou's Maoist period comprises the following texts: *Théorie de la contradiction*, *De l'idéologie* and *Théorie du sujet*. Within these works the problem of philosophy in terms of its status and tasks is resolved, but only for another problem to emerge, that of the scene of philosophy. The problem of the status of philosophy is resolved in favour of the Maoist conception of the class struggle in theory. Indeed, it is resolved to the point of disappearing from the 1975 text *Théorie de la contradiction*, in which philosophy is mentioned very rarely. In the 1976 text, *De l'idéologie*, the first section however is consecrated to developing the notion of philosophy as the class struggle in theory. A Marxist philosophy is defined as one that first serves the proletariat, and second recognizes the primacy of practice inasmuch as theory is both founded on and serves practice. A bourgeois philosophy can thus be defined as one that is founded on the practice of exploitation. Badiou elaborates his strategy as follows:

> To approach the question of class struggle in philosophy in the light of an unquestionable but often forgotten principle: the exploiters are perfectly aware of their interests, and they act and speak in their name. And the exploited of every century know exactly who is exploiting them and how.
>
> (Badiou & Balmès 1976: 4)

The importance of this principle resides in its centrality to the debate over ideology. Badiou's chief concern, in this first section on philosophy, is to distinguish his approach to ideology from that of Althusser, and implicitly from that of his colleagues at Paris VIII, Gilles Deleuze and Jean-François Lyotard. The reason is that the correlate of a mistaken theory of ideology is a failure to take sides in what was then the decisive class struggle – China versus the USSR and the French Maoists versus the French Communist Party. A failure to take sides leads to one's philosophy serving the wrong practice, the practice of exploitation.

The common mistakes made in the theorizing of ideology are three: first, a general theory of ideology is developed with no link to any particular class struggle; second the only ideology recognized is that of the ruling class; and third, like the young Hegelians Marx criticizes in *The German Ideology* for wanting to heal consciousness of its illusions, Althusser, Lyotard and Deleuze want to heal the unconscious of its illusions. In contrast, for the Maoist, ideology is formed within particular struggles, such as a factory occupation, and the struggle leads to a split between the participants concerning what is to be done. Hence not one but two ideologies emerge from a conflictual situation, and only one of them will carry the struggle forwards without capitulating to bourgeois interests. This is the proletarian ideology. The task of theory – of Marxist philosophy – is then to serve the practical struggle by systematizing the thinking of the masses as it emerges in the form of proletarian ideologies around particular conflicts. Theory is thus placed as one moment in the dialectic of class struggle and revolutionary knowledge: it returns knowledge of the rationality of the revolt back to the party and the masses in the form of pamphlets such as *Théorie de la contradiction* and *De l'idéologie*.[2]

In 1977 Badiou contributed part one, "Le Flux et le parti (dans les marges de *L'Anti-Oedipe*)" (2004c), to a collective text entitled *La Situation actuelle sur le front de philosophie: contre Deleuze et Guattari* (Badiou & Lazarus 1977: 24–41). This was the second of two polemical texts – the other directed against Althusser and Lecourt on the Lysenko question – both entitled "The Current Situation on the Philosophy Front". The title indicates the emergence of a second problem for Badiou concerning philosophy. In short, the problem is how to inhabit philosophy, how to take a position within its field, how to even identify its domain via a "front", a line of conflict, while at the same time completely renaming and refiguring it as a predominantly bourgeois ideological service. Badiou practises catachresis with the name of philosophy and yet, in order to struggle, in order to engage in conflict and face off enemies across a line, he needs those enemies to face him; he needs to construct his position as a properly philosophical position rather than pure Maoist activism, as internal to philosophy rather than external. This is the problem of *inhabiting philosophy*: in short, it is the renovator's problem: how do you inhabit what you want to tear down and rebuild?

In Badiou's scathing critique of *Anti-Oedipus*, "Le Flux et le parti (dans les marges de *L'Anti-Oedipe*)", a text that is mainly taken up with a lesson on the correct way of thinking revolt and the ensuing relation between the state, the party and the masses, he devotes just one page to diagnosing Deleuze and Guattari's error:

> For a long time I wondered what exactly their "desire" was, hung up as I was on the sexual connotations and the machinic hardware shop they clothed it in just to make it materialistic. Well, it's the Freedom of the Kantian critique, no more, no less. It's the unconditioned, subjective impulse which has invisibly escaped from the entire sensory order of goals, from the entire rational web of causes. It is pure, unbound, generic energy, energy as such. It is that which is its own law, or its absence of law.
>
> The old freedom of autonomy, hastily repainted to suit what the young, in revolt, legitimately demanded: a few gobs of spit splattered over the bourgeois family.
>
> The rule of the Good in Deleuze is the categorical imperative set back on its feet via an amusing substitution of the particular for the universal: act always such that the maxim of your action is rigorously particular. Deleuze wants to be for Kant what Marx was for Hegel. Deleuze is Kant's overturner: a categorical imperative, but desiring, the unconditioned, but materialist, the autonomy of the subject but as a flow that runs. (Badiou 1977: 30, my trans.)

This is a classic exercise in the use of the history of philosophy: debunking the new by revealing the withered body behind the fancy clothes. The satire is rough, the history sketchy; no argument is offered and the prose is decidedly unacademic, but this critique sets up a properly philosophical scene. Deleuze is not only chosen as a target for being a false radical, for strengthening the wrong tendency in the post-'68 Left. Deleuze is targeted because he is practising a return to Kant under the cover of the new. Kant is thus set up as the figure of a philosopher who does not provide the resources for a philosophy adequate to its times. In very minimal form we thus have a scene of philosophy, inhabited by three figures: the Maoist with the up-to-date theory of ideology, the rival philosopher with an outdated and abstract theory, and the hidden master of the latter, a liberal philosopher.

In 1982, the philosophical scene has altered. In the crystalline Preface to *Theory of the Subject*, not only has Badiou's prose style changed – become more Mallarméan, more Rimbaudian – but the stage resembles the midnight of *Igitur*: a desert. One sole voice in the desert: that of the systematic proletarian. And the desert is not only philosophical, but national, political – in the last century France has known three moments of glory, the Paris Commune, the Resistance in the Second World War, and May 1968. It has also known moments of abjection: the triumph of Versailles after the Commune, of colonialist wars after the Resistance, and the rise of the *nouveaux philosophes* after 1968. Those moments of abjection have lasted longer than the triumphs. They bear the "mark of a failing", which is ultimately subjective: "it concerns the way in which potential forces, amidst the people, have been distanced from their own concept" (TS 13). Badiou writes and acts – not "alone", he insists, while naming one "sole" interlocutor or comrade, Paul Sandevince – in an attempt to remember and continue what occurred in those moments of glory despite the massive forgetting of their promise.

The scene of philosophy is thus deserted. So what does this modern philosopher, alone with his friends, do? He repopulates it with a curious collection of dialecticians: Hegel and Hölderlin; Pascal, Rousseau, Mallarmé and Lacan; Marx, Engels, Lenin and Mao. However, this population was not enough to allow the modern philosopher to inhabit philosophy. As we find out fifteen years later in Badiou's *Deleuze*, the book *Theory of the Subject* surfaced alone: "In 1982 I published a transitional philosophical book ... Deleuze sent me a favourable note which was very touching given the public solitude in which I found myself ... the silence, the absolute disdain for what I was trying to do in philosophy" (D 9). To inhabit philosophy Badiou tears it down – it is a desert – and then rebuilds it, but in his new house he still finds himself alone (with some friends). A new strategy is required.

Philosophy under its conditions

In 1985 Badiou publishes a short text drawn from a series of seminars organized by Jean-Luc Nancy and Philippe Lacoue-Labarthe called *The Withdrawal of Politics* (1983). Badiou's text is entitled *Can Politics be Thought?* Again it is a matter of an absence in the field of politics, of a withdrawal. And again it is the philosopher who is called upon to answer. But this time the status of philosophy will not be left in suspense: it is not simply a front, nor is it a desert; it is a field of enquiry that is capable of progression. In 1989, in his *Manifesto for Philosophy*, in reaction to a series of declarations concerning "the end of philosophy" and "steps not beyond", Badiou calls for "a step further". In doing so he reanimates an Althusserian tactic, and divides the field of philosophy, distinguishing between philosophies of finitude and philosophies of infinity. Later he will divide this latter category – philosophies of infinity – again into the vitalist (Deleuze) and stellar (Badiou) types of multiplicity. But this division is not simply the name of communism as a process, as in the Maoist days, leading to a marginal and unguaranteed future; it is, rather, a return to authenticity via a Heideggerean claim: modern philosophy under the banner of anti-Platonism has not only misrecognized the contemporary actuality and radicality of Plato, but also – *pace* Heidegger and the Platonic forgetting of being – it forgot the Cantorian event that revealed infinite multiplicity in the form of set theory. This claim is both Heideggerean in its form – the field of philosophy is structured by a forgetting – yet anti-Heideggerean in its content – we must have done with the philosophy of finitude. It can also be inscribed as a double denial: Plato did *not* forget being as spoken in the poem, and being was *not* originally and uniquely spoken in the poem by the Greeks. In its affirmative form, being can be inscribed by an idea; in particular, being is inscribed in the mathematical ideas, the axioms of set theory. The first tactic in Badiou's reconstruction of the philosophical scene is thus the call for a step further by rescuing Cantor from oblivion.

The second tactic is the reformulation of the Marxist axiom of the primacy of practice. It is no longer political praxis alone that both precedes and orientates philosophy; it is artistic and scientific and amorous praxes that precede and orient philosophy. These practices are conceived as being woven out of a series of investigations that tease out and realize the consequences of a disruptive event. The investigations in turn make up a "generic truth procedure", where truth is the unfolding of novelty, and the procedure is generic in so far as it escapes capture by any of the established categories of its situation. Philosophy in itself does not produce truths; rather it gathers them after the fact. In thinking the immanent inventions that occur in these truths, and in creating a common conceptual space for them, philosophy will finally render itself contemporary with its own times. This is the doctrine of conditions.

According to this doctrine, it is not every day that a new philosophy is created – a space of compossibility must be conceptually constructed for four truth procedures, one political, one scientific, one amorous and one artistic. Without one of these conditions philosophy dissipates; that is, one may have an apparently philosophical text, but one will not have *a* philosophy (MP 35). This relatively complicated genesis immediately generates some easy diagnostic tools to apply to other would-be philosophies. For instance, a philosopher may have fallen into the trap of attempting to *fuse* philosophy with one of its conditions, resulting in a *disaster*. Such is the case of Althusser, trying to fuse philosophy with politics. It is debatable whether this is also a self-diagnosis with regard to Badiou's Maoist period. In order to avoid a disaster, philosophy must rigorously separate its own names from the immanent names of a truth procedure. Another trap is that of believing that one truth procedure can pass via another: believing that there is such a thing as directly political art, which would imply the fusion of an artistic and a political truth procedure.[3] However, it is debatable how far one can insist upon the separation of conditions: Badiou himself recognizes that one truth procedure can intersect another, and that it is the very intersection between political and amorous truth procedures that forms the subject-matter of an artistic truth procedure in the form of many novels.

What matters here is what kind of philosophy results from the procedure of conditioning: what does a "unified conceptual space" for the "nomination of events" look like (MP 37)? In the introduction to *Being and Event* Badiou claims that philosophy is a "circulation through the referential". By *Logics of Worlds*, he speaks of his "system", infamously leaving the trouble of joining the category-theory construction to the early set-theoretical construction to his exegetes (LW 39). In so far as a conceptual construction is fuelled with material drawn from four different sources, one can imagine that there will be a few problems in joining the pieces together.[4] If each condition demands its own type of philosophical capture – Badiou does not present set theory in the same way that he interprets poems – and produces its own infra-philosophical discourse – "ontology", "metapolitics", "inaesthetics" – then the term "compossibility" refers to a massive problem for the philosopher.

It is precisely this heterogeneity of philosophical discourse that has led to the instability some commentators remark in the status of the illustrations in *Logics of Worlds*.[5] Leaving aside those particular examples, there are two general ways in which this heterogeneity and ensuing instability is domesticated and contained. The first is the assignment of a *telos* to this philosophical construction, namely its contemporaneity. A philosophy will have become *a philosophy of its times* only in so far as it has constructed a unified conceptual space out of truth procedures from *each* domain. Here contemporaneity stands in the same relation to philosophical discourse and its unfolding of figures of truth as the absolute thing-in-itself does to Hegelian philosophical unfolding of figures of spirit.

The second way Badiou saves conditioned philosophy from a potentially centrifugal heterogeneity is by giving it an anchor or a ground: a foundational point in the history of philosophy, Plato. Plato is the first philosopher to practise clearly the conditioning of philosophy: science is there in the shape of geometry, love in the desire of Socrates, politics in *The Republic* and art in both the construction of the dialogues and the expulsion of the tragedians from the luxurious hypothetical city. Thus it is a mistake to read Badiou's calls for a return to Plato or a new Platonism as mere rhetoric or prologemenon to his more systematic work.[6] The reference is vital in so far as if Plato succeeded in creating a conditioned philosophy, he also produced an idea of his times, a Greek contemporaneity. If we accord to Badiou that "there are only three crucial philosophers, Plato, Descartes and Hegel", then the latter will have also generated an idea of their times; they will have conceptualized what is proper to their age; they will have constructed contemporaneities that allow us to grasp what the seventeenth century and the nineteenth centuries were (LW 527). In turn, the Hegelian and Cartesian contemporaneities can serve as measures for the attempt to construct a contemporaneity for the twenty-first century. Evidently Badiou holds that he has constructed a conceptual space of compossibility – for the artistic truth procedure of Mallarméan poetry, for the amorous truth procedure of psychoanalysis, for the scientific procedures of set theory and category theory, and for the political procedure of post-Maoist activism. For this reason his philosophy is at the stage of producing proper names or concepts for its times, such as the name he introduces in *Logics of Worlds*, "democratic materialism", a name for the dominant ideology of our times.

Inhabiting philosophy: scene and theatre

In his *Second Manifesto for Philosophy*, Badiou sets "the philosopher" against "the democrat" (2009g: 33). The philosopher, if not the actual individual philosopher called Alain Badiou, has come to play a larger and larger role in Badiou's philosophy: Quentin Meillassoux speaks of Badiou situating his own figure *qua* philosopher as an "archi-engaged subject", a diagnosis swiftly confirmed by the Preface to *Being and Event*. But this figure is one amidst an entire panoply that Badiou has gradually introduced into the scene of philosophy: once the doctrine of conditions is in place we meet not only the "sophists" – unnamed but ubiquitous – but also the "anti-philosophers" – Paul, Nietzsche, Wittgenstein, Lacan. The philosopher is thus surrounded by multiple antagonists, and the dominant mode of philosophy is polemic.[7]

This is where we find Badiou's solution to the second problem concerning philosophy, the problem of how to inhabit a discourse while attempting to completely transform it, while criticizing all of its predominant institutional forms. One inhabits philosophy by making polemic the very heart of philosophical practice. The redefinition of the field of philosophy, the division of the field into philosophers versus anti-philosophers or philosophers versus the sophists, the publication of manifestos, the discounting of much research as sterile academic specialization – all of these activities are central to the very production of philosophy. More importantly, none of these polemics can be reduced to the status of an expression of one larger extra-philosophical conflict, as was the case under the Althusserian definition of philosophy as the class struggle in theory.

In short, the solution is to create not just a scene of philosophy – already present in *Theory of the Subject* – but an entire theatre of philosophy: a tragic theatre in so far as the unfolding of conflictual action, or polemic, continually separates subjects, and a comic theatre in so far as there are grotesque figures to unmask, the sophist, the anti-philosopher, the reactionary subject, the obscure subject, and ideologies to debunk. A theatre and not only a scene in so far as the doctrine of conditions generates more than one scene and more than one set of characters. Indeed, armed with this doctrine and concepts such as event, fidelity and generic multiple, one can reread the history of philosophy, reorganized according to epochal configurations of truth procedures and their more or less complete recognition by philosophers. This new history of philosophy – a *history of truths* rather than a history of being – generates still more scenes, and even a virtual audience in so far as our contemporaneity will be measured against those of Plato, Descartes and Hegel.

And so the philosopher is no longer the lone proletarian in the desert of theory. The philosopher as archi-engaged subject is also an avant-garde artist, a scientist on the edge of madness, and a lover. The philosopher is a member of a new republic of letters, a transhistorical custodian of the eternal becoming of truths. The philosopher still engages in struggle, but never alone, surrounded by disciples, friends and colleagues. Finally, the philosopher is never alone not only because there are always more young to corrupt, but because the philosophical institution, the proper philosophical education, always remains to be built.[8]

Notes

1. It is worth meditating on the current institutional fate of philosophy from this point of view: are the orthodox categories of analytic and continental philosophy fundamentally anchored by a conservatism with regard to the sole objects of philosophy: a well-formed language and human agency?

2. For a more complete exegesis of the dialectic of revolutionary knowledge see Feltham (2008), ch. 2. Note that *De l'idéologie* was also published in book form by Maspero and signed Alain Badiou and François Balmès.

3. The confusion into which Walter Benjamin plunged thousands of academics via a few sentences at the end of his famous essay.

4. Indeed, in a typically satirical assessment Jacques Bouveresse – as Badiou reports – accuses Badiou of being a hare with eight paws, "running topspeed in the direction of mathematical formalism and then suddenly he turns, incomprehensibly, back in the other direction and runs at same speed in order to throw himself into literature". See Badiou (2008h).

5. For this problem see Clemens (2006) and Feltham's response (2008: ch. 3).

6. One question to explore is which Plato, especially given the immense scholarly debate over the coherence of his views, the variations in the theory of ideas, the Third Man Argument and the problem of the historical Socrates, to mention a few thorny points. A preliminary answer is given by identifying the texts Badiou refers to: the *Republic*, the *Parmenides* and the *Sophist*.

7. See François Nicolas' website consecrated to the transcription of all of Badiou's seminars over the years: www.entretemps.asso.fr/Badiou/ (accessed April 2010). See in particular the 1989–90 course on the *Republic*.

8. See one of Badiou's most important and most neglected essays, "What is a Philosophical Institution? Or: Address, Transmission, Inscription" (2007g).

THREE

The conditions

Justin Clemens

The concept

Perhaps *the* crucial concept in Badiou's work since *Being and Event* (1988) is that of "conditions".[1] The concept is developed between *Theory of the Subject* (1982) and *Being and Event*, and is the marker of an irreversible internal rupture. Its importance is consecrated in the title of a collection of essays *Conditions* (1992), and its implications explored in every significant text from *Manifesto for Philosophy* (1989) to *Logics of Worlds* (2006). This is not to say that there are not abiding interests throughout Badiou's early writings and his post-*Being and Event* work. But abiding interests are not necessarily evidence of real continuity. The rupture in Badiou's work between *Theory of the Subject* and *Being and Event* may be considered a move from assuming philosophy's actuality to reconsidering philosophy's possibility. In doing so, Badiou comes to recognize that "philosophy" is not a synonym for "thought" in general, nor is it the essence or paradigm of thought, nor is it what gives firm grounds to knowledge, nor is it even what interrogates thinking as such.

What does it mean that philosophy is always on condition? First, that philosophy is not an independent discourse. On the contrary, philosophy is *entirely dependent* on its conditions. Philosophy does not and cannot think by itself. Second, philosophy emerges only in response to a certain kind of demand. Philosophy thinks only under pressure. But this pressure is not merely the result of empirical factors. Only the fact that there is already thinking going on and, moreover, heterogeneous kinds of thinking, makes philosophy possible. Philosophy emerges as a belated response to differing forms of thought, each with its own particular claims and modes of operation, as an attempt to articulate what relationships such forms can bear to each other, to identify and explicate their status *vis-à-vis* each other and the world.

Philosophy therefore thinks what it is constrained to think by and about other kinds of thinking. For Badiou, these are the four practices – "conditions", "truth-procedures" or "genres" – of science, love, art and politics. Outside these four conditions, philosophy simply cannot exist, or degenerates into a species of sophistry. Philosophy is, in other words, a dependent, distressed and belated discourse. Why, then, these four conditions? And what does Badiou make of them?

I begin by sketching some problems with *Theory of the Subject*, in order to suggest why Badiou would find that text questionable enough to radically renovate his own thinking, and propose how Jacques Lacan proves instrumental in this renovation. I proceed with an account of how the concept of "conditions" constitutes a rupture in Badiou's thought, and conclude by determining the key traits of this concept and its consequences.

Badiou's problem

Theory of the Subject is an extremely ambitious book. Beginning with an ingenious reconceptualization of the Hegelian dialectic, Badiou moves through a wide range of references, to conclude with a complex formalization of the subject. Yet Badiou's apparatus, despite its materialist insistence on scissiparity, is sustained, paradoxically enough, by an operation that indiscriminates its objects. Badiou implicitly maintains three key positions in this book that will later appear to him the pernicious symptoms of a historically well-determined suture (of which more below). These are:

- logicism, the doctrine that the statements of mathematics are all effectively tautological, that mathematics itself is ultimately authorized by logic;[2]
- politicism, the doctrine that every subject is political, that there is a subject if and only if it is political;[3]
- dialecticism, the doctrine that, if philosophical thinking is an independent form of thought that deals with the "coincidence of opposites", it must nonetheless ultimately be subordinated to praxis.[4]

The Hegelian dialectic is key here, for it underwrites the Marxist revolutionary tradition to which Badiou adheres. Left Hegelianism, moreover, often impels its adherents towards the following positions: a submission of mathematical thought to the *logic* of contradiction (and, with it, a privileging of temporal dynamism over abstract stasis); the thoroughgoing *politicization* of contradiction itself (which founds, within the temporal becoming of the concept, the specificity of revolutionary elements); and the concomitant ambiguity of an absolute injunction to theorize that is nonetheless normed according to the claims of an extra-theoretical real (the imperative to effectuate the communist *eschaton*).

I note the presence of this philosophical Bermuda Triangle in *Theory of the Subject* in order to suggest that Badiou escapes it by means of a savage auto-critique, evidently pursued from 1982 and concluded by 1988. It is this auto-critique that enables him to recognize the sutures he had been labouring under, as it compels him to curb his own politico-philosophical enthusiasms. Paradoxically, it is in curbing such enthusiasms that Badiou can rediscover "philosophy in the fullness of its ambition", as he puts it, and without giving way on the affirmation of radical politics. This rediscovery requires a rupture and a return: a rupture with Hegel, a return to Plato. It also requires a new concept, that of "conditions".

Psychoanalysis is anti-philosophy

According to the Introduction to *Being and Event*, Badiou realized his errors as a result of following a false trail:

> Without noticing it, I had been caught in the grip of a logicist thesis which holds that the necessity of logico-mathematical statements is formal due to their complete eradication of any effect of sense, and that in any case there is no cause to investigate what these statements account for, outside their own consistency.
>
> (BE 5)

But mathematics is not logic, and cannot be reduced to it; what, then, can account for its singular powers? Lacan will prove key for Badiou in providing the resources for liberating the concept of conditions, for "None of this was consistent with the clear Lacanian doctrine according to which the real is the impasse of formalization" (BE 5).

Lacan explicitly announces that "mathematical formalisation is our goal, our ideal" (1998: 119). Badiou independently shares this ideal, and the entirety of his work betrays various attempts to think through the status of mathematics. For Lacan, mathematics is the science of the real, for it grips the real in a way unavailable to any other discourse. Part of the reason why the matheme can do this is through its reduction of signification to letters, themselves stripped of any meaning or any tie to any natural language in particular. In doing so, mathematics also rigorously exposes the stations that it cannot pass.[5]

There is, however, another important aspect to Lacan's project here. First, "ideals" for psychoanalysis are never quite as ideal as they may seem, and Lacan's choice of the word should alert us to a certain ambivalence. Indeed, Lacan constantly affirms the crucial role played by the literary: "How could we forget that Freud constantly, and right until the end, maintained that such a [literary] background was the prime requisite in the training of analysts, and that he designated the age-old *universitas litterarum* as the ideal place for its institution?" (2006: 413). What is crucial for Lacan is that psychoanalysis is a discipline caught between literariness and mathematization. In fact, psychoanalysis is an impossible profession for a number of reasons, not least because it is *conditioned* by having to attend to the profuse chicanery of the signifier, on the one hand, and the abstemious formalizations of the letter, on the other, between poetry and mathematics.[6]

For Lacan, psychoanalysis comes into being only because there is something in the world that demands a hearing, and because as yet there is nothing adequate to hearing that demand. That demand is the hysterical symptom. It is only in response to what Lacan will call "the golden tonsils" of hysterical women that Freud develops psychoanalysis at all. Such "formations of the unconscious" are ever-shifting presentations, irresolvable by any form of dialectics. In attending to this problematic, Lacan gives the most rigorous theorization yet available of the singularity of psychoanalysis. In responding to the hysterical demand, analysis is forced to mobilize both literary attentiveness and rigorous formalization, which pull it in opposite directions; in its attempt to follow through on this irreducible divergence, psychoanalysis brings to its limit the concept of the subject bequeathed to modern philosophy by Descartes. Lacanian analysis is a practice that explicitly theorizes the non-reducibility of heterogeneous discourses, as it seeks to formalize their possible in-articulation. Lacan supposes a separation and heterogeneity of discourses, but also the necessity to deploy them together in a paradoxical way. As such, psychoanalysis is not and will not always be im-possible: one day, for whatever reasons, there will no longer be symptoms that can be treated analytically; and even if there are, it is never certain that analysis can sustain itself given the volatility of its conceptual self-situation between science and literature.

Badiou does not just appropriate from Lacan the very strong propositions about mathematics, nor take up the challenges of Lacan's limit-doctrine of the subject, but also recognizes that thought must be integrally marked by heterogeneity in its operations.

Reconstructing the concept

Between 1982 and 1988, Badiou is confronted with the necessity to break the triple yoke of logicism, politicism and dialecticism, with its fundamentally Hegelian alibi, its internal complications, as well as the necessity to take into account significant shifts in the political realities of the 1980s that render some of his prior theses otiose for Badiou himself. Accomplishing such a break entails the discernment of new conditions of possibility for thought, the construction of a new concept of transcendental condition à la Kant, but which escapes the Kantian subjective juridicy (so to speak). For this, there are the resources offered by Lacan, whereby a particular kind of thought (psychoanalysis) is called into being by a contingent worldly demand (the hysterical symptom), and which can only maintain itself in an impossible way between the matheme and the poem.

If psychoanalysis did emerge in response to hysteria (a singular form of discourse), such a conditioning immediately gives a distinct temporality and topology to analysis, which is not simply empirical nor historical (part of the scandal of the unconscious is its "timelessness"). Psychoanalysis must break with historicism: if it arises in a very particular socio-historical locale, its implications are universal (at least in principle). In a similar vein, why not re-pose the question regarding philosophy's emergence? It is here that the return to Plato becomes critical.

In *Theory of the Subject*, Plato has a peculiar status: he is the founder of idealism, if one whose project can literally be "materialized" by committed political thought (TS 184).[7] Yet he is also clearly the originator, in thought, of the necessity for an exoteric mathematical orientation: "Let no one enter here who is not a geometer" read the sign over the Academy's doorway. Oddly enough, this evinces a strange continuity with Lacan. For if mathematics is the science of the real, what happens if one takes this claim seriously, that is, *literally*? Lacan does not say "logic is the science of the real", despite his own profound Hegelian affiliations. As Badiou proposes in *Being and Event*, why not hold that mathematics inscribes being itself? This is a classical Pythagorean–Platonic conviction. Moreover, if mathematics is not logic, then we need to re-examine the separation between them. What does mathematics do that logic does not? It is axiomatic and deductive rather than definitional. Mathematics makes axiomatic claims (ungrounded fundamental assertions) and then rigorously draws consequences that, before they are demonstrated, can appear preposterous, and yet, after the proof is concluded, are apodictic. Mathematics can therefore be reread as *at once* radical deductive invention that exceeds logical closure (subjective process of invention) and as rational ontology (paradigm of knowledge). Logic is thereby, first, relegated to describing rules for rational thought, and, second, to prescribing possible worlds. Logicism is banished. What I have denominated "politicism" and "dialecticism" are banished in the same gesture.[8]

By taking Lacan as issuing a radical challenge to thought, by taking on his propositions, stylistics and meta-operatory mechanics, Badiou not only learns from Lacan but opens a way beyond him. And just as Lacan effects a "return to Freud", Badiou effects a "return to Plato". It is in returning to Plato through Lacan that Badiou manages to effect a separation between philosophy and the processes that make it think, as well as between those processes themselves. In such a separation, further questions emerge: what is the status of such separations? what consequences do they have for philosophy? what names can be given to these processes? what differentiates these processes from each other?

The key theses that emerge are usefully summarized in the short essay "The (Re)turn of Philosophy Itself", where Badiou declares:

> An attentive examination of Plato … results in the following theses …:
> 1. *Before* philosophy – that is, in a "before" that is non-temporal – there are *truths*. These truths are heterogeneous and occur in the real independently of philosophy…
> 2. Philosophy is a construction of thinking where…it is proclaimed that there are truths. But this central proclamation presupposes a specifically philosophical category, which is that of *the* Truth. (C 10–11)[9]

So we now can speak of truths, the conditions of philosophy; and Truth, the philosophical identification, articulation and affirmation of these conditions. There are also processes, however, that, despite their relationship to knowledge, cannot be considered truths (economics, for instance).[10]

Four aspects of Badiou's position should be emphasized here. First, philosophy can only be philosophy if it takes up the challenge of the four conditions. Every true philosophy deals with these, and only these,

conditions. Second, a corollary: philosophies (in the plural) are singu-
larized by the particular way in which they articulate the conditions.
Third, this articulation is itself governed by *what* of its conditions are
treated in and by any particular philosophy. Fourthly, philosophy must
not confound itself with its conditions.

The conditions

Is it simply on the foundational authority of Plato that these conditions,
and only these conditions, are acceptable to Badiou? A further question
arises: why *these* conditions?

That our relation to truths is "absolute" is fundamental to Badiou's
post-*Being and Event* philosophy, and this is where the issue of the
in-human becomes central.[11] Certainly, the conditions are specifically
human possibilities, but in a very particular sense: not every human
being is always a subject.[12] The conditions are *contingent* in their emergence; that is, nothing in a situation necessitates or determines their
appearance. Not every human situation necessarily harbours all, even
any, of the conditions. This is why Badiou insists that every truth must
begin in an event. Such events are *rare* (you do not have the chance to
fall in love every day), and have neither *substance* nor *consistency* to
them (they cannot be proven to have taken place, and may indeed be
mere illusion or delusion). The conditions are, furthermore, *immanent*
to their situations; that is, they do not proceed from another world, they
do not harbour any transcendent elements. Truths are *self-supporting* in
their elaboration; that is, they are composed of subjects whose struggle
is itself the becoming of that truth. Truths are *indifferent* to all existing
forms of self-interest; that is, the human being that becomes a subject
does not stand to gain anything in the way of goods from its participation in the process and, indeed, in its transformation into a subject, risks
losing all that it already has. A truth must be *egalitarian* in its address:
even if only one person is involved in a process (an artistic process, for
example), the practices that they invent in the course of their work must
be *in principle* able to be taken up by anybody whomsoever in a non-
determining way. Finally, every truth must *restrain* itself. A truth cannot
totalize the others without disaster, that is, by failing itself as truth.[13]

Perhaps most importantly, the conditions found the production of
new knowledges. The predicate "new" is crucial because it enables
Badiou to escape Kantian legislative metaphysics, which constantly discerns transcendental subreptions in the modes of speculative thought,
judging them as exceeding their proper purview and therefore as

philosophically worthless. For Badiou, by contrast, the inventive praxis of the conditions places them at the limits of law and logic, in the realm of the undecidable (regarding which a necessarily lawless decision must be made) and about the indiscernible (whereby two things that presently appear indistinguishable may turn out to be distinguishable according to new criteria generated in the course of the process itself).

In a less abstract vein, one commentator notes, "One can sometimes be at a loss to explain a happening in terms that others will understand; one is lost for words" (Hewlett 2004: 344). This "lost for words" aspect of a subject working under the aegis of a truth condition is integral to Badiou's theory. Since a truth procedure is the production of the new by means of subjective struggle, there is no existing language in which its status can be propounded by any subject of that truth. This inexpressibility is not in any way a mystical apprehension; it is rather the rational consequence of a subject's aleatory trajectory ("is this x connected to the event or not?"), as well as the infinity of the process itself (the process is never "finished" as such, but continues to be elaborated bit by bit). A condition is literally *conditional* for a subject of that truth; that is, *if* this event did in fact take place, *then* what are the consequences for the world at *this* point? There are therefore no existing assurances at any point that an event has taken place, that a truth is indeed in process, that it will indeed have any consequences at all – hence the necessity for courage, terror, anxiety and justice, on the part of any subject.

The four conditions, moreover, each think in their own way. Love deals with the "two of sexuation"; politics with the traumatic infinity of collective human situations; mathematics embodies the power of formalization; and poetry forges new relations between the intensity of sense and formal qualities (see C 44; LW 72–8). Philosophy is the transliteration of the singular injunctions delivered by its trans-material conditions, and the recomposition of these effects in a system under the heading of "Truth". In this respect, philosophy is the only discourse capable of "affirming what the human animal is capable of", a becoming-Immortal that is also an affirmation of a non-humanist Humanity: "Humanity is the historical body of truths" (C 184).[14]

Since philosophy – philosophy worthy of the name – must be conditioned by all four conditions, we can recompose the history of philosophy as the history of the diverse knottings of these conditions. To give two telegraphic examples: Plato uses mathematics as the primary pedagogical device to rupture with the arts, which are banished from the ideal republic in the name of political justice, and which at once presumes and enables the proper love of the idea; in Aristotle, the paradigm of thought is not mathematical (at which Aristotle was reputedly hopeless), but biological; the arts become mimetic and cathartic modes with no stake themselves in truth; politics becomes the study of various organizations in the service of the good life; and love founds the relation to virtuous activity.

Further issues

Because Badiou conceives of the conditions as at once inventive (i.e. forever *new*) and eternal (i.e. *forever* new), several further issues arise. First, what of the apparent obsolescence of truths? Second, what of their external suppression or internal exhaustion? Third, what other things can happen to truths? Fourthly, what of philosoph*ies*' relation to these problems?

Briefly, Badiou holds that truths are *never* rendered obsolete. If each necessarily emerges in a world in time, a truth is absolutely irreducible to its time. A truth has to be infinitely extensible in principle. As Badiou shows, although contemporary mathematics has gone far beyond ancient demonstrations regarding prime numbers, it remains the case that Euclid's demonstrations are well founded:

> In the decisive absence of truly operative numerical and literal notations, and hampered by their fetishism of ontological finitude, the Greeks of course only thought through part of the problem. They were incapable of clearly identifying the general form of the decomposition of a number into prime factors. Nevertheless, they grasped the essential: prime numbers are always implicated in the multiplicative composition of a non-prime number.
>
> (LW 13)

The same goes for the other truth procedures (see in particular Badiou's demonstrations throughout MP and LW).[15] Regarding a truth's exhaustion, it is just as much the case that a particular truth process can be crushed – as with the failure of Spartacus's slave revolt. Nonetheless, although Spartacus is brutally suppressed, "the subjective identity which is fashioned in and by these military movements is not identical with them; it passes through operations of a different kind, which constitute subjective deliberation, division and production" (LW 51). It is the traces of this subjectivization – that is, as an "event which originates for the ancient world a maxim of emancipation in the present tense" – that can always be picked up again, in radically different circumstances, as it was by Toussaint-Louverture in

1796 and Karl Leibknecht and Rosa Luxemburg in 1919 (and Spartacus, lest we forget, was Karl Marx's self-confessed "hero").

Yet a truth can also become "saturated", that is, unable to escape repetition. So classical Greek theatre became saturated when, though hardly externally menaced, it was unable, after Euripides, to accomplish anything really new. As Badiou underlines, however, "the saturation of a configuration ... in no way signifies that said configuration is a finite multiplicity. Nothing from within the configuration itself either delimits it or exposes the principle of its end" (HI 13). Again, the subjective aspects of such a configuration may indeed be picked up at a later date, just as seventeenth-century European dramatists picked up on their classical antecedents.

Our third question is the most complicated, and can be given only the sketchiest treatment here. Moreover, it is necessary to break the question in two, one part concerning the ethics of truths, the other concerning the problem of the suture of truths. Concerning ethics, Badiou maintains there are three main ways that a truth can go rotten: through ecstasy, terror or sacralization. In *Conditions*, he claims that evil is "the desire to name *at any price*" (C 127). Such is a disaster: when one truth attempts to totalize the others (e.g. Stalinist politics forcibly norming love, science and art). But this can also equally be a disaster of philosophy itself – precisely when philosophy *mistakes itself for being a truth procedure in its own right and thereby reduces or dominates its own conditions* (e.g. C 15–20). This is one reason why the concept of conditions is so crucial for Badiou: it is the guardian against philosophical disaster.

Finally, we come to the concept of "suture", most fully developed in *Manifesto for Philosophy*, where Badiou gives an extraordinary interpretation of European philosophy from Hegel to Heidegger as being dominated by "sutures" between it and its conditions. A suture occurs when "philosophy *delegates* its functions to one or other of its conditions, handing over the whole of thought to *one* generic procedure. Philosophy is then carried out in the element of its own suppression to the great benefit of that procedure" (MP 61). Analytic philosophy sutures itself to the scientific procedure; Marxism sutures philosophy to its political condition; Romanticism sutures philosophy to its artistic condition; and so on. It is in such texts as *Manifesto for Philosophy*, *Conditions* and *Handbook of Inaesthetics* that Badiou works out some details of the historical interferences of the conditions.

Conclusion

Being and Event introduces an irreversible rupture into Badiou's work with the concept of conditions, and his work post-*Being and Event* continues Badiou's examination of the consequences of this concept for his philosophy, and for philosophy more generally. Hence he will look at problems of exhaustion and suture among conditions in *Manifesto for Philosophy*, detailed problems within certain conditions in *Conditions*, specifics of the political condition in *Metapolitics*, the artistic condition in *Handbook of Inaesthetics*, and so on. In general, one can consider the trajectory from *Being and Event* to *Logics of Worlds* a process of refinement as well as an extension of the consequences of condition. In *Logics of Worlds*, for example, we see a new emphasis on the problem of contemporary logic, as well as an attempt to describe in more detail the actual appearing and disappearing of truths-in-worlds, with more fulsome examples and new categories such as those of "points" and "openings". We also see an attempt to bring the conditions "forward", as it were. In *Being and Event* all the conditioning truths were essentially modernist (indexed to the names of Cantor, Lenin, Mallarmé and Freud); in *Logics of Worlds*, the truths become more "postmodernist" (indexed to Mac Lane and Eilenberg, Mao, Pessoa and Lacan).[16]

Yet, for Badiou, philosophy must always lag behind its conditions. We are that present, but as yet unable to *know* it.

Notes

1. For brief accounts of the concept of "conditions, see Riera (2005) and Clemens (2006), upon which I draw here; for a more extended account, see Hallward (2003).
2. In *Theory of the Subject* (216), this implicit presumption has the effect of rendering Cantorian mathematics continuous with the general doctrines of philosophical materialism: "The notion that everything can be stated under the sole name of the set, and within the logic of belonging, is equivalent, as far as I am concerned, to the materialist recognition of the One of the name of being. 'Matter' here serves, for being, as universal signifier, just as the set does for mathematics." Previously, Badiou has announced "we consider the mathematical signifier a symptom around which the deductive text, without knowing this at all, attempts an auto-analysis. That is, we take the mathematical text to be in the position of the analyst for some of its own words – as being symptomatic of itself" (TS 148).
3. In *Theory of the Subject* (28), Badiou holds that "every subject is political".
4. Hence "There is not a single major text of Marxism that does not find its mainspring in the question: Where is the proletariat? It follows that politics is the unity of opposites of a topics (the current situation) and an ethics (our tasks)"

(TS 281). This is exactly what *Theory of the Subject* sets out to provide, and precisely what Badiou's subsequent work exceeds.

5. On the problematic of "letters" (as distinguished from "signifiers"), see my "Letters as the Condition of Conditions for Alain Badiou" (2003a).

6. For a more detailed account of this situation, see Clemens (2007).

7. To give a sense of the radicality of Badiou's shift between *Theory of the Subject* and *Being and Event* in regard to Plato, in "The (Re)turn of Philosophy Itself" Badiou will identify this position with that of "Stalinist Marxism", for which "Plato names the birth of idealism" (C 9).

8. As Badiou says of *Theory of the Subject*, "I cut straight to the dialectic, without drawing – in a Greater Logic – all the consequences of the obligatory materialism" (LW 46).

9. Similarly, in "Definition of Philosophy", Badiou writes: "Philosophy is prescribed by conditions that constitute types of truth or generic-procedure", and "Philosophy is the place of thought where the 'there is' (*il y a*) of these truths, and their compossibility, is stated" (C 23).

10. "Love, art, science and politics generate – infinitely – truths concerning situations; truths subtracted from knowledge which are only counted by the state in the anonymity of their being. All sorts of other practices – possibly respectable, such as commerce for example, and all the different forms of the 'service of goods,' which are intricated in knowledge to various degrees – do not generate truths. I have to say that philosophy does not generate any truths either, however painful this admission may be. At best, philosophy is *conditioned* by the faithful procedures of its times" (BE 340).

11. "The fact is that today – and on this point things haven't budged since Plato – we know only four types of truths: science (mathematics and physics), love, politics and the arts. We can compare this situation to Spinoza's statement about the attributes of Substance (the 'expressions' of God): without doubt, Spinoza says, there is an infinity of attributes, but we humans know only two, thought and extension. For our part, we will say that there are perhaps an infinity of types of truths, but we humans only know four. But we do truly know them. So that even if some typical expressions of the true evade us, our relation to truths is absolute" (LW 71).

12. "[T]here is no predestination in Badiou's account. There is nothing other than chance encounters between particular humans and particular events; and subjects *may* be born out of such encounters. There is no higher order which prescribes who will encounter an event and decide to act in relation to it. There is only chance. Furthermore, there is no simple distinction between subjects and humans. Some humans become subjects, but only some of the time" (IT 8: Clemens & Feltham, "Introduction"). Still, a charge of "speciesism" might legitimately be levelled at Badiou in this regard.

13. See also LW 33–4: "7. Distinctive Features of Truths, Persuasive Features of Freedom".

14. See also the last chapter of *The Century*, in which Badiou modulates his vocabulary: "Let us call our philosophical task, on the shores of the new century, and against the animal humanism that besieges us, that of a *formalized in-humanism*" (TC 178).

15. As Badiou has it: "We no longer believe the narratives by which a human group invokes its origin or destiny. We know that Olympia is only a hill and the Sky is filled only with hydrogen or helium. But that the series of prime numbers is unlimited may be demonstrated today exactly as in Euclid's Elements, that

Phidias was a great sculptor is not in doubt, that Athenian democracy was a political invention whose theme still occupies us and that love designates the occurrence of a Two in which the subject is transfixed – this we understand when reading Sappho or Plato just as when reading Corneille or Beckett" (MP 33–4).

16. Or perhaps, after Natacha Michel – Badiou's long-time comrade – these names denote a "second modernity".

FOUR

The subject

Bruno Besana

References and differences

Throughout his work Alain Badiou underlines both the centrality of the notion of subject, and the fact that a subject is neither a specific type of substance, nor the name for the higher functions of human cognition, nor a set of universal conditions *a priori* of experience.

For Badiou, "a subject is not a substance" (OS 26). Against any materialist reduction, a subject cannot be identified with the human animal. And against sociological reduction, it cannot be identified with a "social individual", with an individual component of a given mode of organization of the collectivity (e.g. the subject of the state, or the subject to power). The subject is therefore not a *res extensa*, an object of a situation. But it cannot also be identified with the *res cogitans*: if Badiou somehow identifies the subject with a position (the "empty" position from which one thinks), at the same time he refuses to define it, along with Descartes, as a substance. A subject, in other words, is not a "given", a *datum*, that exists independently of the material contingencies of the situation, but is an *operation* that might or might not appear, an operation the existence of which is not necessarily embedded in the simple existence of a human being.

At the same time, Badiou does not follow the Kantian idea of the subject as "condition of possibility of experience". "A subject is in no sense the organising of a meaning of experience. It is not a transcendental function" (OS 26): similarly to Deleuze (1990: 14th and 15th series), for Badiou a transcendental function is nothing but the sublation to the status of universally valid *a priori* of our contingent, recurrent modes of relation with the world. Then, although dependent on experience, a subject, Badiou claims against Husserl, is not the internal unification of a set of lived experiences. This latter might define the "human", and the genesis of its conscious processes, but there is no necessary inference from this towards the definition of a subject. The subject is neither necessarily activated by a set of perceptive experiences, nor identifiable with man, nor identifiable with the operations of consciousness.

Finally, against the poststructural tradition, Badiou rejects the idea that the subject would be a mere illusion that needs to be deconstructed. Badiou begins with an anti-idealist move, namely the refusal of the idea that the subject would be a specific reality, provided with knowledge, empirically identified with the human animal, standing before the objectivity of the world and able to inscribe in it a sense and a destinality; but although dismissed in its primacy, the subject for Badiou is not dismissed in its reality. There is in fact a clear materialist attitude, inherited both from Marxism – through the mediation of Althusser – and from psychoanalysis – through the mediation of Lacan – that consists in affirming that a subject is a result of a material set of contingent determinations.

Badiou's materialist account of the subject is articulated on one side – as one can read already in *Théorie du sujet* – via reference to Lacan, who is perceived as the most solid point of resistance against deconstruction, specifically because he conceives the subject not as an ideal stance facing the world, but as a specific result of a multiplicity of elements (the symbolic, the imaginary and the real, three instances that are larger than the individual). More precisely, in the formalized analysis of their mutual relation, they appear to produce the unity of a subject only in relation to the inscription – in the form of a symptom – of an excessive element (namely desire), which at the same time displaces its actual configuration. This is why "we must recognize that we are indebted to Lacan for having paved the way for a *formal theory* of the subject *whose basis is materialist*" (LW 48).

On the other hand, with a clear reference to Marxism, the subject is articulated by Badiou as materially determined inside a specific contradiction between a "state of facts" and an intervention that tends to unveil and overthrow the relations of forces upon which such a state of facts relies. At the same time the subject is defined as always at once unitary and collective; it is identified with a unitary sequence resulting from a multiplicity of elements (for instance from a collective construction).

Decision, fidelity, universality

A subject is thus neither solely a material element, nor a warranty of the uniformity of experience. More precisely, "a subject is neither a result, nor an origin. It is the *local* status of a procedure, a configuration that exceeds the situation" (OS 27). In most cases, Badiou claims, when one analyses the objects that compose a given situation, nothing can be found that can be considered as a subject. One cannot for instance call "subject" a voter of a parliamentary democracy, or a painting of a given school of art: they both are completely determined, as such, by the place they occupy; they do not exceed the way in which they can be represented as elements of the situation to which they belong. They are *normal objects*. On the contrary, one will call "subject" a painting or series of paintings or artworks whose existence depends on a radical cut performed in a specific school of art or, politically speaking, a collective of individuals that apply to a given working situation the consequences of a revolutionary event. In both these cases the subject is identified not by the *place* that it occupies in the situation (as for an object) *vis-à-vis* the determinations of its state, but by a set of *actions* that it performs, and that depend strictly upon something that *happens*, that is in excess over the situation.

As such, exposing something a-normal, singular, "the subject is *rare*" (BE 392): it is rare because it is a local, singular configuration of actions that exists under condition of a radical cut in the consistent structure of a situation; because, in other words, it is suspended from the rare occurrence of an event. To this extent a subject cuts, performs a *caesura*, a de-cision, in the situation. A subject therefore exists in a situation, and, given its singularity, it exists even with a particular, singular evidence. But for the same reason it is something that exceeds the *bodies* that inhabit the situation, and the *language* that articulates the sense of their appearance. It is following this argument that Badiou finds a relation between the subject and truth. In the opening pages of *Logics of Worlds* Badiou proposes this motto: "there are bodies and languages, except that there are truths" (LW 4). Both truth and the subject appear to exceed the normal order of a language whose function is to name and classify the bodies and the objects of a given situation.

With explicit reference to Lacan, Badiou argues that a truth is something that exceeds the knowledge that one can have of the current mode in which objects are organized inside an intelligible situation: "truth is not a qualification of knowledge nor an intuition of the intelligible. One must come to conceive of truth as making a hole in knowledge. Lacan is paradigmatic on this point. The subject is thus convoked as a border-effect or a delimitating fragment of such a hole-piercing" (OS 25). If a truth performs a cut into a situation where it appears, it is because "it is the metonymy of the situation's very being" (OS 26). For Badiou, each thing appears as one according to a given criterion of the count, but, as such, is infinitely multiple, is a pure multiple of multiplicity, with no original element. For instance, a certain group of persons can be considered as *one* family, *three* persons, *two* national categories, *dozens* of organs, and so on, but as such, it is a pure, infinite multiplicity that appears as one or several unities, according to a given criterion. A truth is therefore the exposition of two things: on the one side the fact that each element of the situation, as such, is "nothing", it is a pure multiple of multiples void of atomic elements, and on the other that, therefore, the consistent manner in which the elements of the situation are presented, structured, hierarchized is not a necessary reality, but a *contingent* construction. To this extent, the archetypical example of truth is for Badiou that "every one (being a pure multiple) is equal to anyone else, and each one counts as one". Such a statement appears in a given state of facts as a violent cut that breaks the evidence of the structure that attributes a different value to different individuals according to determinate properties (money, culture, social role, nationality etc.) that each one possesses in a different measure. The declaration of equality of each one is therefore the removal of the pretended naturality of such categories, and it is based on the exposition of the indifferent ontological nature of each element of the situation (it is based on the fact that there is no original essence of each thing whereby one might attribute different values to different things, but on the contrary each thing is no-thing specific, is a pure multiple, counted as one): this is why a truth is properly empty of specific content, is purely formal, and is universal. Furthermore, exceeding the current mode of organization of the objects of a situation, a truth cannot appear as a normal part of the situation, but only as a dramatic rupture with the latter.

Therefore, appearing as a radical break of the objective order of a situation, a truth appears as "always new" and it has "a subjective essence" (TS 121, trans. mod.). And conversely, a subject is "the local or finite status of a truth" (OS 25); it is a finite, closed configuration, embodied in a situation, and exposing a truth in excess over the current logic of organization of the situation (for instance, the unequal mode in which each one appears in it). Dependent on a truth that appears as an evental, radical novelty in the situation, a "subject is a forced exception, always coming in the second place" (TS 84, trans. mod.). In fact, set between an event, of which it unfolds the consequences locally, and a truth, a subject is the local, finite form of the consequences of such a truth. The subject, suspended between an event and a truth, is the point at which, on the one hand, the empty, universal truth, carried by the event, is verified and, on the other, is the point through which the event of the appearance of this truth is retrospectively made true, by the unfolding of its consequences.

In this position, the subject is such as long as it carries on the consequences of this caesura, as long as it applies it to the situation. In fact, given that the event *appears* as a de-cision made in the situation, which affirms a truth in contrast with the mode of circulation of knowledge in the situation, it follows that, from the standpoint of the subject internal to the situation, "there are no criteria for deciding whether or not the event is: a pure anomaly; an accident arising from another situation; or a strange product of the situation itself" (Feltham 2008: 101).[1] Therefore the appearance of a truth not only requires a first, evental moment of de-cision, but requires also an infinity of embodiments, an infinity of new acts or enquiries that de-cide (with no proofs) that each point of the situation can be subtracted from the current mode of knowledge, and understood according to the appearance of the truth. Each one of these new acts or enquiries or even "operators of disconnection", which decides again and again about the fact that a truth has started to appear eventally and that therefore such an event really happened, is exactly what we call "subject". In this way, the subjective acts determine the destruction of the encyclopaedic legality of the situation, and this is why "the subject is located at the crossing point of a lack-to-be and of a destruction" (TS 139, trans. mod.).

Further, what a subject exposes is the *equal capacity of each element* of the situation to dismantle the system of evidence upon which the mode of organization of the situation relies: therefore what is proper to the "subject", acting under condition of an event, is the "power of being in excess of the law, of collapsing established differences" (SP 78). The subject is exactly what, at each moment, performs a de-cision, which is the application to a specific contest, to a specific point, of the decision that what happened was not a fact among others, but the real evental appearance of a truth that has produced a de-cision in the consistency of the situation.

A subject is therefore identified by an act of decision that realizes (makes become real) the truth embedded in an event, the *empty* truth that is exactly what makes of the event not a fact among others but a radical caesura. Being not a fact or an element, but a vanishing moment of radical cut in the solid edifice of a situation, an event cannot be judged according to the same criteria by which the state evaluates its objects. One can even say that, from the perspective of the situation, the event does not exist. In fact, as Badiou stresses, revolutionary events are often considered by the state to be mere revolts fully explainable by this or that problem (wages, conditions etc.) that needs to be solved; on the contrary, the event that exposes a truth can become true only retrospectively and progressively (in anticipation) if there is some local configuration – some subject – that acts under the imperative of the decision to assert that what took place has really been an event, and that therefore its truth has to be realized in each single point of the situation.

Although depending on the inconsistent nature of an event, a subject is therefore always specifically located in the contingency of the situation: in this sense, "the subject ... is material" (TS 243, trans. mod.). It is a sequence of actions that cannot be separated from the specific points of the situation on which it acts, and from the specific instruments that enable it to act on them. For instance, a political *subject decides again and again about the truth of an event (a revolution whose immanent declaration concerns the equality of all, thus denying the "natural" division of classes)*, by disconnecting a specific, anonymous and generic part of the situation from its unequal mode of representation. In such acts of disconnection the subject unfolds the consequences of the declarative affirmation that what happened (revolution etc.) was an event. All such disconnections are therefore positive acts in the construction of a new generic sequence, in which the truth opened by the event is realized, embodied, rendered "true" by its inscription in the situation.

Fidelity

At the same time, although rooted in the specificity of the situation, the decision that the subject takes (and is instituted by) depends on something that cannot be "measured" according to the situation (and that is even declared not to exist). The decision necessarily decides on an undecidable: this is why each such action, "if it is a decision" concerning the reality of the event, at the same time "remains undecidable itself" (BE 207). Always relying on a necessary undecidability, such acts that inscribe a truth in specific new points of a situation demand – as Badiou states in *Being and Event* and in *Saint Paul* – *fidelity*, which is the necessary correlate of the impossibility to prove that they are well founded. Being faithful to an event of the truth of which it has no proof, but being rooted at the same time in the specificity of a situation, the subject acts via a series of faithful decisions with which it incorporates the event in the situation, but each of these decisions "is always particular". Therefore "there is no general faithful disposition" (BE 233): fidelity is the specific mode of the rootedness of a de-cision.

To this extent, the faithful action of a subject consists, first, in discerning those elements that are more disconnected from the particular, actual mode of representation and organization of the situation; those elements that, for contingent reasons, are more *singular* – those that, instead of being defined by some essential *particularity* that makes them belong to one or another subset, have on the contrary some aspects that cannot be taken into account by the situation. Second, to *decide* that an element is in excess over the situation means also to de-*cide* it, to *disconnect* it, from the law of the situation, and to connect it to the event that proclaims the contingency of the actual laws of organization of the elements. We see again that the subject is *defined* as "that which decides an undecidable" (BE 407): at each moment, the subject *takes a decision* without the knowledge to do so, and *disconnects* a point from the current mode of organization of the elements of the situation.

This mode of faithful, subjective action is not only a procedure of disconnection, but it also produces a new consistency. In fact, claiming the truth of an event, an act of fidelity decides that, one by one, each point of the situation can be (re)organized starting from the affirmation of the truth embedded in the event. This is why "there is always something institutional in a fidelity" (BE 233): because it *institutes* in the situation a constantly growing, *consistent* portion of it that is disconnected from its present state, for instance the contingent mode of self-organization of all the elements of the situation that, for different reasons, and according to processes that are absolutely singular, declare themselves equals, rejecting at the same time their affiliation to the logic that maintains their unequal positions. Via such operations, "fidelity organizes, within the situation, another legitimacy" (BE 238); it creates a different consistency, or rather a proper space. In this space, fidelity disconnects *and* reconnects elements, but it does not reconnect them according to a new – supposedly more "advanced" – particular criterion. Such new space, far from being a new state of facts that would substitute for the old one, is on the contrary the proper mode of actual organization of the infinite action of dismantling the tendency of the present to re-produce its specific modes of relations between elements. The problem of a revolution, one might say, is not to organize a new, less unequal, state, but to organize the connection between all the elements of the situation such that their equal capacity to disconnect themselves from the present state, whose means of representation foreclose this very capacity, is recognized as such and forms the very basis of the new situation.

Unlike a "normal" part of a situation, which is always limited by some specific characters (only one part of a situation is made by the rich, or by those who have citizenship etc.), the part of the elements connected to an event by a faithful procedure is virtually infinite, because it does not rely on some positive characters that an element would be required to have (by the logic of the encyclopaedia) in order to be counted as part of it: the only characteristic required is an intrinsic one, the equal capacity of each element to perform – under condition of an event and the faithful operator of connection – a disconnection from the actual mode of representation and classification and, as such, to count each element independently of the value attributed to it by the state of the situation. In this process, "fidelity is conjointly defined by a situation ... by the event ..., and by a rule of connection which allows one to evaluate the dependency of *any* particular multiple with respect to the event" (BE 234).

In order to create such a specific space of disconnection, a subject needs to have a body provided with efficient parts and able to operate on the situation: it needs an *organized* body. If "the subject, which is a situated and local configuration ... is the incorporation of the event into the situation" (OS 28), the body (this is a point recently stressed by Badiou in LW) is the specific and necessary instrument of this incorporation: "a body is really nothing but that which, bearing a subjective form, confers upon a truth, in a world, the phenomenal status of its objectivity" (LW 36).[2] This is why the body is not a thing among others, but "this very singular type of object suited to serve as a support for a subjective formalism, and therefore to constitute, in a world, the agent of a possible truth" (LW 451). Such a body "is efficacious to the extent that it is capable of treating some points of the world, those occurrences of the real that summon us to the abruptness of a decision" (*ibid.*); in other words it is efficacious to the extent that it is able to organize the incorporation of an event by deciding which points of the situation, in a given moment, can be disconnected from the mode of organization of the situation, and connected with the event. A subject, in this operation, literally *organizes* itself: it provides itself with organs, with efficient parts, that are able to act in such or such other contingent situation. Against Deleuze, the subject is therefore provided with a "body with organs". And an organ is therefore organized upon two criteria: "its ideal subordination to the trace" of an event, and its "efficacy", which is proved "locally, point by point" (LW 470).[3]

The faithful subject is thus on the one hand a *formalism*, and on the other hand a *body*: it is a formalism because it is not an original entity, but a structural result of the intervention of an evental truth; and it is a body because the truth ex-ists only inasmuch as there is a part of the situation that is provided with the tools adapted to act in the situation, to disconnect and reconnect all the elements of it, to decide on each point.

Universality

A subject is the finite and organized fragment of the exposition of a truth that is universal, that is indifferently addressed to each element of the situation. As such, the subject, although rare, is never isolated: it is under condition both of a situation and of an event, and more specifically it participates in a specific and *finite* sequence of unfolding the consequences of an event. At the same time it is *contingently* finite; it is *essentially* infinite: first of all, the truth of which it is an incorporation is empty, purely formal; it has no specific content, and is therefore eternal; and, second, the event that it carries is addressed to all the elements of the situation, which are by definition infinite. The subjective sequence of inscription of a truth and the subjects that performs it are therefore finite, but their finitude is not intrinsic, always dependent on external, contingent reasons.

It is for these reasons that the procedure of which the subject is a fragment is defined by Badiou as "generic": this term refers to the procedure, purely formal, disjunctive, de-cisive, and not bounded to specific contents, that is applicable to each element of the situation, independently of their particular, positive characters. Therefore the subject that effectuates this procedure, that generically shows the equal, inconsistent composition of each element, is defined as a "local configuration of a generic procedure from which a truth is supported" (BE 391). In this process, the subject demonstrates that "no event can be the event of a particularity" and that "the universal is the only possible correlate to the event" (SP 75).

Thus "every subject, ultimately, is ordained to equality" (BE 409) and to universality, by the very generic procedure that poses at each moment a new de-cision from the particular modes of representation that assign to each element an unequal status. But the generic procedure, which has a universal *address*, is based on the removal of particularities, of the particular mode of division of elements in unequal categories, and not on the removal of singularities. On the contrary, the affirmation of singularities is central: and this because equality itself is based on singularity, that is on the equal capacity of every point to be *singularly* in excess over the laws of the present state, and to realize such excess via a *new* disqualification of the given differences. A subject thus "can bring to bear a disqualification, but never a de-singularisation" (BE 409): supporting a generic procedure, it "forces decision, disqualifies the unequal, and saves the singular" (*ibid.*).

The subject appears under condition of a radical, evental *de-cision* that cuts into the consistency of the mode of organization of the present; it appears, then, embodying in the specificity of the situation, via a series of *faithful acts of decision*, the consequences of an evental rupture; and finally it appears as the point via which is performed a universal address of the consequences of this rupture (it appears as a moment of a *generic procedure*). By the relation of these three modes (decision, faithfulness, genericity), the subject manifests itself as an always *singular* moment, radically subtracted from the ordering of objects, although objectively embedded in the specificity of the situation to which it belongs; and it appears as the moment in which the question of *the universal* appears as an excess over the contingent determinations of the present. It is exactly as a critical articulation of the singular and the universal that Badiou's concept of the subject has a radical influence on contemporary philosophy, because it is in this articulation that philosophy not only thinks its contemporaneity, but thinks it at once *under condition of*, and *towards*, the radical, subjective transformations of this same present.

Notes

1. The fact is that "if one investigates the elements of an event, one finds it contains all of the elements of the evental site, but it also contains itself, its own name" (Feltham 2008: 100).
2. While *Being and Event* focuses on the formal definition of what a subject is, *Logics of Worlds* provides the analysis of the formal modes in which a subject acts in the specificity of a given situation. To this extent it even provides a classification of different subjective figures, and an analytic of the modes of constitution of an efficient body adapted to disconnect one by one each point of the situation from the mode of organization of the latter.
3. We cannot therefore know in advance how many organs a subject will have. It depends from its capacity to face different concrete situations, and to construct a coherent continuity of actions out of it. I owe this remark to Frank Ruda.

FIVE

Ontology

Alex Ling

Mathematization alone reaches a real.   (Lacan 1998: 131)

Fundamental to Badiou's later philosophy is his declaration in *Being and Event* that "mathematics is ontology". Everything that follows from this assertion – from the structure of situations and their states all the way to events and the subjects and truths they can engender – must be understood as the carefully drawn-out consequences of this properly philosophical decision.[1] One could even argue – such is the rigour with which Badiou constructs *Being and Event* – that those who reject Badiou's core philosophy do so foremost because they reject his initial thesis on the equivalence of mathematics and ontology. For if this thesis is unfounded, so too is Badiou's entire philosophy. Conversely, in accepting the equivalence of mathematics and ontology it is hard to avoid its manifold ramifications, meticulously laid out in *Being and Event* and subsequent works.

That ontology – which, since Aristotle, designates the science of being *qua* being – *is* mathematics in no way means that being is mathematical. Mathematics rather figures the *discourse* on being. Or again, "mathematics, throughout the entirety of its historical becoming, pronounces what is expressible of being qua being" (BE 2). It is for this reason that Badiou holds philosophy proper to begin with the Greeks, "because it is there that ontology established, with the first *deductive mathematics*, the necessary form of its discourse" (BE 10). It is however only today – which is to say, after Cantor's invention of set theory and its subsequent axiomatization by Zermelo, Fraenkel and others – that we can truly know this (TO 40–41).[2] Philosophy's "mathematical" foundation is moreover a vexed affair, for the immediate upshot of the equation of mathematics and ontology is that philosophy finds itself primitively split from what had formerly been considered its privileged discourse, in so far as philosophy can only speak "metaontologically": whereas philosophy only offers second-order considerations on the nature of being, mathematics, in its pure intelligibility as much as its apodicticity, is the practice of directly inscribing pure multiplicity, which, for Badiou, is what being *is*. It is in this precise sense that mathematics *is* ontology, because it – and it alone – "makes truth out of the pure multiple" (HI 22).

Ontology of the multiple

The opening gesture of *Being and Event* literally turns the history of ontology – which, from Parmenides on, holds that what *is* is one and what is *there* (or is presented) is multiple – on its head. Considering the famous theses on the one and the multiple in the *Parmenides*, Badiou, in a philosophical *tour de force*, argues that the true Platonic assertion is not "if the one is not, nothing is", but rather "if the one is not, (the) nothing is" (BE 36).[3] At base this means that, if there is no ultimate consistency or unity to being ("if the one *is not*") – this being for Badiou the necessary precondition for any truly non-theological ontology[4] – then being must be that which "in-consists" ("the nothing *is*"). In fact, this is the very kernel of Badiou's "subtractive" ontology: that which is one (or is "consistent") is not, strictly speaking, what *is*. Rather, what *is per se* is multiple (devoid of any instance of the one, radically withdrawn from all possible unification). Which is finally to say that being, thought in its very being (the "being-ness" of being, or being *qua* being), is nothing other than inconsistent multiplicity. This is why Badiou holds that ontology is the science of the *pure multiple*.[5]

While the one is not, there is nevertheless an "effect" of one-ness, which is necessarily posterior to the pure multiple. The fundamentality of this point cannot be overlooked: pure multiplicity is for Badiou anterior to the one; inconsistency precedes consistency.[6] Now, in so far as that which is consistent is clearly one and the same as that which is presented of being, we must conclude that the retroactive "one-ification" of pure multiplicity (or the rendering consistent of inconsistency) is nothing other than the *presentation* of multiplicity as such. Indeed, this fact would appear self-evident given that in everyday life what is presented or brought to experience is in one way or another unified: simply, our experiences are of the one, and in no way of the "multiple-without-one". Such unified presentation constitutes what Badiou calls a *situation*. A situation is thus any presented multiplicity whatsoever. Or again, a situation is the constitution of inconsistent multiplicity: it is literally "the place of taking-place" (BE 24). If the latter is then to have any relation to the place of presentation, it can only be as the "taking-place" anterior to the place itself, that is, the presentation *of* presentation itself (or presentation "in-itself"): pure presentation prior to the structured presentation that is the situation.

As structured presentation, a situation can be anything whatsoever: a July business meeting, Eastern Europe, ontology, several platypuses, a political demonstration, an atom. This concurrently implies that the one and the multiple can quite happily be at the same time both different and the same. Simply, any situation (any presented multiple) admits sub-situations, as much as any situation is itself a sub-situation of another situation (ad infinitum).

Badiou terms the operation by which pure multiplicity is "one-ified" (or "situated") the *count* (or "count-as-one"). The count constitutes the structure of the situation and operates by determining certain elements (multiples) as belonging to the situation. To this effect the situation itself is indistinguishable from the count. The crucial ontological distinction is then found at the level of the situation's being: the pure being of the situation – the "before of the count" – remains beyond the situation itself, inasmuch as its being is uncounted multiplicity. Or to put it another way, the being of consistency is inconsistency. The paradox here is fundamental: the inconsistent being underlying all consistency is itself radically unknowable (inasmuch as all knowledge is necessarily "situated") and to this effect any consideration of what precedes the situation is itself hopelessly compromised by its very situatedness. Inconsistency is therefore the real of presentation, the precise point at which thought butts against its own limit. Which is why Badiou's initial embrace of the multiple (and concurrent assertion that "the one *is not*") is a *pure* decision: the actual status of inconsistent multiplicity is itself properly undecidable. Moreover, this is precisely why Badiou's is a subtractive ontology: in the face of a classical metaphysics defined as an "enframing of being by the one", Badiou decides that ontology can be nothing other than the theory of indifferent, inconsistent multiplicity, radically subtracted from the power of the one (TO 34).

In formulating his ontology, Badiou must still account for the seemingly irreducible and apparently illogical gap between the (known) consistent multiple and its (radically unknown) inconsistent being. Thus we return to his Platonic reformulation of the Parmenidean thesis "if the one is not, (the) nothing is". We must take his words literally here:

Badiou really is asserting that the nothing *is*. This "nothing" is as crucial as it is complex. Inasmuch as the situation and the count are one and the same thing, it is clear that the "inconsistent underside" of a situation is itself fundamentally ungraspable. However, the count itself, being an operation, clearly indicates its status as *result*, thereby necessitating a corollary "must-be-counted" – an uncounted remainder – and it is precisely this before-of-the-count that, in Badiou's words, causes the situation to "waver towards the phantom of inconsistency" (BE 53). Given the seemingly self-contradictory fact that, while everything is counted, the count itself necessitates a "phantom remainder" (namely, the initial "pure" multiple), we must conclude that the pure multiple is simultaneously *excluded* (or subtracted) from the situation – from presentation itself – and at the same time *included* in "the name of what 'would be' the presentation itself, the presentation 'in-itself'" (BE 53). Excluded from presentation itself, included in presentation in-itself, the pure multiple must really be *nothing* in the situation.

However, as Badiou at once points out, being-nothing is not at all the same thing as non-being. Indeed, this nothing subsists within the situation in two immediate guises: in the very operation of the count (which, in its "pure transparency", itself goes uncounted); and in the pure multiple upon which the count operates (which, as we have seen, differs in-itself from its situational result). Thus the nothing, or, to give it a more constructive name, the *void*, ultimately designates the gap between the situation (consistency, presentation itself) and its underlying being (inconsistency, presentation in-itself). To this effect Badiou defines the void as the precise point at which the situation is sutured to its being and asserts that "every structured presentation unpresents 'its' void, in the mode of this non-one which is merely the subtractive face of the count" (BE 55). The pure multiple (*qua* being) thus "in-consists" as the situational void, as the void *in situ*. This in-consistency is, however, absolutely fundamental, in so far as the law of structured presentation is that of the errancy of the void, just as much as its normal regime is "an absolute 'unconscious' of the void" (BE 56). Two immediate and important theses follow from this proposition: first, that, according to the situation, the void is the proper name of being; and, second, that everything that *is* is woven from the void.

Mathematics is ontology

Badiou's position on the multiple leads him to conclude that mathematics is ontology. After all, his two major ontological doctrines – that the science of being *qua* being (ontology) can only be the theory of pure or inconsistent multiplicity, and that all that *is* is woven from the void – are precisely what mathematics – or more precisely, axiomatic or Zermelo–Fraenkel set theory (ZFC) – thinks. Indeed, everything we have examined thus far on the side of both inconsistency (pure multiplicity, presentation in-itself, operation of the count) and consistency ("impure" multiplicity, presentation itself, counted situation), as well as that which bleeds between the two (the void), finds an immediate correlate in axiomatic set theory. For example, a situation (*qua* consistent multiple) is literally a set, inasmuch as a set is ultimately nothing other than "a plurality thought as a unit" (Hausdorff 1962: 11). Moreover, ZFC admits of only one relation, belonging ($\in$), which alone dictates what composes (or one-ifies) a set, meaning the set itself (*qua* multiple) possesses no "unary predicate", no essence other than its being-a-multiple.[7] So too set theory, through the axiom of the empty set, premises existence itself on the void, that is, on the empty or memberless set, on the set to which no elements belong (written $\emptyset$). Thus, rather than affirming a "first" multiple from which all other multiples are derived (and thereby illegally smuggling the one back into being at the level of the multiple) or designating origination at the point of the multiple-counted-as-one (thus overlooking the count's status as result), set theory contrarily substantializes the very "nothing" affecting the purity of the multiple; that is, it literally makes this nothing *be* through the assumption of a proper name (the void, $\emptyset$).

Of ZFC's nine axioms, one is of especial concern here.[8] This is the axiom of the power set, which tells us that if there exists a set χ, then there also exists a set of all the subsets of χ. For example, if we call χ the set $\{\alpha, \beta, \gamma\}$, then the power set of χ – noted $p(\chi)$ – establishes the patently larger set $\{\alpha, \beta, \gamma, \{\alpha, \beta\}, \{\alpha, \gamma\}, \{\beta, \gamma\}, \{\alpha, \beta, \gamma\}, \{\emptyset\}\}$ (note the void is *included* in every set). The number of subsets of a given set can be easily measured by the formula 2^n, where n is the number of elements in the initial set (for example, in the above case of an initial set with three elements we have 2^3 or 8). Thus 2^n measures the *size* (or cardinality) of the power set. This axiom further illustrates a fundamental ontological distinction between belonging ($\in$) and inclusion ($\subset$). For example, each of the elements of our set χ (that is, α, β and γ) clearly belongs to (or is presented in) χ. However, as we have seen, the elements of the set χ also form subsets – namely α, β, γ, $\{\alpha, \beta\}$, $\{\alpha, \gamma\}$, $\{\beta, \gamma\}$, $\{\alpha, \beta, \gamma\}$, $\{\emptyset\}$ – subsets that *include* the initial set χ. The fundamentality of the power-set axiom lies in its providing the schema for the protective mechanism or "riposte to the void" that is the "count of the count" (BE 98). For while existence itself owes all that it *is* to

the void, the latter's errancy necessarily threatens the fabric of structured presentation. Thus the situation must "prohibit that catastrophe
of presentation which would be its encounter with its own void" (BE
93). To avert this "ruin of the one", every situation (with the notable
exception of ontology itself) necessarily subjects itself to a structural
"recount", establishing a *metastructure* whose principle is essentially
that of the power set. Indeed, as we saw above, the void insists within
the situation by virtue of its own structuring principle, inasmuch as,
in its "operational transparency", the count itself fails to be counted,
which means the recount literally involves "counting the count", being
the (successional) count by which the (voided) count is itself counted.
The recount thus "secures" the situation against the void's emergence
in the "vanishing point of consistent multiplicity" that is the very operation of the count, thereby nullifying the gap between inconsistent and
consistent multiplicity (BE 94). This double structuring – ensuring that
there is both presentation and *re*-presentation – by which the structure
of a situation is itself counted as one is what Badiou calls, "due to a
metaphorical affinity with politics", the *state of the situation* (BE 95).[9]
Moreover, it is in this precise sense that Badiou can say that in our
world "what counts – in the sense of what is valued – is that which is
counted" (NN 2).

Things get rather complicated when the situation in question is
infinite. And the fact of the matter is that virtually every situation is
infinite.[10] Certainly, when dealing with finite quantities the domination of the state over the situation is readily calculable (we simply
have to follow the rule 2^n). However, this is not the case when dealing
with infinite quantifications. Key to Badiou's philosophy is his theory
of statist (or representative) domination, whereby the state is seen to
enjoy an *indeterminate* excess over the situation. Suffice to say that
the indeterminate nature of this quantitative excess results from Easton's theorem, which effectively tells us that in order to designate the
value of $p(\chi)$, where χ is an infinite cardinal, it is entirely consistent to
simply choose *any* superior successor cardinal of χ. The ramifications
of such infinite errancy on the relation of the situation to its state
are immediate: in Badiou's words, "however exact the quantitative
knowledge of a situation may be, one cannot, other than by an arbitrary decision, estimate by 'how much' its state exceeds it" (BE 278).
Herein lies the *impasse of ontology*: given an infinite (albeit measur-
able) situation, we cannot know – we can but *decide* – the size of its
state. Between structure and metastructure "a chasm opens, whose
filling in depends solely upon a conceptless choice" (BE 280). This
means in turn that the state – whose very function is that of excising

the void – ultimately serves to facilitate the void's re-emergence at the juncture between itself and the situation over which it presides. Fundamental to Badiou's philosophy is his contention that this ontological impasse "cannot be seized or thought in immanence to ontology itself, nor to speculative metaontology", but rather can be overcome only through recourse to an extra-mathematical anomaly *qua event* (BE 284).

Beyond being

Badiou's axiomatic equation of ontology with mathematics is equally crucial to his more "radical" concepts of the event, the subject and truth. Truth, for example, far from being an adequation or a revelation, designates for Badiou an infinite generic set. That a truth is generic means that it is absolutely a-particular or "indiscernible" with regard to the situation of which it is a subset, being composed entirely of terms that themselves "avoid" every property formulable in the language of the situation. While strictly speaking mathematics has nothing to say about the production of a truth, it nevertheless – through recourse to the work of the mathematician Paul Cohen – delineates its ontological *form*. Indeed, it is Cohen's concept of the generic set that tells us that the being of a truth is ultimately situated in that space opened up by the impasse of ontology. Moreover, Cohen's mathematics shows us how the universality of a truth *qua* infinite generic set resides in the fact that it "has no other 'property' than that of referring to *belonging*" (BE 339). As this property – which is nothing short of *being*, pure and simple – is obviously shared by each and every term of the situation, the generic subset solely possesses the properties of *any set whatsoever*. So too is Badiou's conception of the subject mathematically prescribed. Originating in an extra-ontological event, the generic subset (*qua* truth) does not belong to the situation, and at the same time remains "subtracted" from knowledge (by virtue of its genericity). Thus, in order to be presented, its belonging must first be decided, then *forced* upon the situation, thereby establishing a new situation in which it will be discernible (which is to say "knowable"). Such forcing – the mathematics of which is, once again, provided by Cohen – constitutes "the fundamental law of the subject" (BE 401).

As an "extra-ontological" phenomenon, the event – on which truth and the subject equally depend – presents an altogether different case. In his "transitional" work (bridging *Being and Event* and *Logics of Worlds*) Badiou explains how:

if real ontology is set up as mathematics by evading the norm of
the One, unless this norm is reestablished globally there also ought
to be a point wherein the ontological, hence mathematical field,
is de-totalized or remains at a dead end. I have named this point
the *"event"*.   (TO 60)[11]

Crucial here is the fact that mathematics (ontology) can think the
event only to the extent that it can think its own real *qua* impasse. In
other words, mathematics conceives the event only inasmuch as it axi-
omatizes its own aporetic structure (as we see for example in Gödel's
incompleteness theorems and the work of Easton and Cohen). The
upshot of this ontological detotalization is that, while mathematics
would appear to be able to say nothing of an event's constitution (save
in mathematically illegal formulae), it nonetheless allows a *space* for the
event to, as it were, *be* (a space that lies precisely in its aporias). Indeed,
ontology ensures such an evental space as a rule. We need understand
"space" here in two ways: as an opening *for* an event (not its certitude,
but its possibility, which, strictly speaking, lies in the impossibilities
proper to mathematics/ontology); and as the opening *of* an event, in
the sense of its material ground (what Badiou designates its *site*).

In *Being and Event* a site presents a radically singular multiple, namely,
a multiple such that *none* of its elements is situationally presented: while
the site itself is presented (but not re-presented), the same cannot be said
for any of its elements (all those elements huddled "beneath" the site).
Such a multiple is said to lie "on the edge of the void", inasmuch as,
from the situation's perspective, the site is constituted solely of unpresented multiples (or again, beneath the site there is, for all intents and
purposes, *nothing*). Being a consistent multiple composed exclusively
of that which in-consists (its unpresented or "void" multiples), a site
figures as the minimal effect of structure conceivable and as such is said
to be *foundational*: incapable of resulting from any internal reshuffling
on the part of the situation, the site requires for its existence only the
minimal effect of the count.[12] Simply, the site *founds* the situation of
which it is a term. It is crucial to understand that – at least in *Being
and Event* – there is nothing whatsoever mysterious about the site. To
the contrary, the site is, in effect, the logical consequence of the axiom
of foundation, which tells us that every multiple harbours at least one
element that presents nothing that the initial multiple presents (thereby
prohibiting a set's belonging to itself).[13] As foundational multiples,
sites, which constitute the very material of the event, are fundamental
to the structure of all multiplicity: simply, every multiple is ultimately
founded, and every foundation constitutes a site.

While foundation is a law of being, the event proper eludes mathematical thought as "that-which-is-not-being" because it involves the temporary caesura of these very same laws. Passing over the subtle differences between the structure of the event in *Being and Event* (where the event convokes but never coincides with its site) and *Logics of Worlds* (where the event is effectively considered as a site *in extremis*), we shall simply state that the event's being ontologically "illegal" results from its constituting a reflexive (or auto-belonging) multiplicity – namely, a multiple such that $\alpha \in \alpha$ – thereby rupturing with the axiom of foundation. To this effect the event – whose thought is conditioned by art but whose path is paved by the aporias proper to mathematics[14] – involves an ontological dilemma, inasmuch as it entails the sudden and inexplicable complication of an ontologically prescribed foundation (the site) and an ontologically proscribed anomaly (reflexivity), both of which directly result from the axiom of foundation. Yet such anomalies are precisely what ontology, in its necessary detotalization (or in its axiomatizing of its own real), at once precludes and makes space for. Indeed, in the final meditations of *Being and Event* Badiou relies heavily on one such aporia – namely, that of the undecidability of the measure of statist excess (*qua* impasse of being) – to at once formulate his concepts of the subject and truth and demonstrate how its proof "reproduces within mathematical ontology itself the chance of the generic procedure" (BE 429).

Badiou contends that any philosophy worthy of its name must first come to grips with the ontological question. His own answer is to equate ontology with mathematics – an equation that must be taken seriously if his work is to have any real significance. This gesture founds his philosophy while simultaneously cleaving it from its foundation. In drawing out the manifold consequences of his declaration that "mathematics *is* ontology", Badiou is able to unfold a complex and articulate theory of not only what *is*, but also of what *is not*, as well as what can be.

Notes

1. While Badiou's recent *Logics of Worlds* complements the equation of mathematics and ontology with the parallel claim that "logic is appearing", this later work effectively leaves his ontology untouched. We should also keep in mind that the "logic" Badiou is concerned with is ontologically or mathematically prescribed (as opposed to the ordinary formal or linguistic logic so dear to analytic philosophy).
2. According to Badiou, "with Cantor we move from 'special ontology', which still

links the multiple to the metaphysical theme of representing objects, numbers and figures, to 'general ontology', which sets the free, thoughtful apprehending of multiplicity as such as the basis and destination of mathematics. It forever ceases to constrain the thinkable to the special dimension of 'object'."

3. Cf. Plato, *Parmenides* 166c. Briefly, Badiou's argument rests on a variation in Plato's terminology that shifts between two "kinds" of multiplicity, namely, πληθος (*plethos*) and πολλα (*polla*). Badiou holds the former as designating pure or "inconsistent" multiplicity (or the "multiple-without-one") while the latter figures consistent (or "one-ified") multiplicity. That Plato cannot substantialize these differences – instead resorting to the metaphor of a dream – is for Badiou simply indicative of his pre-Cantorian situation: simply, inconsistent multiplicity is properly unthinkable before set theory allowed us to truly grasp "a multiple disseminated without limits" (BE 36).

4. Badiou holds that any ontology of the one must be theological. Consequently, if God is dead, the central task of philosophy must be that of grasping "an *immanent* conceptualization of the multiple" (D 4).

5. As Badiou puts it elsewhere, "ontology, if it exists, must be the theory of inconsistent multiplicities as such. Meaning that what lends itself to ontological thought is the multiple without any predicate other than its own multiplicity. Without any concept other than itself, with nothing to guarantee its consistency" (TO 36; trans. mod.).

6. We must keep in mind that for Badiou the multiple that ontology grasps is the multiple "reduced without any immanent unification to the sole predicate of its multiplicity" (TO 40). Such a multiple's being radically without-one demands that it consist solely of multiples; it is a multiple of multiples. As this multiple of multiples cannot be subject to any principle of finitude, its multiple multiplicities must themselves be infinitely disseminated. As unpredictable, in-finite multiple of multiples, it is clear that the one is radically foreclosed from being *qua* being.

7. In set theory, "what is counted as *one* is not the concept of the multiple; there is no inscribable thought of what *one*-multiple is. The one is assigned to ∈ alone; that is, to the operator of denotation for the relation between the 'something' in general and the multiple" (BE 44).

8. ZFC's axioms are those of extensionality, power set, union, empty set (or void), replacement, infinity, foundation, separation and choice. A more extensive consideration of Badiou's conception of ontology would necessarily involve an investigation of each and every axiom, something that is impossible here.

9. To this effect Badiou demonstrates (*pace* Rousseau) that "the State is not founded upon the social bond, which it would express, but rather upon un-binding, which it prohibits", and accordingly (*pace* Marx) "one must not lose sight of the fact that the State as such ... cannot be so easily attacked or destroyed ... because even if the route of political change ... is always bordered by the State, it cannot in any way let itself be guided by the latter, for the State is precisely non-political, insofar as it cannot change, save hands" (BE 109–10).

10. In fact, by Badiou's logic, "every situation is ontologically infinite" (M 143). This ontological in-finitude is a necessary consequence of his decision that the one is not, for, as Badiou demonstrates, "given that no immanent limit anchored in the one determines multiplicity as such, there is no originary principle of finitude. The multiple can therefore be thought of as in-finite. Or even, infinity is another name for multiplicity as such" (TO 45, trans. mod.).

11. Badiou continues: "While philosophy is all about identifying what real ontology is in an endlessly reviewed process, it is also the general theory of the event – and

it is no doubt the special theory too. In other words, it is the theory of what is subtracted from ontological subtraction. Philosophy is the theory of what is strictly impossible for mathematics" (TO 60).

12. As Badiou puts it, the site constitutes "a primal-one of the situation; a multiple 'admitted' into the count without having to result from 'previous' counts. It is in this sense that one can say that in regard to structure, it is an undecomposable term" (BE 175).

13. Elsewhere Badiou provides an example of a cat to explain such foundation: "[a cat] is an element of the set of living beings, and it is composed of cells that are in turn elements of this set, if one grants that they are living organisms. But if we decompose a cell into molecules, then into atoms, we eventually reach purely physical elements that do not belong to the set of living beings. There is a certain term (perhaps the cell, in fact) which belongs to the set of living beings, but none of whose elements belongs to the set of living beings, because those elements all involve only 'inert' physico-chemical materiality. Of this term, which belongs to the set but none of whose elements belong to it, we can say that it grounds the set, or that it is a fundamental term of the set. 'Fundamental' meaning that on one side of the term, we break through that which it constitutes; we leave the original set, we exceed its presentative capacity" (NN 71).

14. For Badiou, the thought of the "pure event" lies not with the scientific but rather the artistic condition, principally the poetry of Stéphane Mallarmé. Indeed, Badiou holds that it is uniquely in Mallarmé's "A Throw of the Dice" that the event *qua* event is truly thought, for in this poem "the event in question … [is] that of the production of an absolute symbol of the event", the stakes of the eponymous dice throw being precisely that of "making an event out of the thought of an event" (BE 193).

PART II

Badiou's key concepts or "conditions"

SIX

Science

Ray Brassier

Rationalism and scientism

Badiou is a rationalist: he holds that mathematics captures whatever is sayable about being *qua* being and names science (alongside art, politics and love) as one of the generators of the truths that condition philosophy. It would be difficult to overstate the extent to which this sets him apart from the main stream of post-Hegelian continental philosophy. From Kierkegaard and Nietzsche, through Heidegger and Adorno, up to Foucault and Derrida, continental philosophers have sought to radicalize Kant's critique of reason by exposing the limitations of conceptual rationality in general and of scientific reason in particular. For continental philosophers, scientific reason is congenitally deficient, whether because of its disregard for the concretely existing individual (Kierkegaard); its "religious" reverence for objective truth (Nietzsche); its persistent reduction of time to space (Bergson); its subordination to the prejudices of the natural attitude (Husserl); its inability to understand entities in any terms other than that of present-at-hand actuality (Heidegger); its blind submission to the utilitarian imperatives of instrumental rationality (Adorno and Horkheimer); or its unwitting compliance with power–knowledge complexes (Foucault). This list is by no means exhaustive; it could be expanded to include similar assertions about the debilities of science made by other influential continental philosophers such as Marcuse, Merleau-Ponty and, more recently, Michel Henry.[1]

If pressed about their overwhelmingly negative characterizations of science, continental philosophers are liable to protest that they are criticizing "scientism" rather than science itself (for which, they assure us, they harbour nothing but respect). The facility with which this distinction is routinely brandished invites suspicion. What exactly is meant by "scientism"? On the face of it, the distinction between science and "scientism" points towards the difference between an unobjectionable practice that consists in observing, experimenting and inducing law-like regularities to explain natural phenomena, and an objectionable ideology that presumes to draw broader philosophical conclusions about the nature of reality from this practice. On this account, then, science would be an ideologically innocent practice that becomes perverted into "scientism" when contaminated by the pernicious philosophical presumption that it can limn the ultimate structure of reality.

The trouble with this definition of "scientism", however, is that it ignores the way in which ideology is necessarily implicated in practice and in doing so it unwittingly indicts the scientist's own understanding of her activity. Is it not part and parcel of the scientist's own conception of her practice that her methods and procedures provide a more reliable basis for investigating reality and uncovering truths about the world than the armchair intuitions habitually brandished by metaphysicians? And is not this practice necessarily informed by the scientist's conviction that her theorizing is more credible than metaphysical speculation precisely in so far as it is constrained by standards of deductive and evidential stringency that cannot be matched by any other type of theorizing about the world? The attempt to dissociate the denunciation of scientism from the denigration of science quickly founders upon the observation that so-called "scientism" is inextricable from scientific practice. Such denunciations of "scientism", so prevalent among continental philosophers, cannot but imply an attack upon the autonomy of scientific rationality, insisting as they do that science is internally conditioned by factors that it is intrinsically incapable of comprehending (as when Bergson asserts that quantification depends upon the utilitarian conception of space or when Heidegger claims that chronological time depends upon existential temporality). These critiques mount a direct challenge to the conviction – espoused by educated non-scientists and scientists alike – that mathematized natural science is our most authoritative source of knowledge. Moreover, it is important to note that the "scientism" habitually vituperated by continental philosophers does not target just those who proclaim science to be infallible and indubitable (an indefensible claim that no scientifically literate person would maintain) but also those committed to the more modest assertion that science, although fallible, continues to provide the basic epistemological yardstick by which to measure the credibility of all other cognitive claims. Seen in this light, the distinction between science and scientism is dubious, and invoking it to absolve oneself of the charge of being anti-science is unconvincing.

The common thread running through all these critiques of scientific reason by continental philosophers is the idea that science leaves out something fundamental in its account of the world. This remainder is variously characterized depending on the philosopher in question (self-consciousness, life, being, duration, power, non-identity etc.), but what underlies all these various accounts is the claim that there is something that cannot be captured in scientific concepts and categories. In a gesture that is the exact inverse of the one carried out by those philosophers in the analytic tradition who have sought to realign philosophy with the natural sciences, continental philosophers have opted to fix upon this a-rational residue as the proper concern of philosophy while marking it as forever inaccessible to scientific reason. This leaves us facing a stark alternative: either embrace the positivistic claim that scientific discourse encompasses everything worth knowing about the world; or insist that there is something forever recalcitrant to scientific conceptualization. The choice is between a positivistic conception of immanence and an obscurantist conception of transcendence.

Badiou's rationalism allows him to refuse both horns of this dilemma. On the one hand, Badiou's mathematical ontology, indifferent as it is to the varieties of qualitative particularity – phenomenological experiential, perceptual – fetishized by those who reproach science for disregarding the "concrete richness" of experience, can easily accommodate the claim that mathematized natural science has a direct purchase upon being: "In the final analysis, physics, which is to say the theory of matter, is mathematical. It is mathematical because, as the theory of the most objectified strata of the presented as such, it necessarily catches hold of being-as-being through its mathematicity" (Badiou 1998c: 127). On the other hand, Badiou's conception of generic truth renders transcendence intelligible while ruling out any presumptive erasure of the discontinuity between nature and culture. Thus Badiou proposes a non-positivistic (anti-empiricist) conception of immanence and an anti-obscurantist (rationalist) understanding of transcendence, rooted in the post-Kantian distinction between *what is* and *what is knowable* – the distinction that Badiou recodes as the distinction between truth and knowledge. Accordingly, although Badiou shuns the kind of vulgar positivism that remains completely beholden to the authority of current science while being unable to understand or explain the discontinuities in scientific history, he also abjures every variety of anti-rationalism that would belittle the power of scientific reason while exalting the a-rational as philosophy's proper concern.

Philosophy, science, ideology

Badiou accepts the Marxist claim that science is never ideologically neutral (witness for example the recurring attempts to enlist Darwinism and complexity theory in order to legitimate competition, inequality and the free market as ineradicable natural phenomena). However, he refuses the facile inference that science is nothing but technology *plus* ideology.[2] The challenge is to recognize the imbrication of science and ideology without capitulating to the self-serving conceit whereby philosophy (or "theory") would relegate science wholly to the realm of ideology while arrogating the power of critique to itself by virtue of its allegedly privileged access to some transcendent source of truth: Spirit, Being, History etc. What distinguishes Badiou's stance towards science is its simultaneous acknowledgement of the inextricability of science and ideology together with the novel suggestion that it is science itself, rather than philosophy, that proves to be the most acute diagnostician of those ideological prejudices that hinder its development.

Badiou's most sustained account of the relation between philosophy, science and ideology occurs at the beginning of his philosophical career in four texts published between 1967 and 1969. These are "The (Re) commencement of Dialectical Materialism" (1967), "Mark and Lack: On Zero" ([1967] 1969b), "Infinitesimal Subversion" (1968), and *The Concept of Model* (1969a).[3] Badiou's account unfolds under the aegis of two fundamental distinctions:

1. The distinction between "historical materialism", understood as the Marxist *science* of history, and "dialectical materialism", understood as the latter's *philosophical* counterpart.
2. The distinction between ideological *notions*, philosophical *categories* and scientific *concepts*.

In *The Concept of Model*, Badiou describes philosophy as constituted by its parasitic relation to scientific innovation on one hand, and its subservience to dominant ideological interests on the other. Philosophy is the practice of an "impossible relation" between science and ideology (CM 50). For the most part, philosophy carries out an ideological envelopment of science: philosophical categories denote "inexistent" objects that combine concepts and notions.[4] The task of a materialist philosophy informed by the Marxist science of history (as opposed to a "philosophy of matter", which would merely concoct a spurious category called "matter" through the notional envelopment of physico-biological concepts) consists in exposing the reactionary ideologies implicit in various philosophical appropriations of scientific concepts in order to supplant them with materialist categories capable of being deployed in the service of revolutionary ideology. The proper philosophical index of "materiality" in this conjunction between historical and dialectical materialism is that of the "productivity" of a given theoretical practice. In Badiou's words: "The *reality* of the epistemological materialism which I am trying to introduce ... is indissociable from an effective practice of science" (CM 22, trans. mod.). Badiou's specific aim in *The Concept of Model* is to isolate the scientific – that is, logico-mathematical – concept of model from its notional envelopment by the categories of bourgeois epistemology – central to which is the distinction between the "formal" and the "empirical" – and to construct a philosophical category of model consonant with a materialist history of the sciences. The broader epistemological import of this project is to develop a materialist account of the nature of scientific theory that challenges both the empiricist assumption that scientific theories merely model empirical reality and the idealist claim that reality is nothing but an inert support for scientific theory. In doing so, Badiou lends a specifically Marxian twist to two ideas of Bachelard's: the idea of the "epistemological break" (rechristened "cut", *coupure*, by Althusser), and the idea that science cannot be understood in terms of a relation between representation and reality (Althusser and Bachelard are arguably the two key influences on Badiou's understanding of the relation between philosophy and science, both in this initial stage of his thought and throughout his subsequent career).

The two principal variants of the bourgeois epistemology that Badiou attacks are empiricism and idealism. Both are coordinated around the notional difference between theoretical form and empirical reality: science is deemed to be a formal representation of its object, whether the representation be characterized in terms of the effective "presence"[5] of the object, as in empiricism, or in terms of the primacy of a formal apparatus, that is, of the mathematical code through which the object is represented, as in formalism (the specific variety of idealist formalism that Badiou has in mind here is structuralism). However, the representationalist dualism of fact and form occludes the materiality of science as process of cognitive production. Science neither mirrors nor moulds an allegedly pre-existing "reality"; it is an autonomous process for which mathematics provides the primary means of production: "[U]ltimately, in physics, fundamental biology, etc., mathematics is not subordinated and expressive, but primary and *productive*" (Badiou 1967: 464). Thus mathematics is not an *a priori* formal science grounding the empirical sciences' access to reality, but rather the paradigmatic instance of a productive experimental praxis. This is the specifically materialist dimension of Badiou's Platonism. Mathematical productivity (and scientific productivity more generally) consists in "cutting" or differentiating the notational material upon which it operates: science is the production of "stratified differences". Three questions immediately arise here:

1. How does this stratification operate?
2. What does this differentiation consist in?
3. In what way is this production of "stratified differences" an index of "materiality"?

1. How does this stratification operate?

Stratification is a function of mathematical formalization. A formal mathematical system is stratified in so far as it divides and separates its own means of production, allotting distinct functions to discrete mechanisms. Badiou gives as an example the elementary mechanisms of *concatenation*, *formation* and *derivation*: a formal system must be endowed with well-defined procedures for (a) assembling symbol strings, (b) dividing these into well-formed and ill-formed statements, and (c) deriving proofs or disproofs of these statements. Formal systems vary in their degree of internal stratification; nevertheless, some minimal degree of stratification similar to that outlined above is the structural prerequisite for any formal apparatus. A formal system is a machine that takes strings of symbols as its input, subjecting these to series of differentiations at distinct levels of stratification, before finally outputting statements whose intelligibility (Badiou will have no truck with the ideologically loaded notion of "meaning") is a function of the system's internally articulated differences. Stratification is the condition for *productive* differentiation.

2. What does this differentiation consist in?

Badiou proposes a dialectical conception of scientific production comprising three moments: in the first, science *breaks away* (*coupure*) from its own philosophical self-representation; in the second, this break is *re-captured* (re-presented) by philosophy (this can occur through scientists' own philosophical interpretation of their practice); finally, in the third moment, science breaks once more with this philosophical re-presentation by *reconfiguring (refonte)* itself around new limits that it has independently established and that temporarily defeat philosophical appropriation. The first break is the point at which scientific discourse subverts its current ideological representation by producing a difference that cannot be subsumed by extant philosophical categories. Philosophy then represents this break by de-stratifying (re-categorizing) this stratified difference, thereby re-enveloping the new concepts produced by science within extant ideological notions (these will be novel philosophical categories). Lastly, the moment of reconfiguration is the moment of the second break understood as a re-stratification of what philosophy has de-stratified – a re-stratification wherein the parameters of scientific discourse are re-established independently of science's current philosophical representation. In "Mark and Lack", Badiou illustrates this dialectic with regard to the history of mathematics. He identifies seven moments punctuating the dialectic of break and recapture from Pythagoras to Gödel:

I)   The existence of a historical mathematics (namely "intuitive" arithmetic); one that is open in principle (indefinitely stratified signifier).

II *a*)   The ideological re-presentation of this existence as the trans-mathematical norm of completely controllable rationality (the ideological destratification of the mathematical signifier).

II *b*)   The posing of a question to mathematics about its conformity to this ideological norm, in the form of the axiomatic and formalist *intention*, whose goal is to display a *founded transparency* (this is the ideological motivation of Frege and Russell).

III)   Break: the mathematical treatment of this ideological re-presentation of mathematics via the actual *construction* of formal systems that "represent" historical arithmetic (*Principia Mathematica*).

IV *a*)   The ideological re-presentation of this break: formal systems conceived as trans-mathematical norms of rational closure via the *idea* of a nomological system (Husserl).

IV *b*)   The posing of a question to mathematics about its absolute conformity to the ideological norm of closure: this is the metamathematical *intention*, relative to the *internal* demonstration of a system's consistency (Hilbert).

V)   Break: the mathematical treatment of ideological re-
      presentation via the actual *construction* of a mathematical
      metamathematics (the arithmetization of syntax).
Gödel's Theorem: the structural stratification of the mathematical
signifier does not answer the "question" of closure.
VI)   Ideological re-presentation of this break: Gödel's Theorem
      is experienced as a *limitation* relative to the normative
      expectation.
      Ideological exegesis of this "limitation" as:
      – openness of speech and concealment of being (Ladrière);
      – finitude;
      – splitting, suture;
      – ...
VII) Break: the general theory of the limitation-effect, posi-
      tively conceived as a structural instance of certain math-
      ematical objects (Smullyan's epistemological truth).

The epistemological upshot of this convoluted adventure reminds
us that mathematics *operates upon its own existence such as it is
designated in ideology*; but that this operation, conforming to the
specific constraints of a science, takes the form of a *break*, such
that the (ideological) questions which make up the *material* upon
which mathematics carries out its working reprise, find *no answer*
in the latter.   (ML 172)

The dialectic between scientific production and its ideological representation is one in which science responds to the questions put to
it by philosophy by forging differences that subvert the pertinence of
the categories presupposed by those questions. Science works with its
own ideological representation (the philosophical de-stratification of
what science has stratified), with which it then breaks by deploying a
new layer of stratification (producing a difference for which no category yet exists). Ideology, understood as philosophical categorization,
is not extrinsic to science; but scientific productivity requires constantly
breaking with its own ideological self-representation.

3. In what way is this production of "stratified differences" an index of "materiality"?
But in what sense is science's production of difference "material"?
Clearly, the "materiality" of mathematical practice is not to be under-
stood as an analogue of the specious philosophical category of "matter",

whether physically, biologically, or even economically construed, but rather as an index of the scriptural production of difference. What Badiou means by "scriptural materiality" is somewhat opaque. As Zachary Luke Fraser has pointed out, the materiality Badiou has in mind here cannot be understood in terms of the substance of graphic marks, whether they consist of chalk, graphite, or ink ("Introduction", in CM xxxvi). The materiality at issue can only be understood as incorporeal. Badiou persistently reiterates the Marxian link between productivity and materiality, with the former providing the veritable index of the latter. What renders formal systems productive is their stratification, understood as the differential network through which mathematical symbols and operators are assigned a signifying function and variously combined to produce distinct statements. Thus materiality is to be conceived in terms of this formal capacity for producing intelligible differences independently of the categories of representation. Logico-mathematical inscription circumvents the metaphysical primacy of the linguistic signifier via a "stratified multiplicity" of differential traces such that "no signifying order can envelop the strata of its discourse" (ML 163). Scientific stratification subverts the representational categories of designation and reference – "Neither thing nor object have any chance here of acceding to any existence beyond their remainderless exclusion" (ML 156) – and dispenses with the need for the activity of a constituting subject: "[T]here is no subject of science. Infinitely stratified, regulating its passages, science is pure space, without inverse or mark or place of what it excludes … Science is an Outside without a blind-spot" (ML 161–2).

Here we encounter all the essential features of Badiou's Platonist materialism: scientific thought is "outside", that is beyond the enclosure of ideological representation, not because the subject of science is endowed with a faculty of intellectual intuition that would grant her intuitive access to a transcendent realm of intelligible objects, but, on the contrary, because the remorselessly mechanical "rule governed transparency" of logico-mathematical inscription results in a cognitive practice for which the categories of subject and object are completely superfluous. The non-representational character of scientific discourse is a consequence of its machinic nature, since "[a] formal system *is* a mathematical machine, a machine for mathematical production, positioned within that production" (CM 43, trans. mod.). But the means of mathematical production are themselves produced; the mathematical machine or instrument is also a mathematical product, a result: there would be no formal systems without recursive arithmetic, and no rigorous experimental protocols for such systems without set theory.

Yet it is because this scientific reproduction of the means of production harbours a constitutive historicity that science's self-reproduction is inherently differential. Or rather, it is the inherently differential (dialectical) nature of scientific reproduction that generates its historicity. Scientific re-production is self-differentiating because of the way in which science itself intervenes within a determinate epistemological conjuncture by means of formal experimentation. Thus, for example, by proving the consistency of a model of axiomatic set theory with the axiom of choice and the continuum hypothesis, Gödel demonstrates that these two axioms can be integrated into the formal theory without compromising its coherence. He thereby provides a conceptual sanction for mathematical practice: "In doing so, [Gödel's experimentation] transforms, not the theory, but the status of the theory within the historical process of the production of knowledges" (CM 51). Given a mathematical configuration inscribed within the history of this science, to treat it as a model of a formal system is to situate its specificity by transposing it beyond the narrow ambit of the illusions engendered by its ideological recapture and into the wider mathematical space constituted by the various models of the system. In the history of a science, the experimental transformation of practice via a determinate formal apparatus retrospectively assigns the status of model to those antecedent instances of scientific practice.

For Badiou, then, the materialist category of model designates formalism's retrospective causality upon its own scientific history. The historicity of formalism consists in the "anticipatory intelligibility" of what it retrospectively constitutes as its own model. Ultimately, for Badiou, the fundamental epistemological problem is not that of the nature of the representative relation between the model and the concrete, or between the formal and the model; rather "[t]he problem is that of *the history of formalization*" (CM 54). The materialist category of model proposed by Badiou designates "the network traversed by the retroactions and anticipations that weave this history; whether it be designated in anticipation as a break or in retrospect as a reconfiguration" (*ibid.*). More importantly, Badiou's account of the epistemological dialectic of break and reconfiguration provides a rationalist rejoinder to the anti-rationalist invocation of empirically arbitrary "paradigm shifts" in order to account for the structural discontinuities that punctuate scientific history. The discontinuity of science is not an objection to its rationality since discontinuity is already inherent in the immanent conceptual mechanisms of scientific practice – for "science is precisely that which is ceaselessly cutting itself loose from its own indication in re-presentational space [i.e. ideology]" (ML 165). This is why, for

Badiou, "[T]here are no crises within science, nor can there be, for science is the pure affirmation of difference" (*ibid.*).

Representation, empiricism, naturalism

Ultimately, those empiricist and idealist variants of epistemology rooted in the difference between fact and form are faced with the problem of characterizing the unity underlying this fundamental duality. For vulgar empiricism, the unity of the duality of fact and form is posed in terms of the question of the theoretical model's reproduction or functional simulation of reality. Thus an extrinsic relation of analogical resemblance is invoked in order to bridge the gap between the supposedly inert opacity of empirical fact on one hand, and the active construction of theoretical form on the other. Here, of course, the precise nature of the desired "resemblance", "simulation" or "reproduction" remains vague and ambiguous. For the brand of "naturalized epistemology" spearheaded by Quine, however, the unity of the difference can be unearthed by sealing the gap, by replacing congruence with reciprocal presupposition, by supplanting "resemblance" and "simulation" with isomorphy, and by ensuring the double articulation of fact and form. No longer inert and passive, the structure of the empirical itself generates the form of representation that will account for it. Here evolutionary epistemology and ultimately natural history provide the fulcrum for explaining the relation between empirical fact and theoretical form.

Badiou's own epistemological stance in the period culminating in *Concept of Model* exhibits both surprising parallels and profound divergences with Quinean naturalism. Like Quine, Badiou insists on philosophy's dependence upon science and on the immanent autonomy of scientific thought. Like Quine, he refuses any recourse to a science-transcendent philosophical foundationalism: "One establishes oneself within science from the start. One does not reconstitute it from scratch. One does not found it" (CM 33, trans. mod.). But, unlike Quine, Badiou will have no truck with empiricism and hence refuses to reintegrate the sciences into a broader evolutionary and ultimately biological narrative about the development of human cognitive prowesses. For Badiou, the irreducible variety of scientific practices harbours discontinuous historicities that remain internal and immanent to each practice. These historicities cannot be reabsorbed into an all-encompassing bio-evolutionary narrative about the human organism's "science-forming" faculties.

Badiou's conception of the autonomy of science rules out the possibility of naturalism. "Science" cannot be mistaken for its empiricist representation or conflated with an ambient scientific worldview, a diffuse ideological distillate synthesized from various scientific disciplines (this could serve as a more apt definition of ["scientism")]. It is rather an entirely autonomous, ceaselessly self-differentiating mode of theoretical practice invariably defined by a specific historical conjunction between conceptual demonstration and formal experimentation. The signal merit of Badiou's rationalist conception of science lies in the way in which it manages to reconcile a critical recognition of science's inevitable ideological envelopment – thereby abjuring positivism and empiricism – with an attentiveness to the way in which science is continually breaking away from its own ideological re-inscription. Indeed, for Badiou, scientific progress is fuelled by this constant dialectic between capture and escape, breaking and remaking. At the same time, Badiou's account is one in which there is nothing that science cannot know because, dispensing with every vestige of substance, Badiou's formalist ontology leaves no room for the inconceivable or unconceptualizable. Truth is the sole exception to the order of being, but science is one of the harbingers of truth.

Notes

1. See, for example, Henry (2001), where science is roundly castigated for being one of the primary sources of "the ideology of barbarism".
2. Badiou is refreshingly scornful of reactionary jeremiads about the perils of technology: "We hold these meditations, reckonings, and diatribes concerning technology, however prevalent they may be, to be uniformly ridiculous" (MP 53, trans. mod.).
3. Oliver Feltham and Zachary Luke Fraser have both provided admirably detailed explanations of the role played by these decisive early texts in Badiou's œuvre. See Feltham (2008: 12–31); and Fraser's "Introduction" to his translation of Concept of Model (CM xiii–lxi). English versions of "Mark and Lack: On Zero" and "Infinitesimal Subversion" will appear in Concept and Form, the forthcoming volume edited by Peter Hallward.
4. Badiou gives three examples: the "Platonic" category of "ideal number" denotes an inexistent "adjustment" between arithmetical concepts and hierarchical moral–political notions; the Kantian categories of "space" and "time" combine Newtonian concepts with notions that are relative to human faculties; the Sartrean category of "History" combines Marxist concepts with metaphysico-moral notions such as temporality, freedom and so on. Regarding the second of these examples, it should go without saying that Badiou is here using the term "category" in a sense entirely distinct from Kant's and is perfectly well aware that for Kant space and time are "forms of intuition" rather than "categories".
5. Badiou's use of the term "presence" here is perhaps intended as an allusion to Derrida's work, with which he was certainly already familiar (cf. Badiou 1967: 445). One possible implication here may be that the deconstruction of logocentrism can be enlisted as part of the critique of empiricist epistemology.

SEVEN

Love

Sigi Jöttkandt

The recent interest in Alain Badiou's thought has had an additional, welcome effect of turning critical attention back to the philosophical idea of love. Love, as is well known, constitutes one of Badiou's four "conditions" of philosophy. But with his pronouncement that "no theme requires more pure logic than love", the philosopher contradicts at one stroke the literary-historical tradition that, taking its cues from Plato, sees love as the saving *exception* to logic. For Badiou, love must be regarded in terms of an exceptional logic that simultaneously confirms the philosophical counting operation, while generating another number that is not a product of ordination. Badiou thus begins his investigations of love from a very different place than Aristophanes in the *Symposium*, for whom, "Love is born into every human being; it calls back the halves of our original nature together; it tries to make one out of two and heal the wound of human nature" (Plato, *Symposium* 191d). For Badiou, as for Jacques Lacan, with whom the philosopher is in continuous dialogue throughout his writings on this topic, love is anything but an adhesive substance, a medieval "glue" that binds two tragically divided subjects back to a single loving unity. For Badiou, as for Lacan again, love *supplements* the count-as-one by providing the support for a universalism emptied of the object relation, which the philosopher calls the "scene of the Two".

Unlike the other truth processes (art, science, politics), love has yet to form the subject of a book-length treatment by Badiou. The philosopher's chief writings on love are his two celebrated essays, "What is Love?", published in *Conditions* (1992; reprinted 1998), and "The Scene of the Two", which appeared in the collection, *De l'amour*

73

(1999c).[1] In the first of these two essays, Badiou establishes the foundational axioms or "declarations" of his philosophy of love. Rejecting the "fusional," "ablative" or "superstructural" conceptions of love that he says have characterized until now the most frequent philosophical approaches to love, Badiou (WL 40–41) asserts the following four theses:

1. There are two positions of experience.
2. The two positions are absolutely disjunct.
3. There is no third position.
4. There is only one humanity.

Badiou's theses on love are best approached in reverse, beginning with his fourth declaration, "there is only one humanity". Badiou conceives of humanity as the "support" of the truths created in the generic procedures – the scientific, political, artistic or amorous ways that an eruption of the incommensurable void is taken up and presented by its faithful subjects. Out of step with much of the critical doxa of the twentieth century, Badiou asserts that the truths produced through these four processes are necessarily for everyone. There are universal or *transpositional* truths that are "indifferent" to the particularity of their emergence, thanks to the fact of humanity's unicity.

Nevertheless, as the third thesis asserts, despite there being only this one humanity, it does not follow that humanity therefore occupies an external, "meta" position outside or overlooking the world. There is no third position from which a sort of super-consciousness or omniscient narrator might be capable of reconciling by hidden sleight of hand the two absolutely disjunct "positions" that Badiou mentions in the second thesis. Badiou's debt to Lacan in both this and his first thesis is unmistakable, with his insistence that the two "positions of experience" are irretrievably separate.[2]

One might ask in what respect love fulfils the requirements of a "condition" whose fundamental principle is that it produces truths universal for all. How can two inexorably separated "positions of experience" assert that the truth that love creates for them speaks to both of them – and indeed to the world – *equally*? Badiou's answer is unconventional: love is universal not because it creates a one out of the star-crossed positions of experience, but because love (and it alone among the truth conditions), creates a Two that is, as he puts it, "counted in an immanent way".

I shall come back to the implications that this immanently counted Two might have for humanity later, but let us first look more closely at how Badiou derives this numerical result. As stipulated, the Two of love is not the product of an addition. As he puts it in "The Scene of the Two", this Two neither "counts as one", nor as "the sum of one plus one". It is, rather, the result of a *subtractive* operation, where what is subtracted from the two positions of experience is precisely that which brought them, albeit in an impossibly separated way, together. What is this factor?

In a profound engagement with Lacan's thought, Badiou states in "The Scene of the Two" that the two positions of experience, to which he gives the shorthand Man (M) and Woman (W), do not compose a whole, or a one, because what they share is incomplete. This incomplete element, whose debt to Lacan's object (a) is unmistakable, Badiou names the atomic object, or (u), which he describes as an "unanalysable u of non-being that circulates in the non-relation". This u is the missed point of intersection between the two sexes; the u is the proof of the inevitability by which, like two insects creeping towards each other on opposite sides of a Möbius strip, the sexes will never "meet"; that is, they will never overcome the absolute disjunction of their respective positions with regard to one another. Although Badiou does not give the reason for this absolute disjunction in the two texts we are discussing, it is direct result of the presentational operation that Badiou calls the count-as-one.

Briefly, the count-as-one is founded upon the structuring that, in presenting the void through a nominal decision, originarily specifies which elements of a "set" are in a relation of belonging. The name founds the law of the situation, although Badiou is always quick to point out that, even as it purports to name the void, every eventual naming is inevitably an illegal misnaming. In emphasizing that what passes as a complete representation or identity is only ever a semblance, an "as if", Badiou reminds us that every identity, in so far as it is tied inextricably to that original eventual misnaming, can only be counted "as" one – rather than actually *being* a one.

What interests us here is the way, because of its illegal origins, the eventual name is also responsible for the inalienable fact that under ordinary – that is, non-loving – conditions, every approach to the other will irretrievably be a missed approach, a non-encounter, in which the object that one aims for eludes every attempt to grasp it. This is the inevitability we saw already expressed in Badiou's second thesis regarding the two disjunct positions: "*nothing* in experience is the same for the positions of man and woman. Nothing. That is to say: the positions do not divide up experience, and there is no presentation affecting 'woman' and 'man' such that there are zones of coincidence or intersection" (WL 40).

Nevertheless, despite this stricture, Badiou still maintains that love enables us to step out of presentation's logical structure of non-relation, which would otherwise dictate the entirety of our encounters with others and with the world. Love does so, uniquely of all the truth processes, by subsuming *the object beneath the subject*. The loving encounter "goes straight to that aspect of the object from which the subject draws its little bit of being", explains Badiou. It drives right at the heart of the non-relation of the sexes to enlist the disjunction as the basis for constructing the scene of the Two.

The scene of the Two comes to take the place of the count-as-one in love's "supplement" to the presentational logic that informs the other three truth processes. As mentioned, the Two arises not from an addition but through a subtraction, where the u – the point of the missed encounter – is mutually "internally excised" from the two disjunct, sexed positions. (Note that a certain ambiguity remains regarding whether the disjunction of the sexes precedes the work of love, or if the Two is what (retroactively) causes the lack of coincidence or intersection of the sexes.) Once subtracted from the disjunct positions of experience, however, the u authorizes a different sort of numerical operation. It "pair[s] the two external 'halves' side by side through u (Woman minus u) and (Man minus u)", giving rise to a Two that Badiou says is counted *immanently*. This amounts to saying that the Two is not a product of presentation's usual logic of ordination, which "counts" the subject as a one on the basis of the original misnaming of the void. The Two is rather formed from the subtraction of the remains of that original misnaming that circulates in the situation as what Badiou calls the u. Relieved in this way of the misunderstood object they shared, the Two together construct the world as a scene of enquiry through which they investigate that world from the perspective of the Two. Badiou clarifies that the scene of the Two is therefore not a presentation but "a work" and "a process". Accordingly, the Two are not counted but instead "operate in the situation".

At this point, it is important to note that love in Badiou's conception is not the scene of the Two *per se*. Love, or the amorous event, is rather the "hazardous authorization" given to the "double function" of the u, claims Badiou. For the philosopher, love is where or how the u is thought together in *both* of its functions, that is to say, as the mistaken object of desire *and* as the excess of that object, the "support" of the Two. Hence love is neither simply the first reading of the u, in which the two sexes misunderstand the object, the common cause of their desire. Nor is it properly speaking just the second reading, that is, the "scene of the Two" created by the subtraction of the u from both Man and Woman. Rather, as a truth procedure, love lies in the "limping rhythm" through which the first and second readings are exercised *together*. It inhabits what Badiou describes as the "double reading", which alternates between the contracting movement back towards the object, with its mutual misunderstanding, and an expansive movement outwards through which the Two, subtracted now from the u, faithfully conduct their "enquiries" about the world and its "common practices".

The condition of love in Badiou's work is clearly intended to offer a means of extrication from the otherwise ubiquitous logic of presentation, and is in this sense a "supplement" to that logic. Love manifests itself as a sort of intrapersonal, microcosmic version of the event that, under other conditions, seems a more extensive rupture. In love's truth procedure, the name of the evental encounter is shared only by the couple in love, and yet Badiou still claims that this unique, profoundly personal nomination nevertheless has validity for all. How it succeeds at this is as follows. Badiou explains that in the back-and-forth movement from the missed encounter to the scene of the Two, "something of the scene constructed of the Two 'sticks' to the M and W positions in such a way that it is not exactly in the same configuration that the misunderstanding inscribes". Something brought back from the scene of the Two inflects the missed encounter when, inevitably, the Two return from their "tarrying" in the second reading, to take up their disjoint positions as sexed beings. On this latter point, Badiou is unmistakable: love is a halting movement, a limping rhythm that passes from the first reading to the second, and then again in reverse. One can say that love's "work" amounts to the difficult, hazardous (and usually failed) attempt to somehow hold these two readings together in a creative act – an almost impossible undertaking, Badiou admits, that tries to hold both "readings" of the u simultaneously together.

Yet curiously, and in a manner never fully explained, as they "stick" in this way to the two positions, the results of the creative, constructive "enquiries" into the world conducted by the Two manage to re-situate the sexual non-relation in a different topological configuration than before. The non-relation becomes reoriented in the representational field as a result of the Two's creative investigations such that, as Badiou puts it, the lover becomes "*in excess of himself*, because the uncertain course [*tracé aléatoire*] of fidelity *passes through him*, transfixes his singular body and inscribes him, from within time, in an instant of eternity" (E 45). And as the object relation becomes charged and saturated with the discoveries from the scene of the Two, love's "universalization" literally takes place. The singular, object-directed sexual misunderstanding becomes sufficiently transformed such that a "double reading" of the declaration of love truly does become possible. Simply put, love's nomination, the declaration "I love you", emerges from the scene of the Two to embrace the you of the individual lover *and* the You of humanity at large. In this respect, the unique individual lover becomes at the same time an impersonal subject of truth that bears the "humanity function" (x).

Badiou's concept of an uncounted Two is his stunning contribution to the philosophical dilemma of unity and difference that, in "The Scene of the Two", he phrases in terms of absolute transcendence and the "Trinitarian doctrine". Read from a Lacanian point of view, one would say that Badiou introduces the Two as a creative solution to the impasses of desire – to the fact that, in so far as the subject is a speaking subject, its relation to the world will only ever be through the fantasy. Badiou responds to the desiring impasse by proposing a space that has been purified of the object relation. He proffers the scene of the Two as a world cut loose from its tie to the name, and from the situation's founding law. Badiou is able to propose this "supplement" to the logic of presentation by stripping Lacan's concept of the object (a) all the way down to its atomic form – as the u, which may be added or subtracted in the relation between the sexes.

In essence, Badiou adapts Lacan's account of desire in proposing the u as his own interpretation of the (a). This introduces some important differences with Lacan. For one, unlike Badiou's u, Lacan's object (a) can never be "subtracted" to form the absent support of the scene of the Two. The (a) remains indelibly present throughout both the first (or "phallic") reading *and the second reading*. This is because, once constructed in the original decision of the signifier, the object can never simply be taken away for Lacan, "mutually internally excised", as Badiou puts it, or "subtracted". That is to say, the Lacanian object (a) is not a *term* that can be posited or negated, added or subtracted but, as Lacan was at pains throughout his teaching to emphasize, must be thought as an *object*.[3]

This requirement then introduces the second difference. The universality of love Badiou proposes by way of the Two is conceptually different from that which emerges from Lacan's own "supplement" to desire, and this difference boils down to Badiou's and Lacan's different approaches to language. Where Badiou proposes a universality resulting from the saturation of desire with the (non-phallic) enquiry into the world by the Two in the hazardous double reading that makes up Badiouean love's version of the "duck–rabbit" problem, the impossibility of ever subtracting the (a) from the Lacanian position guarantees that any universal to emerge from love still has to deal with the stubborn and indelible (a). Thus, rather than subtracting the (a), as Badiou does, Lacan *divides* it. For Lacan, the (a) is present both as phallic object that circulates in the desiring fantasy *and* in the form of what Mladen Dolar (2006: 149) suggestively calls the "object in the signifier", the *jouissance* or enjoyment that is attached to nomination, and indeed language, at large. For Lacan, there is an enjoyment that inheres in language which is not subject to castration. Or again, not all *jouissance* is phallic. ⟶ *duh*

This then brings up a third difference. Lacan would certainly disagree with Badiou's insistence that love demands a pure logic. For Lacan – as for the Western literary tradition – love is illogical. It must be, because love is quite literally non-sense. It is by way of nonsense that love supplements the sexual relation and effects a formalization of jouissance through another path than phallic castration and the snares of fantasy. In *Seminar XX* (Lacan 1998), his seminar on love, Lacan declares that, "subsisting only on the basis of the stops not being written (that is, on the 'contingency' of the phallic 'writing' or desire) – love – tends to make the negation shift to the doesn't stop being written, doesn't stop, won't stop" (*ibid.*: 145). We can unpack this as follows: for Lacan, as for Badiou, love is indeed uncounted. However, unlike for Badiou, love depends on, or "subsists" only on the basis of the formalization of *jouissance* effected by the phallic signifier. In a step that can only be briefly touched on here, it is the failure of the sexual relation itself, for Lacan, that forges the path to another means of arriving at the One. While every desiring attempt to reach the One will inevitably fail (as a result of the (a)), this does not mean there is no totality. Some form of an "all", Lacan will hazard, emerges from the very pattern of the repeated failures.

Lacan explains this point in "Seminar XIV (1966–67), the Logic of Fantasy", in his discussion of Russell's catalogue of all catalogues that do not contain themselves, to which he counters the idea of a catalogue that lists all the books referred to in a single volume's bibliography (Lacan 1966–7: lesson of 23 November 1966). Unlike Russell's famous catalogue, there is no question of whether the book whose bibliography is being listed should be included (of course it should not). However, another catalogue that lists all the books that a second book's bibliography contains may well include the title of the first book (although, naturally, not that of the second), and so on. But by effectively grouping books into "sets" in this way, Lacan demonstrates how a totality may be achieved without falling into Russell's paradox. As Lacan explains, although each bibliographic catalogue will not include the title of the book from which it has been derived, once we put these catalogues *together into a series*, it is not unthinkable that, between them, they will succeed in listing *all* of the books in the world.[4]

Although limited in advance by a structural failure that ensures that lovers will, by certain inevitability, fail to reach the desired object, if each of these unsuccessful attempts is placed together into a series, an "all" is created that is more than the sum of its individual parts. This all is what Lacan names a "supplementary One" (*Un-en-plus*), so named because it is an "additional signifier", as he puts it, "one that is not grasped (or, counted) in the chain".

The final difference between the two thinkers on love can now be addressed. As a consequence of the above, for Lacan love will always concern not a two but a one: the uncounted but necessarily *written one* that is best known to us as the crazy nonsense of lovers as they form their lips around and around their beloved's name in love. Both the (a) and the proper name, Lacan suggests in *Encore*, are means of "writing" the absent one, but they do so in the utterly different ways that Lacan proposes: the (a) writes the supplementary one through the failure represented as the fantasies – as "phallic" *jouissance*. The name, on the other hand, as a signifier of "pure nonsense" constitutes a formalization that is not in the service of the signifier – a writing, as Lacan puts it in the following lesson, that "exists already before serving the writing of the word" (Lacan 1965–6: lesson of 5 January 1966).

To conclude, one can say that Badiou invents the concept of the uncounted Two for its power to turn love into as productive a truth as that of the other three conditions. For Badiou, like art, politics and science, love, too, will be a militant act of fidelity with the ability to fundamentally overturn a situation and produce a new founding name. Lacan's position, as is typical, is without such clear situationally transformative implications, although it is also not without them. Love in Lacan gives access to a universal, but the universal is always still tied to the law (of castration), even as it supplements it.

Notes

1. [Editors' note]: Badiou has recently published *Éloge de l'amour* (2009b). This new work would seem to confirm the position elaborated here.
2. In "The Scene of the Two", Badiou even calls his essay a "commentary" on Lacan's claim that love supplements the failure of the sexual relation. Badiou (1999c, 2009f).
3. In the seminars from the mid-1960s, when Lacan was developing his conception of the object (a), he repeatedly claimed that, for him, topology was not a metaphor, not a figure of speech but the Real support of his thinking. See, for example, his opening words in the lesson of 4 May 1966 (Lacan 1965–6).
4. This can be expressed in diagrammatic form, where each letter outside each set represents the title of the "book"whose bibliography is being catalogued:

A (B, C, D)
B (A, C, D)
C (A, B, D)
D (A, B, C)

Between them, every "book" has thus been catalogued (represented), even though there is no single catalogue that contains them all. For further discussion, see Lacan (1966–7: lessons of 16 and 23 November 1966).

EIGHT

Art

Elie During

The relation of philosophy and art, according to Alain Badiou – himself a great stylist and successful playwright – is at once obvious and somewhat twisted. For one thing, they do not communicate directly, but through the relation both entertain with a third term, which they do not reach in the same way: truth. If philosophy does not produce truths of its own, it certainly has something to say about truth: it reaches it through eternity, by formalizing the production of universal patterns of thought. Art, on the contrary, produces truths of its own, but it does so through oblique means, by dealing with sensible images, objects, bodies, or the material dimension of language, the finiteness of which seems to stand in contradiction with the infinite nature of truth.

This intricate disposition of art and philosophy with regard to truth results in the following paradox. On the one hand, art is held to be one of the "conditions" of philosophy, along with mathematics, politics and love: as such, it is only natural to expect it to play a major role in the doctrine (MP 35). As a matter of fact, Badiou's writings make constant use of artistic examples and paradigms, taken from both "high" and "low" cultures. The philosopher's range does not reduce to the familiar icons of modernism, even though his personal preferences more than often draw him in that direction. The image of horses drawn on the walls of a prehistorical cave are discussed along with experiments in painting by Picasso (LW), Malevich (TC) or Duchamp (Badiou 2007d). Poems by Hölderlin, Celan, Mallarmé (TW; BE; HI; C), Rimbaud (TW), Pessoa (HI; TC), are extensively commented upon – and even 'translated' into philosophical prose. References to Schönberg and Webern abound. Badiou's writings on cinema include references to the films of Murnau (TS), Godard, Pasolini, Welles, Visconti (HI), as well as those of the Wachowsky brothers (Badiou *et al.* 2003). Dance (HI) and contemporary performance (TC) (see Badiou & During 2007) are also dealt with, and an entire book is devoted to Beckett (OB), not to mention essays on theatre in general (HI) (Badiou 1990). Art is everywhere present.

On the other hand, however, the *concept* of art tends to be down- graded in favour of the diversity of artistic disciplines and genres encountered by the philosopher. It is as if art in itself was in the end less important than *the arts*, considered as purveyors of "truths" of a particular kind (see Rancière 2004a: 218). As we shall see, this state of affairs is a consequence of elevating art to the status of a "condition" of philosophy. But this only strengthens the paradox, the two sides of which must now be examined in turn.

Art as a condition of philosophy

"We shall thus posit that there are four conditions of philosophy, and that the lack of a single one gives rise to its dissipation, just as the emergence of all four conditioned its apparition. These conditions are: the matheme, the poem, political invention and love" (MP 35). Remarkably, art is introduced here – in a text originally published in 1989 – by means of one of the particular arts, namely, the art of poetry. More than a concern for symmetry between "matheme" and "poem", this lexical choice confirms the *de facto* privilege of poetic examples, and more specifically the particular place occupied by Mallarmé, Badiou's arch-poet. There are good reasons for this primacy of the poetic reference within Badiou's works: it is clear that the arts of language are, of all the arts, those most clearly capable of formulating in their own terms the aporias of nomination encountered by Badiou's ontological project of a pure multiple. However, one should not infer from the special status of the poem anything like a hierarchical scheme ruling over the classification of artistic practices, as in Hegelian aesthetics for example. Arts are not ordered according to their greater or lesser ability to demonstrate art's power, to manifest an extrinsic truth or some aesthetic principle. They enjoy only relative prominence within given philosophical strategies of exposition. Thus poetry is but one among the many arts displaying what Badiou calls "generic procedures" or "truth procedures" (HI 35; BE 335–43).

What counts, in any case, is that art is capable of producing truths that exceed the theoretical or practical knowledge attached to the particular artistic canons of a historically given configuration of the arts. The concept of truth is itself inseparable from that of the event: "The *origin* of a truth is of the order of the event" (MP 36). Truth must indeed be produced: its universality is intimately connected to the novelty it introduces in the world. Thus an artistic truth manifests itself by the way it manages to sustain the consequences of a radical break in an established aesthetic regime. A regime of this sort defines the "world of art" at a given time; it is characterized by "a singular form of tension between the intensity of the sensible and the tranquility of form" (LW 73).

In other words, the world of art organizes a relation between the chaotic disposition of sensibility (always verging on the formless [*informe*]) and what is generally accepted as form (Badiou 2005f).

The event is a break in the established regime of this tension. The trace … of this break is to be found in the fact that what seemed to partake of the formless is grasped as form, whether globally (Cubism in 1912–13) or through a local excess (baroque distortions from Tintoretto to Caravaggio, passing through El Greco).

(LW 73)

Thus a genuine artistic event can be described as "a change in the formula of the world [of art]": it involves "the becoming formal of something, which was not", in other words, the emergence of a "new possibility of formalization" (2005f).

"Inaesthetics"

It is remarkable that Badiou, while constantly referring to "art" in the texts just mentioned, does not feel compelled to offer any independent concept of art – of its essence, of what it should be – over and above the singular configurations of artistic works that fall under his scrutiny. The reason for this should be obvious now: art is a condition of philosophy. But a condition typically does not refer to a domain of objects requiring a specific type of analysis (such as "aesthetics"), or a specific body of knowledge (such as "poetics", as traditionally understood). Accordingly, art is not an area of regional interest, along with science or ethics, to which philosophy could refer as its speciality. Indeed, there is no obligation for philosophy to pay special attention to art as such. More importantly, being a condition of philosophy, art cannot stand in any sense as an *object* for philosophy to reflect upon. What really matters is art's operations, which can be described only with reference to concrete instances. Thus there is no "essence", no "power" of art as such, that would force philosophy into a privileged relation with some external object, which may seem to happen whenever art is celebrated for harnessing the disruptive force of the sensible as such (Deleuze's affects and percepts), for wounding philosophy or violently exposing the limits of its discourse (Adorno's negative aesthetics, Lyotard's touch of the sublime).[1] On this account, Badiou is very straightforward: "philosophy's appropriation and metamorphosis of its conditions cannot be distinguished from the philosophical act itself, which is why one can never object anything to philosophy that is purely and simply exterior to it" (LW 519). When it comes to art, the point then is, as with every other condition, to assess "the degree of compatibility between a philosophical operation and a non-philosophical operation". And this can only be done locally, by examining specific artistic procedures at work.

As a consequence, Badiou's "aesthetics" is nowhere to be found. What is suggested instead is a particular discipline referred to as "inaesthetics":

> By "inaesthetics" I understand a relation of philosophy to art that, maintaining that art is itself a producer of truths, makes no claim to turn art into an object for philosophy. Against aesthetic speculation, inaesthetics describes the strictly intraphilosophical effects produced by the independent existence of some works of art. (HI xiv)

This rather unfamiliar characterization of the relation of art and philosophy leaves room for something like a philosophical poetics attached to "some works of art", as we shall see. But the first thing to observe is the critical impact of this new relation to art viewed as one of the conditions of philosophy. The critical edge clearly appears when this conception is contrasted with other possible schemes: "didactic" (Plato, Rousseau, Brecht), "romantic" (German Romanticism, as well as a certain orientation of Heideggerian hermeneutics), and "classical" (Aristotle and all the proponents of the "cathartic" or "therapeutic" conception of art). Badiou's main target is certainly the "romantic" stance that until today has infused the philosophical discipline known as "aesthetics". This idea connects with the recurring theme according to which philosophy cannot be subordinated – "sutured" – to one of its conditions without destroying itself as philosophy (MP 61–77; IT 91–108). The way Badiou conceives it, philosophy operates a deposition of the poem by ridding it of the auratic and oracular pretenses to access an ineffable and absolutely incommunicable meaning. In fact, as the example of poetry clearly indicates, art produces truths to the extent that it resists the charm of interpretation (image, fiction or narrative) or the lyrical impulse, and operates by purely subtractive means in order to capture the event on the verge of nonsense, in the guise of a vanishing presence. Badiou's underlying poetics is at once anti-mimetic and anti-lyrical (see Rancière 2004a). Hermeneutics and aesthetics are thereby rejected in the same stroke.

What the *Handbook of Inaesthetics* introduces as a "fourth modality of the link between philosophy and art" implies that "art *itself* is a truth procedure" (HI 9). In a way, this amounts to restating that art is a "condition" of philosophy. But how are we to understand the singular nature of artistic truth? One way to answer this question consists in underscoring the sensible dimension of any artistic procedure. Artistic novelty is basically a matter of introducing new ways of formalizing the seemingly formless within the sensible. This much was already granted by Badiou's description of the creative transformation of the "world of art", and this alone would be enough to distinguish the poem from the matheme.

Yet if Badiou is not interested in providing us with a general concept of art, he is equally reluctant to characterize the general operation of art.[2] In the end, it seems that inaesthetics is not so much about art itself as it is about its ability to convey, through the local production of truths within definite configurations, a truth of a more general kind that philosophy "welcomes and shelters" (HI 63), the only truth that matters, namely that *there are truths* – yes, even in art. Admittedly, philosophy should always reveal "a truth of *this art*, an art-truth", but ultimately, the arts, in their very diversity of intents and means, express in various degrees and at various levels of clarity only the simple truth that "art – as the configuration 'in truth' of works – is in each and every one of its points the thinking of the thought that it itself is" (HI 13–14). This rather tautological formulation suggests that there is nothing else for philosophy to *learn* from art, not only because truth fundamentally exceeds the regime of knowledge, but more fundamentally because philosophy's chief mission is to *declare* that there are truths.

But this cannot possibly be Badiou's last word on the issue. At this juncture, two questions arise, difficult to simply brush aside. First, what justifies the singling out of art as a condition of philosophy – rather than, say, religion or games? Second, is there something specific to the "generic" or "truth procedures" displayed by the various arts that may justify capturing their diversity within one single category – that of art or, as Badiou likes to say, "the poem"? In other words: what singularizes art within the set of conditions to which it belongs, beyond the obvious fact that art deals with the sensible (a statement nearly as tautologous as "art is art")? For such is Badiou's claim: not only is truth *immanent* to art – as opposed to the view that truth does not belong in art and must consequently be produced by another discourse (that of philosophy disguised as "aesthetics", for example) – but it is in addition *singular*, in the sense that the truths produced by art belong to it absolutely and cannot be confused with the general ideas or formal schemata that "circulate among other registers of work-producing thought" (HI 9). Thus the truths that art activates are "irreducible to other truths – be they scientific, political or amorous". What are the grounds for such a claim?

Artistic configurations

The key to the whole issue, as Badiou suggests, may well lie in identifying the "pertinent unity of what is called 'art'" (HI 10). The composition of the *Handbook of Inaesthetics*, originally published in 1998, is in itself symptomatic. It is of course nothing like a treatise in aesthetics, but it hardly counts as an essay in the philosophy of art in the traditional sense either. The book is a collection of articles written independently of one another in relation to various artistic figures and disciplines (poetry, dance, cinema, theatre). The opening essay, entitled "Art and Philosophy", focuses on the question of philosophy's task with regard to art. There we understand that what philosophy ultimately deals with is "artistic configurations", rather than singular works of art or artistic figures (authors, creators). An artistic configuration is composed of works only, yet it manifests itself in no work in particular. It is itself a generic multiple: "initiated by an event", it presents itself as "an identifiable sequence comprising a virtually infinite complex of works" (HI 12–13).[3] Such an open-ended structure naturally resists all attempts at totalization under a single predicate.

To sum up: artistic truths necessarily take the form of artistic procedures within particular – yet essentially indefinite – artistic configurations. This compact formula requires some explanation. We have already mentioned that a distinctive character of artistic truths seems to lie in the fact that their production involves a particular disposition of the sensible in relation to the formal, or rather, to possibilities of formalization. In this respect, it is no surprise that the second volume of *Being and Event*, elaborating as it does a "logic of appearance", should throw a different light on the issue of artistic truth, insisting on the active composition and orientation of a "subjectivized body", the function of which is ultimately to create a new "world" from a given artistic configuration (LW 79–89). The example of art is indeed instrumental in Badiou's overall philosophical *montage*; it helps him bind together the notions of "world", "event" and "truth" – along with their corollaries, "trace" and "body".

This line of analysis stands in sharp contrast with the way art – and most notably, the poem – was summoned in earlier works, in order to introduce a doctrine of the event originally formulated against the ontological backdrop of being as pure multiple. In the first volume of *Being and Event*, Mallarmé's *Un coup de dés* was described as a symbolic – or rather, analogical – staging of the event in the guise of a disappearance, vanishing or cancellation of the object. A drama of thought itself obtained by strictly subtractive means, the syntactic machination of the poem was supposed to teach us an abstract and sobering lesson: that thought, as an event, exceeds the expressive capacities of any given art, that it exceeds the logic of expression altogether, as much as that of description (IT 98–107; BE 191–8).

The move to a logical appearing in *Logics of Worlds* may seem to have shifted the focus to the phenomenal manifestation of the work *qua* work. This is not exactly the case, however, for it soon becomes apparent that the fact of drawing its material from the sensible is not as essential to the work of art as we might have thought. The *Handbook of Inaesthetics* already rephrased the problem in a more formal way, describing the work of art as essentially *finite*, that is, both limited as an object in space and time, and closed or accomplished as the individual work that it is. In fact, one may even say that the work of art is the only finite thing that truly exists: owing to the very conditions of its presentation, it is a multiple of an intrinsically finite kind (HI 10–11). This characterization enables Badiou to reformulate the issue of artistic truth in terms of the problematic articulation of the infinite and the finite. In the end, everything comes down to the problem of linking truth as infinite multiplicity with the limited, finite body of the artwork (see TC 153–9). But in order not to get trapped in the romantic schema of the descent of the infinite Idea within the finite boundaries of sensible forms (the very schema at work in the aesthetics of the sublime), it is essential to avoid confining the proper site of truth as a post-evental procedure *within the work itself*. Hence the concept of "artistic configuration" as the pertinent unity for thinking about art as the production of an immanent, singular truth. Only in the configuration can truth as infinite multiplicity find enough room to be borne by art. It is the job of philosophy to show, in each particular case, how a configuration can be seized by the category of truth (HI 13).

It remains to be seen in what sense art serves as something more than a particularly clear exemplification of the general theory of "generic procedures" expounded in *Being and Event*, and further elaborated in *Logics of Worlds*. Even more simply: since Badiou is seeking the "intraphilosophical" effects of certain works of art, what kind of philosophical effects should we expect from a confrontation with art, besides the strictly artistic effects displayed by certain works, and the pedagogical function fulfilled by art within the exposition of a general theory of the event? Again, is there something for philosophy to take from art, something it could not come up with on its own? Or does its role limit itself to recapturing and extracting the localized effects of universal truths that artistic procedures themselves produce while being unable to fully express them by their own means? Such are some of the issues involved in the "encounter" of philosophy and art. Addressing them requires that one carefully differentiate between distinct uses of artistic reference, distinct regimes of philosophical appropriation and transformation of the artistic condition.

Three regimes of artistic reference

Moments of genuine artistic invention can indeed function as models for understanding the general relations of event and being, truth and subject. These relations are not specific to art, although they take a particular form when they are played out in an artistic setting. In this respect, art retains a perfectly valid pedagogical function, to the extent that it is indeed the purveyor of truths, and if we do not merely revel in the sensible, material spectacle it offers. Yet at the same time, art can play a more specific pedagogical function if one focuses on the operations that are proper to it. These have to do, as we have seen, with the fact that the finite scope of the work of art – as opposed to the open-ended, virtually infinite texture of the artistic configuration – involves a particularly obvious play of tensions within the logic of appearance. Experimenting in a creative way essentially means opening up a new world in relation to the trace of an event: it is about finding new access to the infinity of the form itself, beyond the limitations of the work. And this particular dialectics, according to Badiou, is nowhere clearer than in art today – as opposed to a "political question" that remains "very obscure" (2005f).

Thus Badiou's excursions in various artistic domains (poetry and theatre, dance and cinema, to name but a few) can be roughly classified in three categories that correspond to three specific functions of the reference to art in philosophical discourse.

First, an artwork or a body of works can serve to exemplify the mechanism of "generic procedures" in general, in so far as they define conditions as such. Badiou may sometimes give the impression that he is characterizing the proper operation of art – thus providing us with a concept of art in general – when he is in fact merely reflecting on the idea of eternal truths being produced in the context of a particular condition of philosophy. Thus, referring to the horses painted on the walls of the Chauvet cave, which he compares with those painted on Picasso's canvas, Badiou writes:

> This means that – as in the Platonic myth, but in reverse – to paint an animal on the wall of a cave is to flee the cave so as to ascend towards the light of the Idea. This is what Plato feigns not to see: the image, here, is the opposite of the shadow. It attests the Idea in the varied invariance of its pictorial sign. Far from being the descent of the Idea into the sensible, it is the sensible creation of the Idea. "This is a horse" – that is what the Master of the Chauvet cave says. And since he says it at a remove from any visibility of a living horse, he *avers* the horse as what exists eternally for thought. (LW 19)

It is tempting to extract from such a quotation – and others similar to this one – a general definition of artistic operations: "the sensible creation of the Idea". But this "nominal definition", as Leibniz would have it, is hardly illuminating: its main merit lies in overturning a conventional Platonic theme, while distancing itself from the opposite schema, the one identified with Romanticism, in which the sensible (the finite), rather than being subtracted, finds itself exalted and relieved by the Idea (the infinite). In the end, what is important is that art should produce truths. But this can be postulated in the absence of any characterization of what accounts for the singularity of these truths (i.e. what makes them properly artistic truths). As a matter of fact, the passage occurs within a sequence where each condition is in turn examined in order to assess that eternal truths are effectively produced (in art as well as in politics, mathematics and the adventures of the amorous subject).

A second usage of the artistic reference consists, as mentioned above, in the (re)construction of an artistic configuration: art becomes the pretext for a meditation on the very conditions of post-evental action and subjectivation. What is at stake then is the creation, point by point, of a "body" (the worldly dimension of a subject) in correlation with the trace of the event (determining the active orientation of the body), within a particular configuration or "world of art". The coordinates according to which such a process can be described are enumerated in a section of *Logics of Worlds* devoted to the "Schönberg-event" (LW 79–89): through the history of serial music, from Schönberg to Boulez, one can follow the path through which the affirmation of the possibility of a world of sounds no longer ruled by the tonal system was relayed by the constitution and exhaustion of a new subject of serialism. In a similar way, *The Century* describes the fate of various "avant-garde" schools, insisting on the importance of declarations and manifestos, which Badiou considers as essential to the mode of existence of the "trace" (TC 131–47). Here, the reference to art seems justified by its clarifying effect. For one thing, nowhere is it clearer than in art that truths must be actively created and promoted. This is why artistic creation may help us discern "new ways and new means in the realm of politics" (Badiou 2007h). This claim lies at the heart of Badiou's recent upholding of an "affirmationist" stance in relation to the productions of contemporary art (2004b).

Finally, the inaesthetic operation sometimes consists in isolating a particular procedure, one that may be viewed as distinctive of the poetics of some particular art. For example, poetry, more than any other art, appears as an art of the "*deposition* of every supposed object" (TW 236) because it introduces into the domain of language a very specific question: "what is an experience without object?" As Badiou shows through a careful reading of chosen poetic works, the poem operates the "disobjectification of presence". This procedure singles out the active operation of the poem. Yet it can itself take place under different strategies, such as subtraction (Mallarmé) or dissemination (Rimbaud). At this point, it makes sense to say that one may philosophize "under condition of" a poet, writer or artist. Badiou writes:

> What I mean by this is that thinking "under condition of Beckett" has been, in the register of prose, the counterpart of what, for a long while, thinking "under condition of Mallarmé" has been for poetry. To Mallarmé I owe a sharper understanding [*compréhension intensifiée*] of what a subtractive ontology is, namely an ontology in which eventally excess summons lack, so as to bring forth the Idea. I owe Beckett a comparable sharpening [*intensification*] in my thinking of generic truth, that is the divestment, in the becoming of the True, of all the predicates and agencies of knowledge. (LW 548)

Similar investigations lead Badiou into the realm of theatre, where the poetics of disappearance is turned into a prelude to mobilization, inaugurating an altogether different set of relations between art and politics. It is no longer a matter of staging the "passage of the Idea", but its direct encounter. As for contemporary performance art, which Badiou interprets along the lines of a form of generalized theatricality, the issue revolves around experimenting with new links between the finite and the infinite under the notion of "the act", in a way that does not bring us back to the romantic notion of the tormented body as the seat of some deep expressive power, nor to the aesthetic scheme of the incarnation of the Idea in the sensible (TC 153–9; Badiou & During 2007).[4] Here, as elsewhere, Badiou claims the advent of "glorious bodies" [corps glorieux].

These three regimes or modalities of the artistic reference fulfil distinct roles within Badiou's philosophy: (1) averring the generic production of universal truths (art as a happening of the Idea); (2) deploying the resources of the post-evental logic of appearance (artistic configurations); (3) extracting typical operations and procedures at work in particular fields (local poetics), with a view to their general significance for philosophy. None of these approaches directly contributes to a "philosophy of art" in the traditional sense; neither does their combination. In the end, philosophy's relation to art is really a matter of harnessing and incorporating the energy of "some works of art" through a careful montage, in favour of an intensification of philosophical operations.

Notes

1. Badiou acknowledges that art is in a way a "challenge" to philosophy, and probably an "insult" (IT 100–101). But this is the case with all of its conditions. All of them "at once condition and insult philosophy". The job of the philosopher is to turn an insult into a problem: that of truth itself as distinct from sense – as a genuine "hollowing out" of sense (IT 101–2).

2. There are of course notable exceptions to this general rule. One of Badiou's most popular texts on art, "Fifteen Theses on Contemporary Art", contains the following statement: "Art is the process of a truth, and this truth is always the truth of the sensible or sensual, the sensible qua sensible. This means: the transformation of the sensible into a happening of the Idea" (2004b; see www.lacan.com/frameXXIII7.htm).

3. The passage must be quoted in full: "What are we to understand ... by an 'artistic configuration'? A configuration is not an art form, a genre, or an 'objective' period the history of art, nor is it a 'technical' dispositif. Rather, it is an identifiable sequence, initiated by an event, comprising a virtually infinite complex of works, when speaking of which it makes sense to say that it produces – in a rigorous immanence to the art in question – a truth of this art, an art-truth" (HI 13).

4. With cinema, the most impure and hybrid of all arts, Badiou is clearly tempted to give up any particular method of enquiry. In fact, "the basic unit of investigation"

may not even be "the film in its totality as some moments of film, moments within which an operation is legible" (IT 114). At times, the relation of philosophy to film seems to become purely allegorical, as when the narrative of the *Matrix* trilogy provides a ready-made illustration for a new heroism of the Real (see Badiou *et al.* 2003). The identification of operations, as Badiou himself acknowledges, must include "those occurring within films which are globally deficient" (IT 115).

NINE

Politics

Nina Power and Alberto Toscano

In 1985, Alain Badiou published a short but essential book, *Peut-on penser la politique?* (Can politics be thought?) In it, he set out his reasons for deconstructing the "metaphysics" of Marxism–Leninism – a political tradition he had actively sought to shape in the period after May '68 – and introduced some of the concepts that have since come to be associated with his philosophy, in particular that of the event. But the title of book can also be seen to indicate a concern that has defined Badiou's entire philosophical career, from his early attempt to complement Althusserian Marxism to his very recent call to explore and renew "the communist hypothesis" (1967; 2009c). If the conditions of science (mathematics) and art (poetry) determine Badiou's mode of presentation and enquiry, politics plays a motivating role in Badiou's philosophy (TW xvi). Many of the distinctive features of Badiou's philosophy originate in politics: an attempt to formulate a partisan but universalizable conception of truth; an emphasis on the emergence of subjectivity from contingent occurrences, and its persistence in the guise of militancy; a preoccupation with collective forms of action and organization; and an understanding of novelty as a revolutionary transformation in which, following the Internationale, those (or that) which was nought shall at last be all.

Despite Badiou's abiding attempt to think politics, both as a philosopher and as a political militant, isolating a *concept* of politics in his work is problematic. Badiou is firmly opposed to the widespread idea of philosophy as a discipline that would produce judgements about the proper forms of government, enquire into the formation of public opinion or evaluate the moral probity of particular political actions.

In particular, he breaks with two dominant modes of philosophical reflection on the place of politics: political philosophy and ethics (M 10–25; E 18–23). Both imply the idea of politics as a distinct domain that could either be investigated in terms of some general categories (deliberation, consensus, rights etc.) or delimited for the sake of an Other that transcends it. Political philosophy and ethics partake of a broader trend, which involves ignoring singular instances of *politics* for the sake of the "fiction" that there exists a *sui generis* domain of theory and practice, *the political*.[1]

The political has the structure of a fiction for Badiou because it implies the existence of a fully consistent bond (*lien*), something that earlier dialectics of division and later meta-ontology of the multiple undermine by challenging claims to unity and totality. The fiction of the political, as an adequately representable and ordered field of human action, is bound up with the fictions of the social and the historical. Badiou's ontological objections to the existence of any consistent totality (TS 109–11) translate into the declarations that history, community and finally Marxism do not exist as anything but discontinuous, or imaginary, entities (TS 92; see also C 148–51; M 48). Developing an Althusserian intuition, Badiou rejects the idea that the political could be a concept extending over a number of particular instances, a coherent field of human experience or an object of philosophical analysis and judgement (M 62). More specifically, the concept of the political is complicit with the functioning of the state, that "excrescent" entity which operates to stabilize or "represent" the multiples presented in society so as to exclude any presentation of the void that haunts situations. What the statist fiction of the political seeks to foreclose is then "the danger of inconsistency", or what Badiou calls unbinding (*dé-liaison*; BE 109).

Neither a concept with an extension nor an area of human behaviour, politics – as opposed to the political – is instead defined as what breaks through a status quo that is based on a fiction of hierarchical order and is founded on the internal exclusion of invisible or inexistent elements (e.g. "the international proletariat of France" or the *sans-papiers*). In line with the Lacanian adage that truth is what makes a hole in knowledge, political truths involve the upsurge of what an inegalitarian and coercive system of representations forecloses, and the undoing of the rules that structured the initial situation or world (LW 363–80). All political thought for Badiou works "to count as one that which is not even counted" (M 150). Badiou's understanding of political subjectivation and political action can accordingly be seen as a mutable but insistent iteration of two aspects of Marx's conception of communism: politics is not a programme aimed at a blueprint for society, but a movement that seeks to abolish or dislocate the dominant state of affairs; politics is the emancipatory insurrection of a subject that the situation and its statist representation treat as politically non-existent. Any egalitarian politics, if it is not to succumb to impotent reformism, eclecticism or idealism, is obliged for Badiou to address the mechanisms that (re)produce inexistence and to intervene in the *loci* of the unrepresented and uncounted, what in Badiou's meta-ontological doctrine will be called evental sites or sites (BE 173–7; LW 363–80).

In a meditation initially intended for *Being and Event* but published in the political journal *Le Perroquet*, Badiou affirmed the political importance of the factory in terms that illuminate his understanding of the politics of equality and emancipation as a non-statist politics of non-domination:

> The paradoxical statement I am defending is finally that the fac-tory, by which I mean the factory as a workers' place, belongs without doubt to the socio-historical presentation (it is counted-as-one within it), but not the workers, to the extent that they belong to the factory. So that the factory – as a workers' place – is not *included* in society, and the workers (of a factory) do not form a pertinent "part", available for State counting.   (1987b: 4)

Although nothing about it determines the forms that an eventual politics will take, and although its economic function is explicitly side-lined, *qua* event-site, "at the edge of the void", the factory is defined as a place through which any communist politics must pass, and which any new subject will need to transform. This translation of Engels's writings on the factory into the meta-ontology of belonging and inclu-sion of *Being and Event* raises the fraught question of the relationship between Badiou's thinking of politics and Marxism.

Up to *Can Politics Be Thought?* Badiou's political thought is combat-ively placed under the aegis of Marxism. Its development since can be investigated in terms of both its continuities and discontinuities with the legacies of Leninism, Maoism, class struggle and the dialectic (Bosteels 2005c,d; Toscano 2008). A number of Badiou's most important texts on politics were written as documents of the Maoist group of which he was a leader, the UCFML (L'Union des Communistes de France Marxiste-Léniniste) (see Badiou 1975a,b,c; 1978a; Badiou & Balmès 1976; Bosteels 2005c). It is easy enough to identify major differences in the conceptions of politics present in Badiou's "Marxist–Leninist" texts as opposed to his post-1985 metapolitical writings. While in his Maoist phase philosophy seems to be a weapon in the hands of the proletariat, much of Badiou's more recent work is defined by the attempt to "desu-ture" philosophy from its conditions, and from politics in particular. One of the forms taken by this desuturing, which gives political thought its autonomy at the same time as it frees philosophy to work across truth procedures, is a break with a thesis put forward in *Theory of the Subject*: "Every subject is political. This is why there are few subjects and rarely any politics" (TS 28). This is an even stronger break if we note that the subject in that book was the party, and that the latter was bound up with two notions of political collectivity that Badiou's more recent work treats as facets of exhausted modes of politics: classes and masses (M 64, 68–77). Aside from laying out the historical reasons for the saturation of a Marxist–Leninist understanding of politics and the "expatriation" of Marxism, Badiou has also engaged in a more specula-tive self-criticism in the guise of a distinction between a revolutionary thinking of destruction and an evental thinking of subtraction (see, respectively, Badiou 1985; Toscano 2008; Badiou 2005g, TC).

But for all the explicit shifts and caesuras, it is also possible to trace a remarkable consistency of themes beneath the mutations in the stand-ing of Marxism in Badiou's thought. Although earlier, more explicitly militant work lays great stress on the party, this political "subject" is never a canonical Leninist party but is instead defined by trying to draw organizational consequences from the Maoist Cultural Revolu-tion and the political experiments that followed in the wake of May '68. The party was always for Badiou "a party of a new type" and his own organization was tellingly a Group for the Formation of the Union of the Marxist–Leninist of France, setting it apart, for instance, from the Communist Party of France (Marxist–Leninist). Also, while the designation of "imperialist society" and its bourgeoisie as the targets of proletarian antagonism certainly speak of a more totalizing politics than the one indicated in the essays in *Metapolitics*, the earlier *Theory of the Subject* – a kind of dialectical balance sheet of Badiou's political militancy – already formulates a thinking of political subjectivity as revealing, by a kind of "torsion", the inexistence of the Whole. Some of that book's section headings are quite eloquent in this respect: "Eve-rything that belongs to a whole constitutes an obstacle to this whole insofar as it is included in it"; "There are no such things as class rela-tions" (TS 3, 125).

We could also note that Badiou's Marxism has always seen itself as a Marxist politics above all, and paid little note to the critique of political economy (Toscano 2004b). Its concern has always rested with politi-cal organization, as is borne out by recent investigations into military strategy and "bodies of truth" (LW 277–95, 493–503). Other themes testify to a red thread running across Badiou's work, and across his own "destruction" and "recomposition" of Marxism (Badiou 1985; Toscano 2008): the idea of politics against the One, the state, and "existing society" (Badiou 1987a); the notions of force and then forcing as key descriptors of how a subject comes to undo and transform a situation (1975a; BE); the formulation of a dialectic of void and excess (TS; BE); the centrality of the affects of courage and enthusiasm to political action (TS; LW); the polemic against reactionaries and renegades (Power & Toscano 2009); and, most importantly, the idea of the communist hypothesis. It is to this that we now turn, to evaluate some of the ways in which Badiou's thinking has responded to the post-Soviet conjuncture.

In a 1991 paper entitled "Philosophy and Politics" (C 147–76), Badiou asks whether "revolutionary" politics has reached a point where it attests to nothing other than "philosophy's disaster", that is to say, whether politics as thought has culminated only in tragedy. On the surface this seems close to many of the liberal-democratic analyses that accompanied the collapse of the Berlin Wall and the crumbling of Soviet-supported states in Eastern Europe. But far from triumphantly proclaiming the end of history and the inevitability of free markets and democracy, Badiou's conception of politics seeks to reestablish the "existence of politics at the point of its apparent impossibility" (C 151), to base politics on the impossible-real of equality. Badiou's politics is never that of the "lesser evil" (1987a). Although his political ethics of truth tries to define and avert "disaster", understood as the idea of truth's "total power" (E 71), the risk of such an "Evil" cannot mean a retreat into a politics of finitude and modesty. The affirmation against the state of an infinite, generic equality – of a "communism of singularities" – remains Badiou's aim, which rejects the ethical and philosophical consequences drawn by many of his contemporaries from their critiques of "totalitarianism" (2009c). It is this impulse, in the face of the supposed defeat of historical communism, to remain true to the founding impulses of emancipatory politics – equality, collectivity and the "communist hypothesis" – that characterizes Badiou's approach to politics. By contrast with the dialectical thinking of politics that marked *Theory of the Subject*, with its recasting of Hegel and Marx via Mallarmé, Mao and Lacan, Badiou's metapolitical writings of the 1990s and 2000s return in some ways to the problems raised by Left critics of Hegel in the 1840s: how to adequately describe philosophy's relation to politics, how to best understand the emergence and possibilities of communism in the face of inequality, and what it means to remain true to a concept of universality in the face of ever-proliferating social complexity and difference. If the category of class drops out of Badiou's later conception of politics, it does so in a complicated way: class struggle, he argues, "is a category of History and of the State, and only under entirely singular conditions does it constitute a *material* for politics" (C 161). On this point, Badiou comes very close to the Sartre of the *Critique of Dialectical Reason*, where class analysis is for the most part replaced by a critical description of the emergence of atypical political groupings (2009e). If politics is one of philosophy's conditions, then the model of political action is of the order of an event: entirely unpredictable and indiscernible from the standpoint of the situation, and not amenable to an analysis that would see revolutionary change as latent in economic tendencies and social antagonisms.

It is against the backdrop of the collapse of "real socialism" and the set-theoretical turn of the late 1980s, with its assertion of the conditioned character of philosophy and its desuturing from politics, that Badiou's more recent political thought must be understood. Nevertheless, Badiou remains true to certain key elements (justice, universalism, emancipation) that cut across the history of twentieth-century revolutionary politics – a discontinuous history that he periodizes in terms of distinct "sequences" or "historical modes of politics" (M 38–42). Such moments (the French Revolution, the Paris Commune, the Bolshevik Revolution, the Chinese Cultural Revolution, May '68) share certain key features: politics is collective; it exhibits the "infinity" of the situation by rejecting finitude; it invokes subjective universality. In later works, Badiou will claim that there are two communist sequences – from the French Revolution to the Paris Commune and from the 1917 Russian Revolution to 1976, and that following this latter sequence we are in a kind of "interval phase dominated by the enemy" (MS 113). The contemporary challenge for politics is to determine the modality by which we can begin to think through a third communist sequence.

In the Preface to the English edition of *Metapolitics*, Badiou presents four more specific, late twentieth-century periods of political concern that directly relate to his own philosophical and political development. First there is the conjuncture around 1965, where the role of the PCF (Parti Communiste Français) and the problems of colonialism (particularly Algeria) dominated the French political scene. This was followed by the "red decade" of 1966–76, marked by its attempt to draw the consequences of the Chinese Cultural Revolution and May '68, a period where "everyday life was entirely politicised" (M xxxiv). Then we have a long counter-revolutionary period (1976–95) or "Restoration" (see TC), characterized by the rise of an ethical discourse of "human rights" and by "humanitarian" but in practice imperialist interventions under American hegemony – a period that Badiou defines as the "betrayal" of the emancipatory experiments of the 1960s and 1970s. Finally, there is the period from 1995 onwards, which is seen as a complicated and uncertain development from the previous phase, still possessed of many of the same features, but with the addition of popular anti-globalization movements. Whilst Badiou is not sympathetic to the "vain adventurism" of these groups, he nevertheless sees hope in the juncture of a "new political thought" and "organised popular detachments" (M xxxv).

As part of his turn away from a classical conception of revolutionary change and from a Leninist understanding of the relation between party and state, in his recent writings Badiou has stressed the importance of taking what he describes as "distance from the state". This includes a repudiation of parliamentary politics and a harsh critique of political philosophy. Indeed, Badiou's definition of the alternative, "metapolitics", is described as "whatever consequences a philosophy is capable of drawing, both in and for itself, from real instances of politics as thought". "Political philosophy", the academic discipline that in the 1980s and 1990s concerned itself, according to Badiou, with policing politics in the name of human rights and ethics, is in essence the denial that politics has anything to do with thought and truth. While Badiou's claim that a politics worthy of the name should be primarily a question of thinking seems, on the face of it, to be a profoundly idealistic statement, on a continuum with Platonic or Aristotelian claims about the relationship between the *polis* and human nature, about the Good and man as a "political animal", it should be understood as an attempt to resist the pact between academic political philosophy and what Badiou calls "capital-parliamentarianism".

Here politics is only a description of the realm of public opinion – of polls, statistics, advertising and marketing. For Badiou, contemporary politics and the political philosophy taught in universities are entirely inimical to a politics of truth. As he acerbically puts it: "If our knowledge of planetary motion relied solely on suffrage as its protocol of legitimation, we would still inhabit a geocentric universe" (M 15). Likewise democracy, if conceived as a form of government or a norm of consensus, is incompatible with an unconditional affirmation of equality. It is only if considered as an internal criterion of a politics that axiomatically prescribes equality that democracy, like justice, can be a name (or more precisely an adjective) for politics (M 78–95). Otherwise, it is for Badiou an enemy, and, in the guise of what he calls "democratic materialism", the principal ideological obstacle to a politics of truth (LW 1–9).

Building on the work of his long-time associate, Sylvain Lazarus, Badiou's metapolitics explores this idea of politics "as thought". In an essay on Lazarus's *Anthropology of the Name*, Badiou writes: "There is certainly a 'doing' of politics, but it is immediately the pure and simple experience of a thought, its localisation. Doing politics cannot be distinguished from thinking politics" (M 46). Inevitably, Badiou's complicated relationship to Marxism is implicitly invoked in such a formulation: did not Marx break with the idealism of Feuerbach and the other "merely" critical post-Hegelians by turning to the real abstractions of political economy and recasting subjectivity as a matter of revolutionary practice rather than correct cognition? It is true that Badiou explicitly avoids any discussion of the role of the economy in his conception of politics as thought – politics is rare and singular, it is predicated on the rationalist premise that "people think", and that political truths are always the seizing of a collective subject by an event. Objective conditions never determine political action, and as such, true politics for Badiou always happens at a distance from the state. It is clear that for Badiou those who "believe" in the state are little more than mystics:

> for the patient who prays to the Virgin and gets better, all well and good; but if the patient dies it is because She willed it. Similarly, if I implore our State to be good towards workers and illegal immigrants [*sans-papiers*], either it does something, and it's wonderful, or it does nothing, in which case this is put down to the merciless law of reality in crisis-ridden times. Either way, I have done my duty. (M 71)

Badiou's reflections on collective action are marked, especially from the 1980s onwards, by a concern with naming in politics. One of the aims of his enquiry into the terms most typically associated with the history of left-wing movements (party, masses, proletariat, commune) is to break with the "suturing" of philosophy to politics, and to permit forms of naming that would not perpetuate the totalizing fiction of the political. In suturing instead, particular concepts or proper names come to stand in for the whole of political thought and action. The result is:

> the reduction of the diversity of names of politics to a single and primordial name ... But if these names get sutured to the potential eternity of a philosopheme, it then comes to be that there is only one genuine name, and this name inevitably becomes the unique name of politics ... As History has shown, such a name then becomes a *sacred* name. (C 157)

This is why Stalin and Mao can also be regarded as "creations, or creatures, of philosophy". Against this philosophical sacralization of politics, which binds its occurrence to transcendent names and bodies, Badiou defends the precarious emergence of experiences of emancipation that evade totalizing and unifying imaginaries of Class and Party. As Badiou writes, "[a] genuinely political organisation, or a collective system of conditions for bringing politics into being, is the least bound place of all" (M 76).

As a corollary to his critical reckoning with historical communism, Badiou's political writings in the 1990s and onwards are also an exploration of the question of a politics without a party. The party form for Badiou is entangled with the state form and as such is devoid of both collective thought and subjective militancy: "The central subjective figure is the political militant" (M 122). Badiou's alternative to the party form is in no way an anarchistic model but rather "one organised through the intellectual discipline of political processes" (M 122). Badiou's own involvement during this period with L'Organisation Politique, a small group of militants primarily concerned with the struggle and status of undocumented immigrant workers in France, attempts to put this "intellectual discipline" into practice. More recent writings have qualified Badiou's critique of the party form somewhat, for instance by giving a more positive valence to the notion of Terror and enquiring into the figure of the "state revolutionary" (LW 20–27).

By turning to questions of the collective nature of politics ("An event is political if its material is collective"; M 141) Badiou advances a purer and more minimal notion of communism than the one developed in the twentieth century within the horizon of the state and under the aegis of proper names. In his screed against the (meaning of) French President "Nicolas Sarkozy", Badiou declares that "*communism is the right hypothesis*", and that "[w]ithout the perspective of communism, without this Idea, nothing in the historical and political future is of such a kind as to interest the philosopher" (MS 97, 115; see also Badiou 1987a). According to Badiou, then, the current task of philosophy *vis-à-vis* politics becomes the duty to help a new modality of the communist hypothesis to come into being. It is towards outlining this new modality that Badiou's latest work on politics tends, with a frank admission that in many ways we are returning to the problems, not primarily of the twentieth century, but of the nineteenth:

> We are dealing, as in the 1840s, with absolutely cynical capitalists … All kinds of phenomena from the nineteenth century are reappearing: extraordinarily widespread zones of poverty, within

the rich countries as well as in the zones that are neglected or pillaged, inequalities that constantly grow, a radical divide between working people – or those without work – and the intermediate classes, the complete dissolution of political power into the service of wealth, the disorganization of the revolutionaries, the nihilistic despair of wide sections of young people, the servility of a large majority of intellectuals, the determined but very restricted experimental activity of a few groups seeking contemporary ways to express the communist hypothesis. (MS 116–17)

Among the bleakness of the contemporary situation, Badiou sees, however, a duty and a task: "through a combination of constructions of thought, which are always global or universal, and political experiments, which are local or singular but can be transmitted universally, we can assure the new existence of the communist hypothesis, both in consciousness and in concrete situations" (MS 117). Badiou thus attempts to overcome the theory/practice divide in the name of a new approach to an old question: a return to the mid-nineteenth century in the name of the twenty-first.

For Badiou, politics is not a concept that would allow us to classify and judge the social behaviour of "human animals". Rather, as a condition of philosophy, it is a name for a truth procedure that touches on the being of a collective, is immediately universalizing and "presents as such the infinite character of situations" (M 11, 141–2). The task of philosophy as metapolitics is both to do justice to the singularity of politics against the fiction of the political *and* to discern their underlying commonality. As he writes in "Truths and Justice":

These political sequences are singularities, they trace no destiny, they construct no monumental history. ... Yet philosophy does manage to discern a common trait within these discontinuous sequences: namely, the strict generic humanity of the people involved in them. In their principles of action, these political sequences take no account of any particular interests. They bring about a representation of the collective capacity on the basis of a rigorous equality. (M 97)

Politics is for Badiou above all the affirmation of a collective human capacity, which means that more than any other condition it is a matter of thought, since thought "is the one and only uniquely human capacity" (*ibid.*). Indeed, Badiou has even seconded Rousseau's affirmation that the human animal is essentially good, and only corrupting social constraints make it otherwise (Badiou 2009e). At a distance from the state, and defined by an equality that abhors domination, Badiou's politics is at once inhuman in its meta-ontological bases and ferociously humanist in its affirmation of the generic. Viewed in this light, the communist hypothesis amounts to thinking that, to paraphrase the late Althusser, theoretical anti-humanism can serve practical humanism, that the most uncompromising scientific rationalism is compatible with the most unconditional assertion of collective human capacity.

Note

1. On this distinction, see Badiou (1985: 13; TS 85–6; BE 104–5).

PART III

Badiou's engagement with key philosophers

TEN

Plato

A. J. Bartlett

A wise man follows his guide but
is not ignorant of his surroundings. (*Phaedo* 108a)

Alain Badiou identifies his own philosophical project as a "contemporary Platonism". To be a Platonist is to be faithful to both the mathematical *conditioning* of thought – whereby the most rigorous thinking of
being passes through the most contemporary discoveries in mathematics
– and to insist, against the temper of the times, that "there are truths";
that there is something other than opinion, the encyclopaedia, or the
"state" and that consequentially such truths are rigorously *subjective*.
Badiou's Platonism affirms "an ontology of the pure multiple without
renouncing truth".

The resources Badiou derives from Plato are extensive: explicitly,
the Platonic institution of the speculative, aporetic and formal divisions
between being and appearing, truth and opinion, philosophy and sophistry, mathematics and poetry; implicitly, Plato's formal demonstration
of what constitutes philosophical discourse as a *practice* of separation,
division *and* invention. Philosophy, for both, is *subtractive* of all forms
of "sophistic" knowledge, thereby holding in abeyance both "the tute-
lary figure of the One" (TW 37) and the resigned conservatism of the
"rhetoric of instants" (LW 511). That Plato's dialogues are concerned
with mathematics, art, love and politics – Badiou's four conditions for
the existence of philosophy (the discourses wherein truths are played
out) – confirms Plato's foundational importance for Badiou.

The direct consequence is a philosophy that engages in direct, rigorous and polemical confrontation with the greater part of the philosophy

of the past century and a half: from Nietzsche's curative decree against the Plato-sickness, contemporary philosophy has retreated, Badiou contends, to the sophistic logic of despair – the discourse of "ends" with its attendant conceit and varia (MP 27–32).[1] In their various ways the logics of despair – sober and celebratory by turns – prescribe the end of philosophy as a discourse concerning truth, confine it to the vicissitudes of linguistic construction or reduce it to an adjunct of one of its conditions. The term that holds these disparate, even rival philo-sophistries[2] together today, Badiou says, is "anti-Platonism": a commitment to the impossibility of thinking the conceptual link between Being, truth and the subject. For Badiou, to "return philosophy to itself" is to break with these sophistic *varia* – presence, meaning, finitude, objectivism, relativism, vitalism and those for whom the affirmation of multiplicity is the ruin of the category of truth – and to formalize the consequences of this break without occluding the contingent and constitutive necessity of such a break.

Intervention

Badiou's relation to Plato is best conceptualized as an intervention. *Being and Event* closes with Badiou arguing that it is now entirely possible to reinterrogate the history of philosophy in order to expose such categories as "the event and the indiscernible at work but unnamed throughout the metaphysical text" (BE 435; cf. LW 510). To this end Plato's dialogues, the series of enquiries into the *real* possibility of a non-sophistic way of life, so long buried under centuries of received wisdom, practised indifference, linguistic manipulation or regarded as the site of a necessary overcoming, are redialecticized by Badiou's reinterrogation. This intervention is dialogical rather than repetitious, affirmative rather than analytic, decisive rather than comparative. The Platonic *corpus* hereby avoids the fate Plato ascribes to what is written down and is neither silent nor silenced, forgotten nor the place of a forgetting, but once again speaks back and as itself. The Platonic *corpus* resumes again as the place of subjective enquiry.[3] From Plato, Badiou seizes what is proper to philosophy: "to conceive of the present" (LW 514). In this context the Platonic maxim that "friends have all things in common" – a divisive and polemical axiom, rather than a humanist conceit – takes on renewed vigour.[4]

What follows, then, is something of a delineation of the operation of a friendship, wherein two figures, separated, as Badiou (2007–8) wryly notes, by 2434 years,[5] participate distinctly, yet equally, in establishing the same philosophical idea – an Idea consecrated to the problem "what is it to live?" (LW 507–14). We shall explore Badiou's "Platonic gesture" under three terms that exhibit their commonality: orientation, situation and trajectory. First, it is important to note the key conceptual feature of this friendship: participation.

Retroactions *and* anticipations

Participation – the "Platonic concept par excellence" (BE 36) – has been central to Badiou's work since *The Concept of Model*.[6] In an interview accompanying the English translation, Badiou identifies "participation" as that which is at stake in the formalization of a model. Roughly, a model creates both the conceptual space and the formal processes whereby the participation of the sensible in the intelligible can be thought. Platonism, as Badiou conceives it, is both the "knowledge of ideality" and "the knowledge that access to ideality is only through that which participates in ideality" ("*The Concept of Model*, Forty Years Later: An Interview with Alain Badiou", CM 92). Or: "the Idea is the occurrence in beings of the thinkable" (BE 36). Plato, in maintaining the "co-belonging" or "ontological commensurability" of "the knowing mind and the known" is, Badiou says, heir to Parmenides' injunction "that it is the same to think as to be" (TW 49). In *Logics of Worlds* Badiou says: "The universal part of a sensible object is its participation in the Idea" (LW 301–2). What is consistently at stake in this *intrinsic* "dialectic of formalisation" – the generic construction of a present – is the question of universality: how what is, as such – *and* given that the Idea is not One – must *be* for all (BE 37; TW 151–2).[7] In other words, Badiou shares with Plato the indifference to difference, the equal otherness of all others before the Idea, which true subjective participation – the definitive contrary to submission – reveals in the realm of the sensible (E 25). The ramifications of participation – the activation in thought of the Idea – are present in all efforts to think real universality for which, unlike thinkers of totality or presence, there are no privileged subjects even as there is always *some* subject. For Plato, and this from the *Republic*, anyone, subject to the contingency of an event, has the capacity for truth (*Republic* 518c–d; cf. IT 71). To translate this into *Logics of Worlds*, participation names the "affirmative joy which is universally generated by following consequences through" (LW 514).

Orientation

The *orientation* Badiou and Plato share is two-fold. Philosophical practice is not concerned primarily with definition or interpretation but with transformation. This is not to say that philosophy has transformational effects "outside itself". Rather, it is the discourse of the possibility of transformation – that truths are real, that truth is possible. Philosophy composes the *form* of transformation, preserving the infinite or eternal truth of the various finite and particular procedures that "change the world". This is a question, then, of the constitution of philosophy: "Philosophy does not produce truths"; it is provoked into being by events outside itself. It is the discourse that seizes and composes the being-*there* of the truths of its mathematical, political, artistic or amorous conditions. Badiou asks "who can name one single truth of philosophy?", thus echoing Socrates, Plato's exemplary avatar, who in maieutic mode declares "I cannot claim as the child of my own soul any discovery worth the name wisdom" (*Theaetetus* 150d). For both, the "things" of the world – the aporias they signify, the decisions they demand – are provocations *to philosophy*: For Plato, the trial and death of Socrates, the only *non-sophist*, at the hands of what he all but calls the "sophistic state" (*Republic* 493a), provokes the singular prescription of Plato's turn to philosophy; "how are we to live?" Badiou, similarly provoked by conservative renegations of all types, reinvigorates this polemic when he declares that he has "only one question: what is the new in a situation?" (Badiou & Bosteels 2005: 252–3). These questions convene a practice and not a space of reflection.

This thinking of the generic, the new, the ideal or true requires the thinking through of "the old situation" from the perspective of the universal prescription inherent to *what happens*. In order to track the trace of the new – at the site of an event – in any *situation*, both the *state* or encyclopaedia – which gives order and currency to what exists therein – and the very situation itself *qua* "structured presentation" must be (re)thought or "worked through". In the *Cratylus*, Plato – beginning decisively with things and not words, the ideas and not discourse – provides the generic, dialectical formula: "I think we have to turn back frequently to what we've already said, in order to test it by looking at it backwards and forwards simultaneously" (*Cratylus* 428d): thus *back* to the situation – its logical construction and its ontological predication – and forward from the Idea whose truth manifests itself in accord with, yet as aleatory exception to, that which is elemental to its situation.

Situation

In Plato's dialogues the "exemplary figure of thought", Socrates (or an avatar), confronts one or several figures of "knowledge" – orators, dramatists, professional men, demagogues, generals and so on. Plato collects this seemingly diverse array of interlocutors under the term "patrons of the flux".[8] Socrates is constantly provoking them to speak in their own name because it is clear to him – and once the appearance of things is stripped away it will be revealed as such – that his interlocutors speak for some doctrine or other. Invariably – when they are not the figures themselves – they represent the doctrine of the poets (Homer, Hesiod, Pindar, Simonides) or Heraclitus and his followers; or Protagoras and Gorgias. Parmenides alone escapes this gathering but his commitment to the One is equally problematic for Plato. Badiou notes that Plato rejects the Parmenidean ontology of the indivisibility of the One in favour of a division in being that admits that "the nothing is" (BE 37). Thus, as is demonstrated in the *Sophist*, what is not has being. For Badiou, this turns on the distinction made in the *Parmenides* between two types of multiplicity: *plethos* and *polla*, the first being inconsistent multiplicity, the second "consistent" or "structured" multiplicity. For Badiou, Plato deductively "intuits" the former but lacks the means to its formalization. Instead, Plato has recourse to the "astonishing metaphor of a speculative dream" (BE 34). For Badiou, it is Cantor who will turn the dream into a paradise.[9] In general, for the patrons of the flux (or becoming), in their various ways, to claim the truth of a distinction was an error against the right of perception. The two categories of knowledge for these *Protagoreans* are ultimately "better" and "worse" (*Theaetetus* 152e, 167a). Relation is constitutive and no "fixed point" not "measured by man" anchoring a situation to its being can legitimately be conceived.

In *Manifesto for Philosophy*, Badiou notes six categories of anti-Platonism that he repeats and extends in his recent seminars.[10] He says, "ultimately the 20th century reveals a constellation of multiple and heteroclite anti-Platonisms". Taken together, "their anti-Platonism is incoherent", but what unites them is that each ostensibly accuses Plato of being ignorant of something essential to philosophy and "this something is identified with the real itself" (change for the vitalists, language for the analytics, concrete social relations for the Marxists, negation for the existentialists, thought, inasmuch as it is other than understanding for Heidegger, democracy for the political philosophers). In his most succinct presentation of contemporary anti-Platonism, Badiou not only outlines its general thread but notes that it is itself constitutive of what is understood by "Platonism".

This "Platonism" is that common figure, the contemporary montage of opinion, or configuration that circulates from Heidegger
to Deleuze, from Nietzsche to Bergson, but also from Marxists
to positivists, and which is still used by the counterrevolutionary
new philosophers ("Plato as the first of the totalitarian master
thinkers"), as well as by neo-Kantian moralists. "Platonism" is the
great fallacious construction of modernity and post-modernity
alike. It serves as a type of general negative prop: it only exists to
legitimate the new under the heading of anti-Platonism.

(D 101–2)[11]

From this anti-Platonist collective Badiou derives three predominant
"philosophical" tendencies: the hermeneutic, whose central concept
is interpretation; the analytic, whose concept is the "rule"; the post-
modern, concerned with the deconstruction of totalities in favour of the
diverse and the multiple. Badiou shows that what they have in common
is: a commitment to language, its capacities, rules and diversity such
that language is the "great transcendental of our times" (IT 46; C 20).
The obvious consequence is a commitment to the end of metaphysics
and thus philosophy since Plato (IT 45–6). Plato thus marks the point
of an inception that must be reversed. Contemporary "philosophy" or
anti-Platonism, he says, effectively "puts the category of truth on trial"
(IT 46).[12] Badiou agrees with two claims that arise from the contemporary critiques: being is essentially multiple (MP 85); and Plato marks a
singular and decisive point in the history of thought. Here Heidegger as
much as Deleuze is the central reference. However, in regard to the first
point of agreement, to say being is multiple today is to say it falls under
the regime of mathematics *qua* ontology and not "language". In regard
to the second point, Plato is to be understood today as an *incitement to
thought*, through whom thought is given "the means to refer to itself as
philosophical" and thus "independently of any total contemplation of
the universe or any intuition of the virtual" (D 102). Plato is decidedly
not the moment at which thought turns to despair; rather, it is Plato's
conception of what *there is* that matters and what *there is* are truths,
"a regime of the thinkable that is inaccessible to th[e] total jurisdiction
of language". What is required therefore is a "Platonic gesture" whose
condition is a "Platonism of the multiple" (MP 97–109).

Trajectory

The notion that truth is "on trial" is entirely prescient. In the *Apology*
Plato makes it clear that Socrates is both a singular figure[13] and that

what he represents is intolerable and must not be. Socrates concentrates in a single point what the state, in Badiou's terms, exists to prohibit – unbinding (BE 109). Plato, personally effected by the event of the trial – or rather "the life of Socrates" it brought into relief – takes this as his central point of articulation, deciding thereby that an encounter between two incommensurable "ways of life" has "taken place" and thus undermining the sophistic (and later, Aristotelian) inflection of difference as a global trait. In dialogue after dialogue – and by work-ing through the various articulations of the "encyclopaedia" – Plato elaborates the *indiscernible* consequences of Socrates' *non-sophistic* discourse. The universal form of this non-sophistry is given ultimately in the *Republic* – the ideal city, the place where sophistry, under the condition of love, is, like everyone, "assigned to its place" (C 73).[14] The trajectory is familiar – from (the) nothing (that is) to everything – but the step-by-step articulation of this "immanent universalism" marked by "Socrates" crosses *and* subtracts itself from the contempo-rary sophistic city.

Plato's dialogues each engage the "encyclopaedia", taking their cue from the sophists and anti-philosophers in order to begin to think *through* what it is they propose in order to make it possible that this thought be thought otherwise: specifically, with regard to its *Form*. Likewise, Badiou notes that to return philosophy to itself *today*, one must take from Heidegger the importance of the ontological ques-tion, from the analytics the "mathematico-logical revolution of Frege–Cantor", from deconstructive-postmodernism (wherein Nietzsche lives posthumously) the inexistence of the one of totality, and from Lacan's anti-philosophy, a modern doctrine of the subject (BE 2). Badiou seeks to free what is essential in these discourses from the predicates that con-strain them – and this includes refuting the consensus on "mathematical Platonism" (TW 49–58) – in order to compose a new philosophical form contemporary to its time but concerned, ultimately, with what phi-losophy "had for a long time decided to be, a search for truth" (IT 47).

For Plato and Badiou, philosophy, to be anything other than a branch of sophistry, needs recourse to a discourse that cannot be reduced to the vicissitudes of opinion, dissemination without limit, the temper of the times, judgement or the play of languages. For both, mathematics is "foundational". It is *the* singular discourse that, "in one and the same gesture, breaks with the sensible and posits the intelligible", thus deny-ing *by* its formal existence the right of *doxa* to elevate its knowledge into the "truth of [an] era" (TW 30). Mathematics allows Badiou and Plato to rethink the situation, beyond what logically constrains it, to grasp the form of its being, thus elaborating its consistency without recourse to the vicissitudes of language.[15] The *goal* in doing so is neither expertise nor retreat but, discursively, to "not know what sophistry knows", which is to say, "*to* know that what sophistry knows is not all": on this basis it seeks to formalize under condition of its subjective manifestation the "exceptional" and thus "eternal" Idea of that which sophistry is not (LW 511).

In what we might call the "contingency of recommencement", each time Plato opens a dialogue it is in some way already *decidedly* faithful to this mathematical idea that discerns the split between the *noetic* and the *somatic*, between thought as a disciplined procedure of participation in the Idea and *doxa* as the ingenious reconstruction of the continuity of the state as a stable and fixed body of knowledge.

Let us note that *justice* is what is at stake: wherein only that which is not sophistic – partial, interested, bound in its conceit to the determinations of the state – can be "for all". Plato's "recourse to the matheme" – as aporetic as it *had* to be – is not so much a "mathematical turn", but the realization that only mathematics can consistently support thinking what is otherwise *indiscernible* to a situation. Plato deploys the force of its demonstrations to extend the intuitions and implications opened up by the Socratic *encounter* with the sophistic state. For Badiou, the risk of philosophy amounts to accepting that a discourse exists that does rationally and consistently *think* the being of situations, thus providing the anterior, apodictic and formal Idea of the truths that "found" them (TW 47–8). Philosophy, then, the thinking of truths – as event, as subject, as revolt, as logic – must be conditioned *by* such "thinking". Its role is to compose, in a discourse specific to this composition and to its time, the implications for all thought of the possibility of a discourse – and even, perhaps, a "way of life" – that is not subject to opinion or *doxa* alone.

Philosophy: mathematics of love; politics of poetry

To "return philosophy to itself" – thus to combine in a singular discourse the thinking of the act of interruption *and* the formalization of its consequences within and beyond its situational site – is to be singularly (at first) faithful to Plato. However, fidelity is neither repetition nor mimesis. Nor is it slavish, but rather the practice of a "continuous constraint" (HI 26). For Badiou, given "our situation", it is necessary to do what Plato did. But to do what Plato did is to do it pursuant to contemporary conditions. For Badiou "contemporary conditions" require a different conceptual attitude to mathematics and poetry. We know what Plato thinks about poetry (and its sophistic variants), how its

114

charms are precisely what must be guarded against – for the *coincident* good of the individual soul *and* the polity – and for Plato it is this very affect which means that poetry cannot ultimately be considered as a thought (*dianoia*) of its own. For Badiou, simply, poetry thinks; and philosophy, as the thinking of this thought does not, as Plato suggests, annul it *as* thought (HI 27). For Badiou, poetry can both think the sense of its own situation and, within the space of philosophy, command a position equal to mathematics in so far as poetry names the event – the very sign of the mathematical impasse – and opens the fictional space within which the situated indiscernible or generic (love of) truth will come to "be-there".

While Plato endorses the interruptive capacity of mathematics, his problem is that mathematics cannot be anything other than this. This is to say, mathematics has no *choice* but to break with opinion.[16] For Plato, this signifies a lack of freedom in mathematics; there remains a certain obscurity in regard to its understanding of what it thinks, and this prevents it from being "*noetic*". How can the truth of the break that mathematics establishes without question with opinion – in all times – be thought in such a way that the obscurity it bequeaths to philosophy be illuminated in terms of a principle that serves thought at its most extensive? Plato cannot answer this question and so for him dialectics names a second break: the break with the "obscurity of the first" break (TW 31). For Badiou, this *breaking* with the obscurity of the first break is not required because mathematics thinks *its* situation (as presentation of presentation): it is autonomous and in no way in need of philosophy's *imprimatur*. Gödel's theorem demonstrates that mathematics, as with all situations, is structured *and* incomplete – thus an inconsistent multiplicity, precisely in so far as it forms a consistent discourse. As set theory demonstrates, the former – "the nothing that is", let us say – is essentially the very condition of the latter, and as such this "obscurity" does not annul or condemn mathematics to non-knowledge but instead comes to define its internal rigour and consistency. Philosophy, then, situates this thought as the very site of its own capacity to think the universal trajectory of what is generic to situations – a truth being precisely that which is generic and therefore must *address* every element of the situation for which it is a truth. Thus the impasse or aporia of ontology – that being is not One – is crucial to philosophy's *multiple* composition. With regard to philosophy, poetry is rescued from sophistry (as love is from the sophistry of sex and sentimentality, politics from the sophistry of administration and demagogy, and art from the sophistry of academicism) precisely by the constraining rigour of a mathematical ontology that, being incomplete to itself, induces the decided specificity of poetry's place. At the risk of sentimentality, Badiou returns philosophy to the conditions of Plato's speculative dream and thus to the question of that which is "for all" but is not *one*. However, thanks to what Plato lacked (in a word, Cantor), the dream is now *intelligible*.

Notes

1. In *Plato's Metaphysics of Education*, Samuel Scolnicov notes that aporia has two consequences: despair or incitement (1988: 50). It is very clear that Plato uses aporia as incitement (cf. D 58). Unless otherwise stated, all translations of Plato will be taken from *Plato: Complete Works* (1997). We use the standard abbreviations for all references to Plato's dialogues.
2. This is Barbara Cassin's (1995) term.
3. Debra Nails argues that "Plato's dialogues are and were in Plato's lifetime occasions to philosophise further, not dogmatic treatises" (1995: 4).
4. If Badiou's recent seminars are any indication, the commonality, conceptual and formal, has become even more decisive, extending in one direction as far as a new translation of the *Republic* and a film project called *The Life of Plato*, and, in another, traversing the new concerns of *Logics of Worlds* – most particularly as concerns the status of the Idea – and directly and polemically linking the concerns, categories and disciplinary structure of Platonic enquiry to the contemporary reduction of thought to parliamentary cycles and the attendant disaster of "capital time" – "the normal *speed* to which the subject must *bend*". The seminars entitled "Pour aujourd'hui: Platon!" were given at the College of France over three years: 2007–8, 2008–9, 2009–10 (to come). We should add to this the 1989–90 seminar series on the *Republic*. The 2007–8 seminars and the 1989–90 seminars are reproduced in full on François Nicolas' excellent website. The notes that reproduce the seminars are by Daniel Fischer. See www.entretemps.asso.fr/Badiou/07-08.htm (accessed April 2010). All translations are my own.
5. Cf. *Theaetetus*, where Plato comments on "time" being the privilege of free men (172c+). Here, time is a revolutionary construction. The philosophers invent their own time – the time of truth, to be precise – in express opposition to the "man of the law" courts or the slaves to the state who speak subject to the clock and to a master. "Revolutionary time", Plato remarks, can be "a day or a year"; it does not much matter, the only concern is to "hit upon that which is" (172e).
6. This includes *Theory of the Subject* and the work preceding it, even if there it signifies under a different dialectical register. In this work Badiou marks Plato as the founder of idealism (184) – the ideology of conservatism. He nevertheless puts Plato at some distance from its "history" when he says that Plato designated idealism as a *topos*. It is, perhaps, via this notion of *topos*, suitably "mathematized", that Plato becomes for Badiou a thoroughgoing materialist founder of an "assault philosophy" (185).
7. "When one abdicates universality, one obtains universal horror" (TS 197).
8. In the *Theaetetus* (160d–e) Homer and Heraclitus are linked with Protagoras in that they have converged on the single idea that knowledge is perception. In the *Cratylus* (402b–d) Plato links Heraclitus to both Homer and Hesiod.

He claims that in their treatment of the Gods named Rhea and Cronus can be seen the same concept of "everything gives way, nothing stands fast". The link is through the names, as this dialogue deals with the knowledge associated with etymologies. Thus Rhea sounds a lot like *rheuma*, "stream", and Cronus is meant to be heard as *krounos*, which is "spring".

9. Given our Platonic context, it is interesting to note that the mathematician and senior colleague of Georg Cantor, Leopold Kronecker, described Cantor as a "corrupter of youth". And in terms exactly those of Nietzsche describing Plato, Poincaré described transfinite numbers as a "disease from which he was certain mathematics would someday be cured" (Dauben 2004).

10. These are: the vitalist (Nietzsche, Bergson, Deleuze) the analytic (Russell, Wittgenstein, Carnap), the Marxist, the existentialist (Kierkegaard, Sartre), the Heideggerean, and that of the "political philosophers" (Arendt, Popper).

11. After praising Deleuze as "the most generous" anti-Platonist, "the most open to contemporary creations", Badiou concludes: "All that Deleuze lacked was to finish with anti-Platonism itself". Cf. Badiou (2006j).

12. In his recent seminars Badiou also notes another form of contemporary Platonism, "la Platonisme mystique", which he links to the events of May 1968 and, he says, is manifest in the work of Guy Lardreau and Christian Jambet. See the seminar of 5 December 2007.

13. The only one who speaks the truth (*Apology* 17b) and the only one in all Athens who does not educate (25a).

14. Barbara Cassin, taking up this very phrase, argues, on the contrary, that it is a mistake to seek a place for sophistry within philosophy or as somehow determined by philosophy. Cassin argues that sophistry be understood as a thought of its own, thus making it impossible for sophistry to be "assigned its place" *by* philosophy. See Cassin (2000: 116–17; 1995).

15. "[T]o rethink the situation beyond what logically constrains it" is precisely what is at stake when in the *Meno* Socrates introduces the slave-boy to the diagonal. That the existence of the incommensurable is mathematically demonstrable is the grounding for the hypothesis concerning "recollection".

16. Cf. "Surely you would not regard experts in mathematics as masters of dialectic" (*Republic* 531d). Plato has Socrates add that he has met a few exceptions to this rule.

ELEVEN

Spinoza

Jon Roffe

The various engagements with the history of philosophy that can be found throughout Alain Badiou's work present not just incisive and fascinating encounters motivated by his own philosophical concerns, but also figure as cases in a serial and topical approach to Western thought. It is possible to envision, for example, a history of the infinite in the style of Badiou in which the treatment of Hegel in *Being and Event* is an iconic instance. Likewise, one might speculate on a history of fidelity where Pascal and Beckett are joined in a rigorous fashion. Taking this approach, Badiou's *œuvre* would be traversed by a number of virtual series, manifest in only a few particular cases.[1]

Such a view allows us to appreciate in a summary fashion the proximity of Spinoza to Badiou's work, since the latter finds in Spinoza's metaphysics evidence, licit or otherwise, of almost all of his main ontological concepts: the mathematical access to being, the void, the subject and the generic are all instanced in the pages of the author of the magisterial *Ethics*.

In fact, what Badiou presents in his main readings of Spinoza is a sketch of the work of an *obscure precursor*. In his own way, Badiou takes up the famous Hegelian claim according to which "to be a follower of Spinoza is the essential commencement of all philosophy" (Hegel 1974: 253).

The Spinoza who is a precursor to Badiou's own project is not the Spinoza of Althusser, Negri or Deleuze; nor indeed is it even Spinoza's own Spinoza. In *Being and Event* and Badiou's *Court traité d'ontologie transitoire*, we find the sketch of an "implicit, paradoxical Spinozism" (TW 93),[2] a hidden Spinozism, not without its flaws, which invokes a network of conceptual connections in tension with what lies on the surface of Spinoza's metaphysics.

In more geometrico

Introductions to Spinoza's philosophy inevitably begin by invoking the great themes of his thought. His primary thesis, which flowers from a problematic rift in the work of Descartes, is that there exists only a single being, *Deus sive Natura* – God or Nature – that Spinoza characterizes as infinite, eternal, necessary and self-caused.[3] Those things that we readily identify as the plural occupants of reality (human beings, ponds, stones – the milieu of what a certain analytic philosophy would characterize as middle-sized dry goods) are not themselves to be counted as substances, but as modifications or modes of this single substance. Being is thus strictly speaking predicable of only one subject.

While Badiou's significant pieces of commentary on Spinoza do engage directly and penetratingly with Spinoza's ontology, as we shall see shortly, the basis for the admiration extended to Spinoza lies elsewhere, in Spinoza's conception of mathematics, specifically as it comes to bear on the form of his writing,[4] which is the famous *mos geometrico*, or geometrical method.[5] This method – the most obvious characteristic of Spinoza's *Ethics* to those who open it for the first time – involves presenting his philosophy in the manner that one would present a mathematical argument. Book one of the *Ethics*, for example, opens with eight definitions and seven axioms, which Spinoza draws upon in formulating and proving the thirty-six propositions of the first book. Thus the opening paradox of Spinoza's *Ethics* is precisely that its form seems quite foreign to its content, a paradox already encapsulated in the full title of the work: *Ethica Ordine Geometrico Demonstrata – Ethics demonstrated in geometric order*.

In order to understand Badiou's admiration for Spinoza, we need only see that the paradox here is merely apparent. At the level of Spinoza's project, this is because reality itself is rationally organized, and thus our highest ethical achievement would be to live in accord with this organization, available to all through rational thought. Further, though – an elementary conviction that lies at the centre of Badiou's thought and marks his irreducible hostility towards any romantic doctrine – rationality can never be the enemy of ethics, but is rather the only mark of its effective reality. This is why the attack on irrationality in the appendix of the first book of the *Ethics*, a text held in the highest regard by Louis Althusser, is at the same time an attack on unfounded moral ideas, superstition and prejudice. Of the cure for these constructions drawn from an imaginary relation with the world? "Mathematics."

Now, it is important to be clear that for Badiou Spinoza does not simply take mathematics as the paradigm of knowledge, a theme we often find in modern philosophy. Nor is it just the case that mathematics marks a philosophical and ethical commitment to rigour that Spinoza takes as a hallmark of adequate philosophical thought, although his translator Edwin Curley is certainly right to claim that "Spinoza's choice of the axiomatic method represents ... an awesome commitment to intellectual honesty and clarity" (Curley, "Editorial Preface to the Ethics", in Spinoza 1985: 402).

Nor again is it sufficient to invoke, as I have above, the critical rigour that Spinoza brings to bear upon the many ways in which knowledge, bereft of a deductive foundation and therefore a critical power, leads us to disaster. For few philosophers is the attack on superstition in the name of rationality – inspired more by the Stoics in this case than by Plato – as central as it is for Spinoza. When Badiou movingly invokes mathematics as "a fearsome machine of thought, a catapult aimed at the bastions of ignorance, superstition and mental servitude" (TW 16), or writes that "mathematics alone allowed for the inaugural break with superstition and ignorance" (TW 22), Spinoza is among the very first philosophers who ought to come to mind.

Beyond these quite legitimate claims, it is central to Badiou's appreciation of Spinoza's manifestation of his commitment to mathematics in the form of the *mos geometrico* that it involves a *positive* commitment to an approach to being. Spinoza's commitment to such a method springs from the very nature of being itself. This is part of what is at stake in a famous proposition in the *Ethics*: "The order and connection of ideas is the same as the order and connection of things" (EIIP7). To produce ontological claims according to such a method is not to introduce a foreign apparatus into philosophical thought (a claim that we find, more or less, in Heidegger), but rather involves an inaugural decision to think ontology *rationally*. This is why Badiou is right to insist that Spinoza "sees salvation as residing in the ontology that underlies mathematics, which is to say, in a conception of being shorn of every appeal to meaning and purpose, and prizing only the cohesiveness of consequence" (TW 15).

The geometrical method is thus finally not just a model of thought or a paradigm of epistemological certainty – something to be emulated in other fields or admired from within the hazy environs of human life – but the only concrete means to think being. This is why, in an unforgettable phrase that Badiou cites with admiration, Spinoza writes:

"For the eyes of the mind, by which it sees and observes things, are the demonstrations themselves" (EVP23S).

The ineluctable void

Now, the balance of Badiou's explicit treatment of Spinoza is based on a careful analysis of the Spinozist conception of causality. The nature of causality and the issues that surround it concerning knowledge, freedom and constraint play absolutely central roles in Spinoza's metaphysics. While there are a number of important details this chapter is unable to touch upon, we can see what is at stake for Badiou by thinking once more of Spinoza's substance. If there is to be only one substance, of which everything else is but a modification, then there cannot be any causal interactions that exceed its enclosure. It follows then that substance cannot be the product of anything else, and nor can it be causally engaged with anything else: "God acts from the laws of his nature alone, and is compelled by no one" (EIP17). Substance is the cause of all particular modal expressions of being, and the particularities of the existence of each mode can be exhaustively treated by the specific causal relations they interact with.

Put in terms more germane to Badiou's approach, we can say that Spinoza's account of being necessarily involves the foreclosure of the possibility of the event. While things certainly happen at the level of particular modes (Adam eats the apple, one spider kills another), from the point of view of substance itself – the infamous point of view *sub specie aeternitatis* – the network of causal relations is entirely comprehensive, allowing nothing to come about other than what follows from the nature of substance, and in turn what follows from the nature of particular modes.

It is surprising, therefore, that Badiou's initial critical attention towards Spinoza, as found in the tenth meditation of *Being and Event*, bears not on the event but on the category of the void. In this text, Badiou will argue – in a fashion reminiscent of deconstruction – that in fact Spinoza cannot entirely secure the causal fabric of being, and that the void, a lacuna in causality, symptomatically re-emerges.

The void returns in what is at first sight a peculiar location, that belonging to what Spinoza calls "infinite modes". As we have already seen, a mode is an expression of the single substance, a reconceived notion of "thing" in accordance with the demands of a rationally examined notion of substance. As a mode, it is inextricably entangled with the entire network of causal relations that criss-cross and structure substance, to the extent that what makes a given existing mode (itself always composite for Spinoza) a unified or singular thing is the fact that it has unified effects (EIID7). In Badiou's words: "A composition of multiple individuals (*plura individua*) is actually one and the same singular thing provided that these individuals contribute to one unique action, that is, insofar as they simultaneously cause a unique effect (*unius effectus causa*)" (BE 112).

Now, Spinoza argues that what is finite can be caused only by another finite existing thing:

> Every singular thing [*res singulares*], or any thing which is finite and has a determinate existence, can neither exist nor be determined to produce an effect unless it is determined to exist and produce an effect by another cause, which is also finite and has a determinate existence. (EIP28)

Such is the world of existing modes – a regime exhaustively structured according to causal relations. But this world is also to be characterized in terms of *finitude*. For Spinoza, every existing thing is finite, which is to say, limited by other things of the same kind. This is what lies at the root of the single axiom at the start of book four of the *Ethics*: "There is no singular thing in nature than which there is not another more powerful and stronger. Whatever one is given, there is another more powerful by which the first can be destroyed" (EIVA1).

The problem emerges when we discover, contrary to this line of argumentation, that Spinoza believes a certain class of things exist that are *infinite* in nature. These are what he will call infinite modes, for example God's infinite intellect. These infinite modes cannot of course be caused by already existing finite modes, but rather follow directly from the infinite nature of substance itself, according to Spinoza (see in particular EIP21–3).

Badiou detects here the creation of a strange chimera, one that draws upon the causal nature of existing finite modes on the one hand and the infinite nature of substance itself on the other in order to stitch together a hybrid existent, the infinite mode. Given the precarity of this existent from the point of view of Spinoza's deductive philosophy, Badiou does not hesitate to assert that something illicit has taken place. Given that "the immediate cause of a singular finite thing can only be a singular finite thing, and, *a contrario*, a (supposed) infinite thing can only produce the infinite", the name "infinite mode" can only be given to the void that emerges here in the causal chain: that is, "the void would be the errancy of the incommensurability between infinite and finite" (BE 116).

In place of another deducible element in his systematic metaphysics, Spinoza's infinite mode is rather a "nominal artifice" that "inscribes errancy into the deductive chain" (BE 120). This errancy is nothing other than the void itself.

Spinoza's implicit subject

For Badiou the ineluctable return of the void is, however, not the only problematic admission that Spinoza's philosophy forces us to make, and nor is it necessarily the most significant. Already in *Being and Event*, Badiou links his critical conclusion to the fact that "one can no longer avoid the supposition of a Subject" (BE 113). This line of argument is pursued in a piece published six years later under the revealing title "Spinoza's implicit ontology", a title later changed to "Spinoza's closed ontology".[6] Both are apt: the latter marking Spinoza's goal and the former his illicit achievement. It is with respect to Spinoza's implicit ontology that Badiou is able to argue, in his second essay, that it is only by exceeding the limitations of his own statutes that the great philosopher is able to manifest the requirements for a theory of the subject even in a metaphysics that seemingly has no room for one.

Badiou comes to argue that there are operations theorized by Spinoza that cannot be accomplished without the existence of a subject, operations irreducible to the unfolding of causal consequence. To see what is at stake here, we must introduce the third great ontological category of Spinoza's thought, *attribute*. The category of attribute is central to Spinoza's repudiation of Cartesian dualism. In place of the substantial division between mind and body posed by the latter, Spinoza will argue that the difference is *formal* in nature. The upshot of this is that thought and extension, to mention the two attributes most commonly referred to by Spinoza, a mind and a body, are not two substances but rather the same thing (ie. the same existing modal expression of substance) grasped from two different points of view – or, to be more precise, under two different attributes, or according to two "qualities" of substance itself. In illustrating this idea, Spinoza writes:

> For example, a circle existing in nature and the idea of the existing circle, which is also in God, are one and the same thing, which is explained through different attributes. Therefore, whether we conceive nature under the attribute of Extension, or under the attribute of Thought, or under any other attribute, we shall find one and the same order ... (EIIP7S)

Thus a human being is not composed of two unequal halves, as in Descartes, but is rather one singular thing grasped from two points of view. When changes occur to my body – when I eat, or fall ill – they are equally changes within my mind, and inversely, when I change my mind, I indeed change what I am on the strictly material level.

As a resolution to problems insoluble within the Cartesian framework, Spinoza's use of the category of attribute is radical and original, but it is not without its own problematic consequences. The (famous) problem that Badiou will investigate emerges when we put even this rudimentary account of Spinoza's human being alongside the technical definition of attribute as we find it at the start of the *Ethics*: "By attribute I understand what the intellect perceives of a substance, as constituting its essence" (EID4). What he seems to be claiming here is that one attribute provides the capability of thinking all of the other attributes (which Spinoza argues are infinite in number [EIP11] even if we as human beings are only able to conceive two), seemingly elevating the activity of thought above all other attributes with which they are supposed to be in a strictly parallel relationship.

How can this be the case? Badiou's reply is that, while Spinoza's explicit ontology cannot provide a solution to this vexed issue, he provides an account of an *implicit* operation. This operation is required not to hastily shore up an ill-formed category, but to provide a foundation for the reality and significance of thought as such.

Badiou will call this operation *coupling*, a non-causal union of thought and its object, an operation unique to the attribute of thought. It is worth noting at this point that Spinoza himself characterizes thinking in just these terms: "The object of the idea constituting the human Mind is the Body, or [*sive*] a certain mode of Extension which actually exists, and nothing else" (EIIP13). An idea and its object are, in keeping with Spinoza's radical monism, identical in substance but distinguishable in thought. Badiou's point, however, is on the one hand that this kind of relationship is in excess of causal connection and cannot be reduced to it. Thus Spinoza is in the position of having to surreptitiously endorse the reality of a non-causal operator of connection in order to explain how we can come to know reality. In other words, he must embrace the possible being of the subject.

A final problem remains, however, and it once more concerns the relationship between finite and infinite. As thinking beings, we are finite in nature, and thus our access to reality is limited. And, while Spinoza's account of knowledge is extremely complex, we are already in a position to see that true knowledge for Spinoza cannot emerge from my case alone, but by bridging the gap between my particular case and what I have in common with other beings. This is because, strictly speaking, what I am as an individual is already invested in causal relations with others. Thus it is through what is common to all that what is true for me is guaranteed, and this access to the common cannot be thought according to the strictly local causal relations in which I am engaged. From this it follows that local knowledge requires a relationship with the level of what is true for all possible intellects: the finite, in so far as it attains to truth, must be engaged with the infinite. This is what leads Badiou to posit a third mode of relation beyond causality and coupling, which he calls *inclusion* (this set-theoretic term is used here in a way that differs from its role in *Being and Event*). The finite intellect is included in the infinite intellect, which is nothing other than substance itself under the attribute of thought for Spinoza.

What is key, however, is that these two relations of coupling and inclusion are extra-causal in nature, which is to say irreducible to the regime of structure in being. As such, they are exemplary figures of what Badiou will call the indiscernibility of the subject and the generic character of truth.

Conclusion

We might, by way of conclusion, divide Badiou's elementary concepts as we find them in *Being and Event* into three categories with an eye to the way in which they appear in the work of his obscure precursor Spinoza. In the first case, we have an explicit and fundamental agreement on the unique status of mathematics in relation to being. The philosopher for whom "mathematics = ontology" (BE 6) is in the company of an ally in Spinoza, for whom the *mos geometrico* provides us with the deductions that are "the eyes of the mind" (EVP23S). Both thinkers "accept mathematics as multiple-being", which makes Badiou, in his own words, a "Spinozist" (TW 93).

In the second category are those concepts that have obscure and implicit counterparts in Spinoza's metaphysics. Despite his attempt to account for being according to an exhaustive network of causal relations, Spinoza nonetheless admits the void and the subject into his system, the first as a symptomatic lacuna, and the second as implicit operation of genuine thought.[7]

There is, however, a third category that has no complement, explicit or otherwise, in the great pages of Spinoza, and it includes a concept of supreme importance for Badiou: the event. In Spinoza, the vast hum of occurrence is never undone by the advent of a radical novelty.

In Spinoza, we find time without history, a time governed by a single unbroken divine metric, a time of pure geometric order, a time without temporality:

> What is lacking is a founding category [that] would constitute an exception to, or supplement for, the "there is". It is precisely at this juncture that we need to introduce what, in the wake of others, I have called "the event". This event is also what grounds time, or rather – event by event – *times*. But Spinoza, who according to his own expression wished to think "without any relation to time," and who conceived freedom in terms of "a constant and eternal love of God," wanted no part of it. (TW 93)

So it is to others that we must look in order to find the midwives of the Badiouian conception of the event. And in making this point, Badiou illustrates a philosophical imperative of some import, an imperative that separates philosophy from psychoanalysis on one side and mere scholarship on the other: that one must always strive to have *more than one master*.

Notes

1. For a sympathetic account of Badiou's reading of Spinoza more technical than I provide here, see Sam Gillespie (2001b). A critical assessment of Badiou's treatment of Spinoza's infinite can be found in my "Badiou and Deleuze on Individuation, Limitation and Infinite Modes in Spinoza" (Roffe 2007).
2. Throughout I refer to Badiou's two essays on Spinoza: Meditation 10, in *Being and Event*, and "Spinoza's Closed Ontology", R. Brassier & A. Toscano (trans.), in *Theoretical Writings* (2004e: 81–93).
3. These claims are found, respectively, at EIP8, P19, P11 and P25S; throughout I will quote from *The Collected Works of Spinoza* (1985) according to the standard means of reference, which is itself set out in the Curley edition (*ibid.*: xix).
4. In a presentation to the "Wandering with Spinoza" conference held at the School of Creative Arts in the University of Melbourne in 2006, Badiou spoke in detail and with great passion about the strictly deductive nature of the *Ethics*. A version of this text, entitled "What is a Proof?", will be available shortly in a collection of essays dedicated to this event edited by Dimitris Vardoulakis, whom I thank for granting me access to this important text.
5. A good summary of the various possible reasons why Spinoza chose this method as the means to present a number of his works, including the *Ethics*, is provided by Aaron Garrett (2003). As will be clear from what follows, Badiou adopts the strong, intrinsic reading of the geometrical method, rather than treating the form of Spinoza's work as merely pedagogical.
6. The piece was originally published as "L'ontologie implicite de Spinoza", in *Spinoza: puissance et ontologie*, M. Revault d'Allones (ed.) (Paris: Kimé, 1994).

We must imagine that Badiou changed the title upon its inclusion in his *Court traité d'ontologie transitoire* (1998d).

7. Badiou's own list is longer, making inclusions that we cannot in this short chapter adequately account for: "indeterminacy, difference, subject, undecidability, atypicality, coupling, doubling, inclusion, genericity of the true. And a few others as well" (TW 93).

TWELVE

Kant

Peter Hallward

Of all the modern philosophers that Badiou engages with, Kant occupies an exceptionally ambiguous position, at once distant and congenial. If on balance Badiou affirms a qualified fidelity to Hegel, his explicit relation to Kant is generally critical, if not dismissive. Badiou's main concern is with what might make the "impossible" possible – with events that cannot occur, with decisions that cannot be resolved and with actions that cannot be carried out or continued within the existing limits of a situation. But in his conventionally "watered-down" form, at least, Kant is precisely the thinker of stifling "limits, rights and unknowables" (LW 8);[1] any "return to Kant" is the symptom of "closed and morbid times" (Badiou 1995: 14). Kant seems to exemplify a tendency to restrict philosophy to scholarly if not idle reflection on the various (logical, linguistic or biological) dimensions of a mere "capacity of cognitive judgement", on the assumption that the "laws" that limit this capacity are more or less constant (2006i: 21). Badiou has long associated a certain "average Kantianism" with the dominant ideological configuration of the day, a tepid "idealism, centred on Man, and no longer on God: consciousness as the focal point of experience, the subject as guarantee of truth, morality as atemporal formalism" (TS 187).

It is easy, then, to enumerate a series of obvious differences between the two thinkers. Where Badiou himself seeks to affirm the primacy of a "subject without object", Kant imposes their irreducible correlation. Where Badiou affirms the exceptional and subversive quality of the subject as the local operator of universal truths that exceed demonstration, Kant confirms its transcendental status as an enabling condition of *all* possible experience. Where Badiou insists on adequation of being and thought, Kant confines knowledge to the representation of appearances. Where Badiou urges the "laicisation of the infinite", Kant figures (especially in the wake of Heidegger's mediation) as "inventor of the disastrous theme of our 'finitude'" (LW 535). Where for Badiou a subject forces the apparent "impasse" or "impossibility" of a situation, Kantian "critical incarceration" obliges all subjects to respect the humbling sanctity of the law. In short, as Badiou admits in an evocative note to *Logics of Worlds*, "everything about Kant ... exasperates me, his legalism above all". Kant obliges a respect of constraints and limits,

> always asking *Quid juris?* or "Haven't you crossed the limit?" ... . The critical machinery he set up has enduringly poisoned philosophy, while giving great succour to the Academy, which loves nothing more than to rap the knuckles of the overambitious – something for which the injunction "You do not have the right!" is of constant help ... . The solemn and sanctimonious declaration that we can have no knowledge of this or that is always a preparation for some obscure devotion to the Master of the unknowable, the God of the religions or his placeholders: Being, Meaning, Life ...   (LW 535)

It would be much too simple, however, to reduce Badiou's relation to Kant to one of antagonism pure and simple. Badiou acknowledges Kant as a vital precursor in the effort to devise an adequately "subtractive" ontology, a properly logical account of the object, and a suitably uncompromising approach to ethics. In many ways Badiou's theory of the subject resembles Kant's rationalist voluntarism more than it does either Hegel's account of spirit or Marx's account of class. Like Badiou, Kant affirms the immortality of a true subject and insulates this immortality from the given configuration of the world, from the apparent norms of nature or society, or from any (necessarily incoherent) reference to a "whole". Overall, therefore, Badiou reads Kant as a "paradoxical philosopher whose intentions repel, whose style disheartens, whose institutional and ideological effects are appalling, but from whom there simultaneously emanates a kind of sepulchral greatness, like that of a great Watchman whose gaze you cannot escape" (LW 536). A great deal of Badiou's work, in and after *Being and Event*, is shaped by his quasi-Kantian acknowledgement (against both Hegel, Heidegger and Deleuze) that what can be said of truth and being cannot be said in one and the same discourse. It is hardly surprising that one of the most frequent critical moves made against Badiou's later work, most notably by Slavoj Žižek, is precisely to characterize it as, in the end, more Kantian than Hegelian (or Marxist).[2]

Badiou's effort to engage with and elude Kantian super-vision, so far, has proceeded along two main fronts: ontologico-epistemological and ethico-political.

Ontology and epistemology

Perhaps the most obvious difference between Badiou and Kant concerns their respective understanding of the relation between being and knowledge. Kant accepts that, after Hume, there is no going back to the classical ontological presumptions of a Spinoza or Leibniz: knowledge applies only to what appears and as it appears, within the spatio-temporal confines of our passive and sense-bound intuition, via the synthetic operations of the understanding. By interrupting the classical ontologists, Kant proposed for the first time a philosophy made fully autonomous of the play of *substantial* reality. He subtracts the categories of pure reason from any constituent relation with noumenal realities or "things in themselves", and thereby provides a sort of "subtractive ontology" that anticipates Badiou's own lack of concern for the apparent nature or "essence" of things (TO 132). But for Badiou, subtraction applies to any form of essence (including its most abstract form, that of the "one" as such) but not to being itself. No less than his contemporary rival Gilles Deleuze, Badiou's own ontology returns to the classical assertion that thought engages directly with true reality or being, rather than merely supervising the orderly analysis of phenomena or appearances. "Not only is it possible to think Being, but there is [ontological] thought only insofar as Being simultaneously formulates and pronounces itself therein" (D 20, cf. 45).

In direct contradiction with Kant, when Badiou equates ontology with mathematics, he does not mean that mathematical analysis in some sense represents (let alone measures or quantifies) a reality external to it. He means that mathematics articulates being itself, being as such. Mathematics does not describe, represent or interpret being, but is, in itself, what can be thought of being *tout court*. "The apodicity of mathematics is guaranteed directly by being itself, which it pronounces" (BE 6, trans. mod.). The analysis of number is not merely a matter of representation; "it is a matter of realities .... Number is a form of Being", and the most fundamental such form is simply zero as such, the void of an empty set (NN 7, 211).

Rather than grasp realities in themselves, Kant limits cognition to knowledge of objects of possible experience. Seeking a secure foundation for knowledge against (Hume's) scepticism and (Swedenborg's) delirium, Kant argues that cognition can be sure of itself only when it links sensory intuition and conceptual understanding in the synthetic unity of *an* object; it is a short step from here to a definition whereby "thinking *is* the action of relating given intuitions to an object" (1997b: A247/B303–4, emphasis added).[3] After condemning his "childish" ignorance of mathematics, Badiou recognizes that "Kant is without doubt the creator in philosophy of the notion of object", where the term "object" applies to "that which represents a unity of representation in experience" (LW 236, 231). It is precisely Kant's insistence, at the centre of his doctrine of cognition, on "the category of the object, the guideline and absolute limit of the Kantian critique" that blocks any reference here to "fundamental ontology" (MP 73).

Badiou's reaction to Kant's cognitive limitation is characteristically ambivalent, involving ontological defiance and an epistemological concession. For Badiou, it is not the rational correlation of subject and object that serves to ground awareness of "heterogeneous existence"; the void, or "nothing, rigorously (mathematically) subsumed under a concept, is precisely what upholds *the heterogeneously existent*" (Badiou 1991b: 9, emphasis added). Badiou cannot agree with Kant that "being-in-itself is unknowable. On the contrary, it is absolutely knowable, or even known (historically-existing mathematics)". In *Logics of Worlds*, however, he is happy to accept that whether or not it is accessible, "this knowledge of being (*onto*-logy) does not entail that of appearing (onto-*logy*)" (LW 102). Whatever we might know of being *qua* being (if anything), such knowledge cannot inform our knowledge of being-there, that is of what "appears" or "exists" in a given world.

Here then is the basis for a new convergence with Kant. "What Plato, Kant and my own proposal have in common is the acknowledgment that the rational comprehension of differences in being-there (that is, of intra-worldly differences) is not deducible from the ontological identity of the beings in question." Kant compensates for this gap by introducing the "transcendental subject, which binds experience in its objects"; Badiou appropriates similar vocabulary in order to name the elaborate logical machinery that, though detached from the constitutive and subjective functions it retains with Kant, can still "account for the intra-worldly cohesion of appearing" (LW 122). Whereas Kant associated the transcendental conditions of experience with the invariable limitations of an abstract subject of thought, what Badiou calls the "transcendental" of a given world is entirely immanent to the objective configuration of that world, in which it serves to differentiate, order and rank the infinitely many degrees of appearing that are compatible with its prevailing logical configuration (LW 118–19, 199–201).

Where Kant insists on a single transcendental logic, grounded in the synthetic cognition of a universal subject, Badiou's new "logics of worlds" recognizes an infinite multiplicity of transcendentals, such that "the intra-worldly regulation of difference is itself differentiated; this is one of the main reasons why it is impossible here to argue from a unified 'centre' of transcendental organisation, such as the Subject is for Kant" (LW 120). But where Kant's insistence on the object as the abstract form of all possible representation was previously just an obstacle to ontological speculation, Badiou is now happy to

> concede to Kant, not only the distinction between thought and cognition, but also a kind of antecedence of transcendental thought over the contingent singularity of being-there. There must be concepts a priori "as conditions under which alone something is not intuited, but thought as an object in general". There must exist a formal identification of the object, such as it is constituted in its worldly being-there, or such as it appears. And this identification is thought – as Kant remarkably puts it – with respect to transcendental operators as such. (LW 239)

Badiou can now "agree with Kant that existence is nothing other than the degree of identity (of permanence) of a being 'in the phenomenon' (according to being-there-in-a-world)" (LW 238). He can also agree that the need to think the difference between the pure logical form of an object and any actual or empirically given object evokes an essential onto-logical difference, between "the invariance of the multiple and the variation of its worldly exposition". In the Kantian framework, Badiou points to an "empirico-transcendental undecidability of the notion of object" itself, indicated by Kant's need to distinguish between the pure or abstract logical notion of an "object in general" (the object form as such) and "any object whatsoever" as encountered in experience, that is, the object or phenomenon as actually given via intuition. In his own framework, Badiou explains that "my goal too is not that of making visible what is known in a world, but that of thinking appearing or the worldliness of any world whatsoever – whence the affinity with the Kantian idea of possible experience" (LW 232).

Despite this newfound proximity, Badiou continues to insist on two essential differences that distinguish him from his old antagonist. First, because "he was unable to think through the (mathematical) rationality of ontology itself", Kant is unable to think the relation *between* being and appearing. In the most elaborate sections of his "greater logic", Badiou seeks to show that, however great "the gap may be between the pure presentation of being in the mathematics of multiplicity, on the one hand, and the logic of identity which prescribes the consistency of a world, on the other, a twofold system of connections exists between them". At the local or "atomic" level, Badiou demonstrates that "the smallest component of being-there is prescribed by a real element of the multiple that appears". At the global level, "by means of the retroaction of transcendental logic on the multiple composition of what appears, there exist relations immanent to any being which is inscribed in a world", and which enable "exactly what Kant searched for in vain: an ontico-transcendental synthesis". (Badiou does not assess Kant's later attempt, in his *Critique of the Power of Judgement*, to evoke the "supersensible" basis for an apparent reconciliation of being and appearance, of noumenal freedom and phenomenal necessity). Badiou formalizes his version of this synthesis, in the daunting scholium to book three of *Logics*, as the *"transcendental functor"* (LW 277–95): regardless of whether or not this version is persuasive – it seems to depend on a combination of pure postulation on the one hand and unpresentable retroaction on the other[4] – it allows him to reassert his post-Hegelian fidelities, against Kant. Because he insists on the irreducible mediation of sensibility, "what Kant does not see is that thought is nothing other than the capacity synthetically to think the noumenal and the phenomenal; or – and this will be the Hegelian ambition – to determine being as being-there" (LW 240). To grasp the truth of the object requires the "overturning of Kant's prudence: the concept of object designates the point where phenomenon and noumenon are indistinguishable, the point of reciprocity between the logical and the onto-logical" (LW 241).

Second, if like Kant Badiou seeks to think the "appearing or the worldliness of any world whatsoever", he does so in order to help prepare us to get that further post-Hegelian point that Marx would make, half a century after Kant, about our world: "the point is to change it". This brings us to the other main dimension of Badiou's rivalry with Kant – the dimension of practice and ethics.

Ethics and politics

Most of Badiou's explicit references to Kantian ethics are again unequivocally hostile. For Badiou, decisions about how to act and how best to continue such action can proceed only (like everything else) in a situation, drawing on the resources and opportunities of that situation and in opposition to the limits that structure and constrain it in certain ways. True ethical decisions proceed from the point of a "constrained action", under the pressure of events, without any sort of overarching guarantee. He associates Kant, by contrast, with the assertion of an absolute moral imperative transcending all matters of mere political circumstance or strategy, along with the reductive notion of a "radical Evil, identified as indifference to the suffering of the other" (Badiou 1995; cf. LW 240). In the context of Badiou's own political trajectory, a "return to Kant" evokes, first and foremost, the stridently apolitical moralism of the *nouveaux philosophes*, their appeal to an abstract and hypocritical discourse of human rights and ethical guarantees.

The urgency of this polemic leads Badiou to downplay some obvious similarities here, which have often been noted by his readers and critics. Kant's moral philosophy is precisely an attempt to formalize universally binding subjective "truth", made in the absence of any reliable knowledge as such (Kant 1997a: 47, 49).[5] If for Kant we are indeed finite as phenomena, as moral agents we *act* as infinite noumena (and through these actions, we illustrate the noumenal, that is, unknowable, basis of our freedom, our immortality and so on). Precisely because practical reason is free of any "heteronomous" or "empirical motives" (1997c: 390), so Kant's moral philosophy holds "firm even though there is nothing in heaven or on earth from which it depends or on which it is based" (*ibid.*: 425–6). Is there not then an important sense in which the supremely Kantian effort – "to deny knowledge in order to make room for faith" (1997b: Bxxx) – anticipates, if we swap "fidelity" for "faith", a central preoccupation of Badiou's philosophy?

Like Badiou, Kant abstracts questions of ethics from all "sensibility", and like Badiou, he posits the universal as the sole legitimate dimension for subjective action (1997c: 443, 438). In so far as Badiou's approach is one that acknowledges the ability of *everyone* to become a subject, it is consistent with Kant's refusal to treat people as means rather than ends. It was Kant who first evacuated the ethical command of any substantial content, so as to ground ethical "fidelity" in nothing other than the subject's own *prescription*. "The unique strength of Kant's ethics", as Žižek explains,

> lies in this very formal indeterminacy: moral Law does not tell me what my duty is, it merely tells me that I should accomplish my duty. That is to say, it is not possible to derive the concrete norms I have to follow in my specific situation from the moral Law itself – which means that the subject himself has to assume the

responsibility of "translating" the abstract injunction of the moral Law into a series of concrete obligations .... The only guarantor of the universality of positive moral norms is the subject's own contingent act of performatively assuming these norms.

(Žižek 1997: 221; cf. Lacan 1988: 315)

Kant's very procedure – the evacuation of all heteronomous interests and motives, the suspension of all references to "psychology" and "utility", the refusal of any calculation required to obtain "happiness" or "welfare" (Kant 1997c: 391, 394) – bears some resemblance to Badiou's. What remains paramount for both is a specifically *subjective* (and explicitly "infinite") power, that is, the force of our will as such. When Kant says "I ought never to act except in such a way that I could also will that my maxim should become a universal law" (*ibid*.: 402), the active willing is an essential component of the criterion (*ibid*.: 424). In some of his most recent work, on communism, Badiou himself seems quite happy to approach the notion not as a concrete programme so much as "an Idea whose function, to speak like Kant, is regulative" (MS 99, trans. mod.).

The obvious difference of Kant's arrangement from Badiou's is that he grounds his practical reason less upon the random incidence of an event than upon the constituent attribute of freedom as the property of all rational beings. Badiou sees true freedom as an exceptional achievement; Kant sees it as a necessary presumption. Although Kant accepts that we cannot *know* freedom as "something real in ourselves and in human nature", we do at least know that "we must presuppose it" as the dimension of practical reason (1997c: 449). Kant thus lends rational universality an emphatically law-like character, grounded in the literally regular employment of a general faculty. In Kant's hands, moral behaviour becomes the realm of a general legislation or supervision, a matter of public "duty" and "obligation". Where Žižek sees in Kant's insistence on the formal indeterminacy of the law an invitation to take a further step towards (post-Hegelian) political self-determination, Badiou sees in it a retreat from politics altogether, a retreat from direct political participation to the comfortable perspective of the indignant moral spectator. Kant's moral

Law is without content, and it is its being evacuated of any assignable reference that constitutes it as commandment ...[;] the moral meaning of the act lies in the universally presentable nature of its signification, and the universality of signification is itself grounded in the formal void of the Law.   (C 204)

What Badiou objects to in Kant, in other words, is not the association of truth with an infinite reality "independent of animality … and the whole world of sense", but the association of this reality with an abstract transcendental *normality*. Kant grounds the authority of *the* moral law in the *fact* of freedom and the faculty of reason (1997a: 91–2). Having banished the transcendent One from his ontology, Kant resurrects it in his morality (1997b: Bxxx, A641–2/B669–70, A828/B856). By contrast, Badiou argues that only ontological infinity is "normal": every subjective intervention is an exception to pre-existing limits and rules, including moral rules. Badiou's ethics is incommensurable with the whole Kantian register of legality, duty, obligation and conformity, and his notion of the subject has nothing to do with a will determined by purely *a priori* principles. Between Kant and Badiou, on this score, there is the distance travelled by two centuries of militant engagement and revolutionary politics.

Notes

1. In his *Theory of the Subject*, one of the many aspects of Badiou's defence of an adequately "historical" (as opposed to a merely structural) dialectic involves "taking sides with Hegel against Kant" (TS 187). Kant and Hegel oppose each other, here, as alternative ways of moving from the sphere of the mind to the sphere of reality in itself. For Hegel, "the interior produces its own exteriority", in keeping with the presumption that there can be "no guarantee of the truth except in the Whole". Kant (unlike Berkeley) acknowledges an outside to knowledge but only on condition that such external reality "in itself" must remain forever unknowable and inaccessible. "What does Kant gain by recognizing that there is an outside", Badiou asks, "if the constituent legislation of the inside suffices to gauge experience?" He gains two things: "first, the opening of a territory for morals and religion that is in excess over the delimitation of knowledge. And, second, a minimal productivity" in the domain of knowledge, in so far as knowledge, equipped with a capacity for "synthetic a priori" judgement, acquires a limited ability to engage with a novelty in excess of mere analytical repetition or redundance, that is, a "topological ability of generating the new according to a trajectory in which the real exteriority, even though it cannot be traversed, nonetheless imposes from afar upon the subjective interior the strangeness of a production on itself" (TS 119–21).
2. See for instance Žižek (2002: lxxxiv–lxxxv). On the alternative "Kant or Hegel'", as it plays out in *Logics of Worlds*, see Clemens (2006: 134–40). Clemens notes that Badiou overtly sides with Hegel against Kant, but suggests that he has "far more profound affiliations with Kant" (*ibid.*: 138).
3. References to Kant's works here use the conventional German pagination. Cf. Badiou (1991b: 6).
4. For more on this aspect of *Logics of Worlds*, see Hallward (2008: 118–20).

THIRTEEN

Hegel

Bruno Bosteels

Of all canonical philosophers aside from Plato, Hegel is without a doubt Badiou's most constant interlocutor. "In effect," he writes, "I think there are only three crucial philosophers: Plato, Descartes and Hegel" (LW 527). At least in his published work, no other philosopher is read with the same fervour as the author of *The Science of Logic*: "I have never ceased measuring myself up to this book, almost as unreadable as Joyce's *Finnegans Wake*" (LW 529). Both *Being and Event* and *Logics of Worlds* contain important sections devoted to Hegel, and there are a sufficient number of references to Hegel scattered throughout Badiou's recent publication to warrant the claim that he continues to see himself as a dialectical thinker who works in the shadow of Hegel.

In *The Century*, Badiou argues that the re-evaluation of the dialectic is very much a self-assigned task of the whole twentieth century: "The century is a figure of the nondialectical juxtaposition of the Two and the One. Our question here concerns the century's assessment of dialectical thinking" (TC 59, trans. mod.). Instead of the more familiar schemes for the sublation of contradiction, much of the twentieth century is said to be dominated by what Gilles Deleuze would have described as "disjunctive syntheses", that is, non-dialectical or even anti-dialectical solutions to the problem of articulating not only the old and the new, the end and the beginning, the instantaneous act and the creative duration, but also truth and semblance, life and the will, historicism and vanguardism. The highest aim of many of the most innovative political, artistic and even scientific experiments of the past century is to come face to face with the real in an instantaneous act or ecstatic break, rather than in an internal overcoming of contradictions: "The question of the face-to-face is the heroic question of the century" (TC 15). In fact, it is precisely the absence of any dialectical sublation that is compensated for by the violent "passion of the real" that characterizes so many of these artistic and political sequences: "Violence comes in at the point of the disjunction; it substitutes itself for a missing conjunction, like a dialectical link forced into being in the place of the antidialectic." Only on a few occasions in these lectures are we given a glimpse into what might constitute a more properly dialectical understanding of truth as the articulation of an ongoing process, over and against the primacy of the violent and instantaneous act.

The reassessment of the "valences of the dialectic", to adopt Fredric Jameson's title, not only applies to the twentieth century; it also casts its shadow over all of Badiou's own writing: "You could almost say that my entire enterprise is one giant confrontation [démêlé] with the dialectic" (TC 31–2, trans. mod.). On one hand, this body of work seems slowly but surely to have moved from a dialectical to a mathematical outlook, to the point that we might be able to read the later writings in light of what the author says about Hegel in *Being and Event*: "Mathematics occurs here as discontinuity within the dialectic" (BE 169). On the other hand, as late as in *Peut-on penser la politique?* all Badiou's major philosophical concepts are still presented as the building blocks for a new dialectic: "I hold that the concepts of event, structure, intervention, and fidelity are the very concepts of the dialectic, insofar as the latter is not reduced to the flat image, which was already inadequate for Hegel himself, of totalization and the labor of the negative" (1985: 84). If anything, *Logics of Worlds* only further highlights this continuity, as Badiou now labels his entire philosophical project – or at least the ideological atmosphere surrounding it – a new "materialist dialectic" as opposed to the dominant ideology of "democratic materialism" (LW 21). However, it is above all in Badiou's earlier works, most notably in the article "Infinitesimal Subversion", in the prefatory remarks and footnotes to the translation of *The Rational Kernel of the Hegelian Dialectic*, a text by the Chinese philosopher Zhang Shiying, and in the first part of *Theory of the Subject*, that Badiou argues in a detailed and painstaking way for the possibility of a materialist reading of Hegel's dialectic.

The sheer fact of this continued interest in Hegel in and of itself deserves some comment in so far as Badiou is formed in a school of thought dominated by the influence of Louis Althusser, for whom Hegel is the philosophical curse that weighs down on Marx and Marxism, threatening both with the temptation to relapse into one form or other of idealism. Badiou's Hegelianism thus completely runs counter to the accepted wisdom of orthodox Althusserians. We are also far removed from the image of Hegel popularized by Alexandre Kojève, whose introductory lectures on the *Phenomenology of Spirit*, particularly the section on the master–slave dialectic, heavily marked French thought from André Breton to Jean-Paul Sartre to Jacques Lacan. Finally, Badiou's most recent invocations of Hegel have little to do with the image of Hegel as a thinker of finitude – an image of thought that runs the gamut from Adorno to Žižek by way of Jean-Luc Nancy and Catherine Malabou.

In *Peut-on penser la politique?* Badiou remembers how fiercely divided the French philosophical scene was in the 1960s and 1970s, as witnessed by the polemic between Sartre and Althusser. Hegel, in this context, was often little more than a code name to denounce the persistence of humanist and idealist elements in the early Marx, even if the anti-humanist trend according to Badiou is not wholly incompatible with a return to Hegel of its own, provided that we abandon the dominant influence of the *Phenomenology* in favour of the *Science of Logic*.

Sartre, on one hand, found inspiration for his critique of Stalinism by turning to the arch-Hegelian topics of alienation and the struggle for self-consciousness, whose influence is most strongly felt in the Marx of the *Economic and Philosophic Manuscripts of 1844*. For Badiou, however, this effort, while in many regards heroic, in the end betrays both Hegel and Marx. "In the *Critique of Dialectical Reason* (but after the young Lukács, after Korsch), Sartre in a single movement greeted Marxism as the insurmountable horizon of our culture and undertook to dismantle this Marxism by forcing it to realign itself with the original idea that is most foreign to it: the transparency of the cogito," Badiou writes in *The Rational Kernel of the Hegelian Dialectic*. Furthermore, he concludes: "Both this Marx and this Hegel are equally false, the first for being reduced to the second, and the second for being separated from that part of himself that precisely cleared the path for the first: the *Great Logic*" (Badiou, "Hegel en France", in 1978b: 13–14, my trans.).

Althusser, on the other hand, wanted to reclaim Marx's radical discovery of a new, structural type of causality by stripping it of all Hegelian elements: "Althusser restituted a kind of brutal trenchant to Marxism, isolating it from the subjectivist tradition and putting it back in the saddle as positive knowledge", and yet this project, too, in the end involved a double avoidance: "Marx and Hegel, even though in opposite terms, found themselves as much foreclosed as in the previous moment: the materialist Hegel of the *Great Logic* is equally mute for Althusser and for Sartre" (*ibid.*).

This grandiose but also debilitating alternative between Sartre and Althusser is precisely what Badiou's retrieval of the Hegelian dialectic seeks to overcome, all the while remaining loyal to the two major referents of French Maoism. "What the Cultural Revolution and May 1968 made clear on a massive scale was the need for something entirely different from an oscillation of national intellectual traditions (between the Descartes of the cogito, Sartre, and the Descartes of the machines, Althusser), in order to reinvest Marxism in the real revolutionary movement," Badiou writes, and concludes: "The Maoist aim was to break with this alternation, with this avoidance" (*ibid.*: 15). Thus, as a major recourse to trace a diagonal across the Sartre/Althusser debate, Maoism also means a return to the conflict of interpretations surrounding Hegel. Hegel's very own division, in fact, seems to be the only remedy against the temptation to submit his work to either a positivist or an idealist reductionism: "Hegel remains the stake of an endless conflict, because the belabored understanding of his division alone is what prohibits, in thinking the relationship Marx/Hegel, both the idealist-romantic deviation and the scientist-academic deviation, as well as, finally, the hatred pure and simple of Marxism" (*ibid.*: 17).

Hegel's fate, according to Badiou, is to be neither inverted nor discarded, but split from within. In fact, the dialectic itself comes to be defined as a logic of scission, to the point that all its concepts are in turn internally divided between a dialectical and a non-dialectical side: "The dialectic itself is so to speak dialectical, insofar as its conceptual operators, which reflect reality, are all equally split" (1975c: 81; 1985: 84). This interpretive principle applies in the first place to Hegel. "Thus, it is the style of transformation at work in Hegel that we must also question and divide: in a way, we must seize the Two of the Two, the dialecticity of the Hegelian dialectic, and see what in this movement finally leads back to the One," Badiou concludes; and later, he seems to reiterate the same principle: "The dialecticity of the dialectic consists precisely in having its conceptual history, and to divide the Hegelian matrix up to the point where it turns out to be in its very being a doctrine of the event, and not a regulated adventure of the spirit. A politics, rather than a history" (1978b: 91). This is not the same old story about the rational kernel hidden within an idealist shell so much as the idea that the kernel itself must be split: "It is the kernel itself that is cracked, as in those peaches that are furthermore so irritating to eat whose hard internal object quickly cracks between one's teeth into two pivoting halves" (TS 3). It is only by cracking in two the rational kernel of the Hegelian dialectic that we can begin to understand how this dialectic presents a doctrine of the event – one that precisely articulates a theory of the subject onto the fundamental crack in the ontological edifice of being – that anticipates Badiou's own.

Hegel himself already hints at the possibility to see the first role of the subject, of spirit or of the "I", not as a schoolbook example of synthesis and sublation but as the power to split reality into the real and the unreal. "For it is only because the concrete does divide itself, and make itself into something non-actual, that it is self-moving. The activity of separation is the power and work of understanding, the most astonishing and mightiest of powers, or rather the absolute power", Hegel writes in his Preface to the *Phenomenology*, and concludes:

> The circle that remains self-enclosed and, like substance, holds its moments together, is an immediate relationship, one therefore which has nothing astonishing about it. But that an accident as such, detached from what circumscribes it, what is bound and is actual only in its context with others, should attain an existence of its own and a separate freedom – this is the tremendous power of the negative; it is the energy of thought, of the pure "I".
>
> (Hegel 1977: 13–14)

Rather than opposing subject and substance as two self-enclosed circles without intersection, as so often happens in textbook versions of the opposition between humanism and structuralism, the real task of the dialectic as a theory of the event, or a theory of what Hegel here calls an accident, consists in coming to grips with the articulation of both these terms through their inherent scission. Finally, much more so than in the *Phenomenology*, Badiou finds the interpretive keys for his materialist reading of the dialectic of scission in Hegel's *Science of Logic*. "To restore Hegel in his division is not a vain task," Badiou concludes, "Yet this requires that we give back the power of speech to the Hegel who has been gagged, the essential Hegel, the one feverishly annotated by Lenin and the one about whom Marx declared that his reading governed the intelligibility of *Capital*: the Hegel of the *Logic*" (1978b: 17). Even more specifically, given the primacy of the activity of the understanding over and above speculative reason, it is only to be expected that the dialectic would manage to avoid the trappings of its idealist capture above all in the early steps of Hegel's arguments. "As so often, we will admire in Hegel the power of local dialectics, the precision of the logical fragments in which he articulates some fundamental concepts (in this instance, being-there and being-for-another)", Badiou declares in *Logics of Worlds*, repeating an insight already stated much earlier: "What is manifested here is a typical contradiction between the local and the totality of Hegel's work", so that, even if this work as a whole "makes a circle" in so far as globally "he ignores the differed retroactions", we should add that "Hegel is as always capable of locally forgetting his global forgetting" (LW 146; TS 47–8; see also Badiou 1978b: 76).

We are now in a better position to understand why Badiou can define himself as "a philosopher of the post-dialectical dialectic (for this is, pardon me, how I would like to define myself)" (2007j: 151). This dialectic is *post*-dialectical in so far as it reiterates some of the more hackneyed criticisms thrown at Hegel. Badiou first of all claims on numerous occasions that Hegel's dialectic tends to be circular – presupposing the end at the beginning and leading back in the conclusion to a speculative restating of the initial presupposition. "It would not be an exaggeration to say that all of Hegel can be found in the following: the 'still-more' is immanent to the 'already': everything that is, is already 'still-more'" (BE 162). For Badiou, the materialist answer to this looping-back mechanism responds to a periodization by way of breaks and leaps, followed by qualitatively new retroactions: "Hegel, on this point, must be divided once again. He must be divided in terms of the procedures he proposes for looping back the whole process. To be brief, we will oppose (materialist) *periodization* to (idealist) *circularity*" (TS 18). The Hegelian circle, thus, is undone in favour of an image of the dialectical process as a spiral, combining the circle and the leap in an ongoing series of symptomatic torsions.

Second, Badiou's dialectic is also critical of Hegel's tendency to subordinate the logic of scission to the notion of the true as totality. "Hegel is without the shadow of a doubt the philosopher who has pushed furthest the interiorization of Totality into even the slightest movement of thought", whereas Badiou's materialist dialectic – like Adorno's negative dialectics – starts from the principle that the Whole is the false. "One could argue that whereas we launch a transcendental theory of worlds by saying 'There is no Whole,' Hegel guarantees the inception of the dialectical odyssey by positing that 'There is nothing but the Whole.' It is immensely interesting to examine the consequences of an axiom so radically opposed to the inaugural axiom of this book", Badiou writes in *Logics of Worlds*, and concludes:

> Of course, we share with Hegel a conviction about the identity of being and thought. But for us this identity is a local occurrence and not a totalized result. We also share with Hegel the conviction regarding a universality of the True. But for us this universality is guaranteed by the singularity of truth-events, and not by the view that the Whole is the history of its immanent reflection.
>
> (LW 141–3)

Third, perhaps the most original criticism of the Hegelian dialectic appears in *Being and Event*, when Badiou shows how the con-
demnation of the "bad infinity" of mathematics as opposed to the
"good infinity" of the subjective dialectic actually showcases the
pre-Cantorian nature of *The Science of Logic*. The argument in this
instance is a good example of the dialecticity of the dialectic. "After all,
the bad infinity is bad due to the very same thing which makes it good
in Hegelian terms: it does not break the ontological immanence of the
one; better still, it derives from the latter. Its limited or finite character
originates in its being solely defined locally, by the still-more of this
already that is determinateness" (BE 165). The infinite, thus, would be
intrinsic to the finite – indeed, it can be wholly inferred or generated
out of the latter, as its immanent passing over into its opposite. For
Badiou, this generative ontology, in which quantity and quality are said
intrinsically to pass into one another, cannot hide the central disjunction between the two – a disjunction or split that the word "infinity"
covers up with a false homonymy. "The 'good quantitative infinity' is a
properly Hegelian hallucination", Badiou concludes, before announc-
ing for his part a subtractive ontology, based on a Cantorian understanding of multiple infinities, to replace Hegel's generative ontology:
"It was on the basis of a completely different psychosis, in which God
in-consists, that Cantor had to extract the means for legitimately naming the infinite multiplicities – at the price, however, of transferring to
them the very proliferation that Hegel imagined one could reduce (it
being bad) through the artifice of its differentiable indifference" (BE
169–70).

While thus in many ways decisively *post*-dialectical, Badiou nonetheless remains at the same time a post-*dialectical* thinker writing in the
wake of Hegel. This positive legacy, too, can be summarized in three
main points. For Badiou, truth is first of all a process or a labour, rather
than an act of revelation or a propositional attribute:

> At least in this regard I remain more profoundly Hegelian. That
> is, I am convinced that the new can only be thought as process.
> There surely is novelty in the event's upsurge, but this novelty is
> always evanescent. It is not there that we can pinpoint the new
> in its materiality, but that is precisely the point that interests me:
> the materiality of the new.   (In Bosteels 2005b: 253)

The practice of philosophy, second, amounts to thinking the truths of
one's time, truths that have already occurred before the arrival of the
philosopher on the scene of the event. "I have assigned philosophy the

task of constructing thought's embrace of its own time, of refracting newborn truths through the unique prism of concepts", Badiou claims.

> In this aspect, too, I think that I am fairly Hegelian. In certain regards, philosophy would rather have a tendency always to arrive too late. Ultimately, the owl of Minerva only takes flight at dusk. I understand this fairly well, even though obviously not for the same reasons as Hegel. I understand that the major problem for the philosopher is to arrive early enough.
> (TW 14; see also Badiou in Bosteels 2005b: 254)

Unlike for Hegel, though, this thinking of the truths of one's time does not presuppose an intrinsic temporalization of the concept. Put otherwise, the concept is not the effectuation of history's immanent rationality. This is precisely the point where the notion of rupture, introduced by the extrinsicness of a contingent event, breaks with the subjective circularity of the Hegelian dialectic. This also means that for a philosopher of the post-dialectical dialectic, such as Badiou sees himself, thinking must break with the romantic paradigm of the historicity of thought in which philosophy is typically called upon to compete and – nowadays at least as opposed to the heyday of the owl of Minerva – plead guilty in the tribunal of world-historical reason whose blindfolded goddess seems to hearken to the call of finitude. "There is a very tenacious and profound link between the disentanglement of mathematics and philosophy and the preservation, in the inverted or diverted form of finitude, of a non-appropriable or unnameable horizon of immortal divinity", which can only be overcome through a radical secularization of the infinite: "Only by relating the infinite back to a neutral banality, by inscribing eternity in the matheme alone, by simultaneously abandoning historicism and finitude, does it become possible to think within a radically deconsecrated realm" (TW 26–7; MP 29–31; C 16–22). Despite his pre-Cantorian deposing of the bad infinity of mathematics, Hegel's most precious gift to the twenty-first century, according to Badiou, and over and against the previous century's complete domination by Kant's analytic of finitude as retrieved by almost every major philosopher from Heidegger and Foucault to Nancy and Malabou, might well have been the search for a secular or a-theological infinity.

Badiou's ongoing confrontation with Hegel's dialectic, in other words, announces a battle on two fronts: against the dogmatism of the metaphysics of theological infinity, on one hand, and against the perhaps no less theological scepticism of the analytic of finitude, on the other:

The decisive point here is that, for Hegel, mathematics and philosophical speculation share a fundamental concept: the concept of the infinite. More particularly, the destitution of the metaphysical concept of infinity – in other words, the destitution of classical theology – is initially undertaken through the determination of the mathematical concept of the infinite. (TW 10)

The destitution of the traditional metaphysics of the infinite, however, should lead not to an embrace of radical finitude but to a thorough immanentization of infinity. "I think Hegel saw it before anyone else: ultimately, mathematics proposes a new concept of the infinite" and "teaches us that there is no reason whatsoever to confine thinking within the ambit of finitude. With mathematics we know that, as Hegel would have said, the infinite is nearby" (TW 18). This is a promise not limited to mathematics but announced by certain art forms as well. "There is no separate or ideal infinite. The infinite is not captured *in* form; it *transits through form*. If it is an event – if it is *what happens* – finite form can be equivalent to an infinite opening", Badiou writes, and in an explicit return to the argument over bad infinity from *The Science of Logic* previously criticized in *Being and Event*, he concludes this time with a word of praise for the immanent power of the infinite as displayed in art:

> The infinite as pure creation is thereby attained by taking hold of that which makes the obdurate activity of surpassing count 'in itself,' and not by virtue of subsequent repetitions. It is this immanent creative power, this indestructible capacity to overstep boundaries, which is the infinity as *quality* of the finite.
>
> (TC 155–8)

Hegel against Kant, the dialectic of infinity against the analytic of finitude, the constant passing beyond against the obsessive fixating of boundaries: such would be, finally, the philosophical battle of the new century against the old one.

FOURTEEN

Heidegger

Mark Hewson

In setting out the position of his work within the contemporary philosophical environment, Badiou states that his philosophy belongs with that of Heidegger in that it recognizes the necessity of the question of being to the renovation of philosophy. Comparison between the two enterprises is therefore inevitable.

The intervention of Heidegger's first works was to restore ontology to the central place that it had held in the philosophical tradition, showing that, approached from the right angle, its questions reveal a closer link between philosophy and human existence than the theory of knowledge that had displaced it. Despite Heidegger's efforts, it is not clear that ontology has regained its former status within the wider field of philosophy: such force as it retains remains largely tributary to Heidegger's direct influence. This had been the case, at least, until *Being and Event*.

If Badiou, too, restores the primacy of ontology for an understanding of what philosophy is, he does so, I would suggest, in a largely autonomous way. His project is not conceived primarily as a critique of Heidegger. Badiou's reconception of the questions of ontology goes back to the Greek sources, and to the (relatively marginal) philosophical work in which this tradition was preserved, rather than to Heidegger's thought. This explains why, despite the similarity of the titles – *Being and Time*, *Being and Event* – these works do not stand in the kind of close communication and dialogue that one might expect.

Being and Event does not attempt to answer the questions that Heidegger poses for reflection. For Badiou, ontology is not a question of the "meaning" of being: the "content" of ontology is rather located wholly within the work of mathematics, and philosophical work is hence directed towards the event-character of truths belonging to science, love, art and poetry.[1]

Badiou's engagement with Heidegger comes, as it were, after the occupation of this basic position, and serves primarily to clarify it by contrast. One sees this externally in the absence of a concern to engage with the details of Heidegger's text. There is a chapter in the *Manifesto for Philosophy* that does about as much as could possibly be done in the space of a few pages to identify the direction and the sensitive points of the later Heidegger's philosophy; but here as elsewhere there is little sign of a genuine absorption in the work. Badiou's writing on Heidegger seems primarily intended to redraw the map of contemporary philosophy by dislodging Heidegger from the eminent position he occupies.

The fact that Badiou proceeds from a fully formed ontological thought allows him to assess Heidegger from a point of exteriority to his work and, at the same time, to be open to the questions that animate his philosophy. This gives his writing on Heidegger an especial interest. Since Badiou grants the greatest importance to the question of being, his critical approach is entirely different, even when it is at its most sharply polemical, from the kind of critiques that have issued from the Anglo-American context, where Heidegger's work is found wanting as measured by logical, ethical or political imperatives that shape the critics' own work, but do not lead into Heidegger's concerns. On the other hand, Badiou's work does not have the close internal relation to Heidegger that one finds in a whole tendency of contemporary philosophy, above all in France, represented, among the best-known names, by figures such as Levinas, Blanchot, Derrida, Nancy and Agamben.

One could well situate Badiou's work in relation to the conjuncture represented by these names in terms of the relation to Heidegger. For each of these writers and philosophers, there is a sense in which Heidegger constitutes a turning point in philosophy, defining the space within which contemporary thought has to move. In Badiou, by contrast, one finds an attempt to see Heidegger's work as representing a decision between two or more alternatives, as one possible direction among others.

We can see this stance in *Being and Event* in Meditation 11 entitled "Nature", which is the main treatment of Heidegger in this book. Here, the alternatives consist in the possible relation to Plato. This Meditation proposes a revision of the historical picture and the philosophical self-understanding presented in Heidegger's essay "Plato's doctrine of truth". With Plato, Heidegger argues, there occurs the historical transformation in the "essence of truth" that institutes the interpretation of truth as conformity to the idea, and supplants the understanding of truth as *aletheia*, as taking out of concealment. Heidegger argues that this latter conception is still present in parts of the myth of the cave, but that it is displaced in the movement by which Plato gathers his thought together as "doctrine" (i.e. the doctrine of the Ideas). This textual crux in Plato is taken as indicative of an epochal transformation, by which the understanding of being, articulated by the Presocratic thinkers, in their manipulation of key words, such as *aletheia*, *physis*, *logos*, *polemos*, and others, is submerged by Western metaphysics. A number of Heidegger's texts are devoted to recovering the experience of being preserved and transmitted in these words through close analyses of the fragments of the Presocratics. The wider significance of this hidden reserve of early Greek thought is set forth most comprehensively in Heidegger's 1935 course, the *Introduction to Metaphysics*. It is to this course, which was published in book form in 1953, long before the more recent project of the collected publication of Heidegger's lectures, that Badiou primarily refers in *Being and Event*.

The debate that Badiou initiates with Heidegger, then, concerns how we understand the beginning of philosophy, and how this beginning programs our own relation to philosophy. This general question is already embedded in the more narrowly philosophical–historical question of how one should formulate the relation between the Presocratics and Plato. Let us here refer to Badiou's version of the transition in *Conditions*, where we find an admirably clear and stark formulation of the alternatives that confront any interpretation of this sequence:

> When Parmenides places his poem under the invocation of the Goddess, and begins with the image of an initiatory cavalcade, I think that it is necessary to maintain that this is not, that this is not yet philosophy. For every truth that accepts its dependence in regard to narrative and revelation is still detained in mystery; philosophy exists solely through its desire to tear the latter's veil.
>
> The poetic form, with Parmenides, is essential; it covers with its authority the maintenance of discourse in the proximity of the sacred. However philosophy can only begin by a desacralisation; it institutes a regime of discourse which is its own earthly legitimation. Philosophy requires that the *profound* utterance's authority be interrupted by argumentative secularisation.
>
> (C 36)

The decisive moment, the real transition, then, occurs with Socrates and Plato, with a discourse based on argumentation, subject to the test of critical reason, and aspiring to universal intelligibility. In many ways, Badiou's version of the transition is closer to the traditional understanding than that of Heidegger. The distinctive strategy of Badiou's attempt at a re-foundation of this ideal consists, of course, in the recourse to mathematics, as the guarantee of a purely secular and universal order of truths. Mathematical reasoning provides the fixed point, the point of interruption, that allows purely secular and argumentative procedures to dissipate the authority of mystery, and to create the universal space, in which there is no longer any reserve for the "profound utterance" to shelter:

> It is essential to see that the support for such an interruption can only be of the order of the matheme, if one understands by this the discursive singularities of mathematics. Apagogic reasoning is without doubt the most significant matrix of an argumentation that does not sustain itself on the basis of anything other than the imperative of consistency, and which turns out to be incompatible with any legitimation by narrative, or by the initiated status of the subject of enunciation. (C 36–7)

Against Heidegger's archaeological recovery of the unthought of Platonic and hence Western thought, Badiou defends the legitimacy of the Platonic intervention as the real inauguration of philosophy, and underlines the essential place of mathematics as its enabling condition. Moreover, through the refusal of the analysis of "Plato's doctrine of truth", it becomes possible to sketch out a basic alternative, a divergence of paths open to philosophy, depending on whether one has recourse to the naming power of language, or whether one rather refers to mathematics, and to the universality, not essentially bound to language, that it represents. Let us return to Meditation 11 of *Being and Event*, for Badiou's statement of the alternative that is placed before us, by Heidegger's work.

> It is clear then that there are two paths, two orientations, commanding the whole destiny of Western thought. The one, referring to nature in its original Greek sense, receives in poetry appearing as the emerging presence of being. The other, referring to the idea in its Platonic sense, subjects the lack, the subtraction of all presence, to the matheme, and thus separates being from appearance, essence from existence. (BE 125, trans. mod.)

For the one orientation, being signifies the initial openness, the evidence of things, prior to any kind of human ordering and mastery of the given: for the other, being is the void, "the lack, the subtraction of all presence", the pure multiple, of which mathematics is the progressive exposition. Correspondingly, for the one, ontology (or thinking, since Heidegger later abandons the word "ontology') is a reflection on "simple relations" (*einfache Bezüge*) that bind us to the most initial dimensions of evidence, in advance of any knowledge (cf. "Letter on Humanism"): for the other, ontology is rather "a complex and rich science" (BE 8, trans. mod.).

One can pursue this contrast to the point where the differences between Badiou and Heidegger appear so great that one has to conclude that it is simply a matter of two quite distinct philosophical enterprises, each with a basically different question, which only somewhat contingently and misleadingly cross paths on the word "being". For Heidegger, being demands our attention, our response, and is the only possible repository of our hopes: in an at-times rather wild essay from the 1940s, he even suggests that the truth of being is what has to be preserved, no matter what happens to humanity or to anything else.[2] For Badiou, on the other hand, being in terms of discourse is a matter for the specialized operations of the mathematicians, a matter of deductive consistency rather than a demand for existence, capable of transforming it.

sic

But one could also suggest that the coexistence of these alternatives on the philosophical scene invites us to preserve the sense in which they represent a fundamental alternative, a struggle in which the antagonists can take on their real shape (to borrow the pattern of Heidegger's interpretation of *polemos*, *Auseinandersetzung*, the conflict that opens the space of thought). One can perhaps discern something of this conflict in the way that Badiou recurrently returns to Heidegger, giving similar and yet slightly modified versions of their relation, sometimes wanting to dismiss his problematic entirely, more often seeking to partition and localize it, as if he still felt a kind of fascination for the problem of being, in the Heideggerean sense, even from the position that claims to have bypassed it.

In *Being and Event*, as in *Conditions*, Badiou's strategy is to consign the thought of the Presocratics – so important to Heidegger's later work, since it contains the evidence of a thinking of being, prior to Platonic doctrine – to the status of "mysteries", a thought still linked to narrative and revelation. This does not, however, seem to reduce it to a mere seductive rhetoric without content:

> I can readily admit that the absolutely originary thought moves in
> the element of poetics and the letting be of that which comes into

presence (*laisser-être de l'apparaître*). This is proved by the imme-morial character of the poem and of poetry, and by its established and constant suture with the theme of nature. ... Ontology in the proper sense, as the native figure of Western philosophy, is not and could not possibly be the advent of the poem in its attempt to name, in its power and luminousity, appearance as the coming to light of being, or unconcealment. This is much older in time, much more multiple in its site (China, India, Egypt ...).

(BE 125, trans. mod.)

The Presocratics, as a thinking of presence, cloaked in mystery and revelation, cannot represent what is specific and epochal to Greek thought, it is claimed, since their thought has analogues in many dif-ferent cultures or traditions. It must be said that this analogy is merely declared, not something that is shown or "established", and as such it cannot be taken to affect the extensive analyses of the early Greek thinkers, in many of Heidegger's texts. In part, the similarity is made plausible by the reduction of the early Greek thought to the key term *physis*, which then becomes "the theme of nature", and starts to sound less like the being of beings, in the Heideggerean sense, than the eternal emerging and disappearing that characterizes nature in the modern sense (i.e. vegetal and animal life, considered as a totality). Badiou seems to be attempting here to reduce Heidegger's thought, or at least his principal witnesses, to the status of a kind of pantheist mystery reli-gion. It is hard to see such an approach as more than merely polemical. Above all, what it does not attend to is the sense, in Heidegger, of early Greek thought as an *event*, as the first opening up of being, which is then transformed and effaced with the advent of metaphysics. If one can say, with Badiou, that the "poetic ontology" of the Presocratics (in Heidegger's presentation) is an ontology of presence, an ontology of the One, it is essential to add that this is a "one" that is constituted, opened up in poetic thought as the "setting to work of being" (*Ins-werk-setzen-des Seins*), not a theological One, that can be supposed to be the same noumenon, celebrated in the song and ritual of all lands and peoples.[3]

When Badiou comes back to the *Auseinandersetzung* with Heidegger in the *Manifesto for Philosophy*, the approach is somewhat different, although the basic strategy moves in the same direction – to limit the monological discourse of the thinking of being and its polarizing authority-claims by positioning it within a wider field of possibilities. This time, however, Heidegger's work is situated in relation to the historical pressures of modern thought, rather than to the decisions of the Greeks. The Heideggerean thought of being is now seen as the philosophical expression of the impulses that transform poetry from the beginning of the nineteenth century.

Badiou's thesis here, though only given in sweeping outlines, is of great potential interest to literary studies, since it offers a novel conceptualization of an area that is still in need of historical paradigms for its interpretation. For the historical formation, he proposes the title "The Age of the Poets" – a sequence beginning "just after Hegel" during which "poetry assumed certain of philosophy's functions" (MP 69). The basic phenomenon at stake here is that which is concisely encapsulated by Jean-Luc Nancy as "the specifically modern possibility that literature and/or literary theory (criticism, poetics etc.,) is conceived as the locus of truth" (1993: 260). In the literature – and above all in the poetry – of this period, the literary or the poetic is understood, not in terms of a certain kind of language, a certain modification of the language we use in everyday business and conversation, but rather in terms of a truth-potential proper to the poem. The truth of the poem would not be its subject matter, but would be produced solely to the extent that the poem realizes itself as a poem, and nothing else.

For Badiou, the motivation for this remarkable tendency in the history of poetry derives from philosophy, rather than from within the poetic domain itself: an "intellectual pressure" weighs on poetry because of a lack of "free play" in philosophy (MP 69–70). This "pressure" is traced back to what Badiou calls the "sutures" by which philosophy, in the nineteenth century, delegates its functions to one or other of its "generic conditions" – the scientific condition in positivism, the political condition in Marxism. The domain of truth staked out by poetry is opened up by the limitations of the philosophical thought of the period. This thought is dominated by the imperatives of logic and verification (positivism) or by the subordination of thought to political imperatives (Marxism). More generally, it is opened up by the domination of the category of objectivity that prevails within both these forms of thought. The truth of the poem, announced by poets such as Hölderlin, Rimbaud and Mallarmé, announces the decisive separation between truth and knowledge. It is this truth that Heidegger's thought then thinks through, in uncovering the foundations of knowledge in truth as unconcealment.[4]

For Badiou, however, this means that Heidegger's work – and the whole conjuncture of contemporary philosophy that it commands – can be grasped as a "suturing" of philosophy to poetry. Now that it no longer represents a nascent resistance to the sutures of the nineteenth century, now that it has been thought through by Heidegger, the age of the poets can also be seen as a historical formation that has reached its end:

The only fundamental critique of Heidegger is that the age of the poets is finished. It is necessary to de-suture philosophy from its poetic condition. This means that disobjectivation, disorientation no longer today have to be formulated by poetic metaphor. Disorientation is now conceptualisable.   (MP 74, trans. mod.)

good

What is needed, in other words, is something like the renewal, after an immense historical trajectory, of the initial interruption that was worked by Plato with reference to the Presocratics. In order to renew the philosophical field, it must once again be freed from the auratic authority, the mystery and the revelation, that is now identified with Hölderlin, Mallarmé, Char – and first and foremost, one can think, with Heidegger, in whom the themes and motifs of these poets are put to work and given their latent philosophical force.

the greats

perfect!

But what are the demands, what are the constraints on an "interruption" in this situation? And what will its character be? Will it be merely a repetition of the Platonic gesture, such as Heidegger describes it, a turning away and a forgetting, anticipated perhaps by the turning away of being itself? For Badiou, mathematical reasoning provides the "fixed point" from which to interrupt the rumour of the profundity of Heidegger – but must one not also hear and belong to this interminable questioning, in order for the interruption to be genuine, in order for a true silence to be created, as opposed to a mere diversion, behind which the voice of being continues its murmur? How does one in fact *cease* to attend to being in the Heideggerean sense – the "wonder of wonders" – that things are? In the violence with which, at times, Badiou seeks to neutralize Heideggerean thought, one can see a desire to tear philosophy out of hearing range of "the voice of being". In the claim to mark the beginnings and the ends of "the age of the poets" one can see a historical justification for this desire. On the other hand, in the care with which Heidegger's thought is preserved as an alternative, even if the wrong one, and in the recurrent return to poetry that has marked Badiou's work one can see the concern still to belong to an order of questions – the initial evidence of things, opening up before us – entirely free from any kind of formalization, immune to the demand of universality, and accessible only to the language that belongs to it.

Notes

1. Justin Clemens and Jon Roffe sketch out this transformation of the question of being and hence of the task of philosophy in "Philosophy as Anti-Religion in the Work of Alain Badiou" (2008).

2. See the "Afterword" to "What is Metaphysics?" in *Pathmarks* (Heidegger 1998).
3. For the Heideggerean sense of Greek poetry and thought as an "evental" opening up and gathering of being, see *Introduction to Metaphysics* (2000: § IV, pt 3, "Being and Thinking").
4. For a critical discussion of Badiou's theses on "the age of the poets", see Lacoue-Labarthe (2007), esp. ch. 1, "Poetry, Philosophy, Politics", 17–37.

FIFTEEN

Lacan

A. J. Bartlett and Justin Clemens

Lacan for us is essential and divisible.   (TS 133)

It would be difficult to overestimate the impact of Jacques Lacan's work on Badiou. In the "Formulas of *L'Étourdit*", Badiou is blunt: "my guiding thread is going to be, as always, Lacan's relation to philosophy. Ultimately, this is the only thing that interests me" (2006d: 81–2). With regard to philosophy, then, Badiou heeds Lacan – "Psychoanalysis gives us a chance, a chance to start again" (Lacan 2008: 76) – precisely in order to return philosophy to itself. Given that Badiou is not an analyst, an analysand, a theorist of literature, film, culture or the psychology of the social, any examination of Badiou's relation to Lacan has to take this orientation as its guiding thread. In short, Badiou's confrontation with Lacan, the exemplary anti-philosopher, is *for* philosophy alone.

The scene of the Two

Lacan is the immediate precursor and contemporary whose life and work continually shadow Badiou, the thinker whose own turbulent acts are one model of a form of political activism (E 6–7), whose constant renovation of his own doctrine provides an exemplary prac-tice for thought more generally, and whose radical propositions are to be remorselessly re-interrogated for their import. Badiou admires Lacan's rejection of social consensus, of analysis as normalization, of the pursuit of happiness, and so on. Badiou admires Lacan's institu-tional courage: Lacan was famously expelled from the International

Psychoanalytic Association in 1963 for his clinical innovations, notably the notorious "short-session"; Lacan later set up and then dissolved his own school. Badiou admires Lacan's constant re-elaboration of the distinction between "truth" and "knowledge", the concomitant de-substantialization of truth, as well as Lacan's voracious enthusiasm for mathematical formalization as well as linguistic invention. For Badiou, Lacan's own practice was not just a matter of generating new content (new theorems, methods, etc.), but itself a radical ethics. Badiou even occasionally assumes the form of Lacan's characteristic presentation, as in the "seminar" that eventually became *Theory of the Subject*.[1] As Badiou confesses in his notes to *Pocket Pantheon*, "I have written on, or about Lacan very often" (PP 189).

Badiou discusses Lacan at length in *Theory of the Subject*, *Being and Event* and *Logics of Worlds*, that is, in all three of his "big books", in essays collected in *Conditions*, in many other occasional essays, and as one of the subjects of a year-long seminar in 1994–5. Moreover, covert allusions as well as explicit references to Lacan can be discerned throughout Badiou's text, making any summation of the former's influence on the latter literally impossible.[2] Yet, unlike Plato, Descartes and Hegel – the three confessed crucial philosophers (LW 527) who are an inspiration and a model to Badiou, whose propositions and procedures he ceaselessly returns to and cites approvingly, if sometimes critically – Lacan's propositions are first to be confronted, then passed through.

Finally, Lacan's self-identification as an "antiphilosopher", a term he picks up from the Dadaist Tristan Tzara, is linked to the strongest possible contemporary challenge to philosophy.[3] As Lacan puts it in a late interview, "I detest philosophy; it's been such a long time since it's said anything of interest" (Lacan & Granzotto 2004: 25). Among the great anti-philosophers – Badiou lists St Paul, Pascal, Rousseau, Kierkegaard and Nietzsche – Lacan is the one who literally "completes" contemporary anti-philosophy (see Badiou 1994b: 19). This certainly does not mean that there are no longer anti-philosophers; on the contrary – only that, in the contemporary situation, they can go no further than Lacan. Lacan is, for the moment at least, the anti-philosopher who has offered the most radical challenges to philosophy.[4]

The field

In order to delimit this "set of elements of their relation" it is useful to consider this *polemos* in terms of Badiou's own contemporary language. What Lacan establishes as the discourse of anti-philosophy

– the discourse of the unconscious and, as such, that which for Lacan is "maximally alien" to "philosophy"[5] – Badiou will try to *reverse*.[6] Badiou will try to retrieve from Lacan the thought of that thought (the unconscious) that, for Lacan, "would rather relinquish itself than be thought" (by philosophers) and that philosophy – primarily under the names of Plato and Hegel – therefore could not think (see Lacan 2008: 103).

At the heart of the philosophical enterprise for Lacan was its certainty as to the sense of truth, which provides the philosopher with a comforting wisdom, the knowledge of the whole. Lacan's rejection of the philosopher's happy "correlation" turns on the real of sex, on the man–woman disjunction and, as such, the psychoanalytic discovery that there is no relation to the real. The real thus marks the impossibility of sexual relation.[7] In *Theory of the Subject* Badiou – declaring that "Lacan is ahead of the current state of Marxism and we must take advantage of this advance so as to improve our Marxist affairs" (TS 115) – imposes this "idealist" doctrine directly on to the real of class: there is no relation between classes.[8] Critically, there where the subject comes to be outside all knowledge is, essentially, the very – anti-philosophical – thought of the real.

For Badiou, philosophy today must begin in this place, designated by the antagonism of anti-philosophy. In accepting Lacan's analysis of philosophy as "the discourse of the master" – which give the stakes of Lacan's anti-philosophical reversal – Badiou simultaneously affirms that "philosophy" is *not* that discourse of sovereign expropriation Lacan describes in *My Teaching* as the discourse whose knowledge of its thought determines its indivisibility. Badiou's strategy in reading Lacan is in fact somewhat Lacanian. For Badiou, Lacan's definition of philosophy literally still leaves something to be desired, and it is precisely the subject of this residue – that which is nothing – that Badiou seeks to extract from Lacan's anti-philosophy. The void point from which philosophy will begin again as philosophy will have to be distinct from both the discourse of the master and the analytic discourse. This is to say that the relocalization of this void point will be crucial in order that the *subject* of Plato can truly become "our contemporary".

In *Conditions*, Badiou makes a brilliant anti-anti-philosophical joke regarding the relation between philosopher and psychoanalyst. Referring to Plato's "speculative parricide" of Parmenides, Badiou confesses that it is as "a faithful son of a parricide" that he comes to philosophy; moreover, it is not therefore as a parricide that he comes to psychoanalysis, but with "filial respect". He is indeed a "son of philosophy", that is, "a son of Plato", but – despite this "criminal heritage" – he comes to psychoanalysis not under the condition of some "end" but in order to "take one more step in philosophy" (C 201).[9] In this sense, Lacan is understood as "the educator for every philosophy to come" (C 129; TW 119; LW 523). Lacan's anti-philosophical animus is thereby given a philosophical freighting by Badiou himself, who turns it into a central category of his own thought.[10] In sum, "Ontology or not, psychoanalysis according to Lacan imposes a general rectification on philosophy, which touches upon nothing less than the way in which truth leans up against the real" (TS 135).[11]

What is crucial for Badiou about anti-philosophy is that it offers challenges to philosophy that philosophy ignores at its cost; it is only by confronting the real of anti-philosophy that philosophy has any chance at all of establishing something at once new, yet still philosophical. This is the sense in which we invoked the category of "the reverse of the reverse" that establishes the existence of that which – within the situation of psychoanalysis – could not exist except as the minimal condition of its own act of reversal.

A return to the scene of the crime

Taking up Badiou's example of the philosophical criminal, we shall attend to the charges Lacan makes against philosophy. In particular, Lacan charges philosophy with the following. It is: (i) a discourse of the master, that is, one that exploits the practice of workers by transforming *savoir-faire* into *savoir* (a crime of power); (ii) an ancient discourse fixated on the whole, and therefore incapable of dealing with the challenges of modern, post-Galilean science (a crime of knowledge); (iii) for the most part incompetent to deal with the problematics of desire and enjoyment (a sex-crime). Moreover, most modern philosophy is also characterized by its stupidity, above all, its capture by what Lacan called "the discourse of the university" and a concomitant reduction of the radical particularities to which psychoanalysis attends and affirms.[12]

Lacan's determination that his discourse is an anti-philosophy obviously presupposes the existence of "philosophy". Yet Lacan's engagement with philosophy is something of a secondary effect. Lacan's entire discourse is grounded in clinical practice, and so engages with philosophy only in so far as what is said in the clinic can be in some sense considered to mark the place of truth – a truth that philosophy is determinedly incapable of recognizing as such.[13] In turn, Badiou's definition of philosophy is at once classical and contemporary. Philosophy is the love of truth, the pursuit of wisdom, but, for Badiou, philosophy as the love of truth can be no such thing if it fails to submit itself to the truths of its own times. The difficulty for the "philosopher" is that these truths are not themselves philosophical.

Badiou notes that for Lacan the pretension of philosophers is to corral the love of truth within the conceit of a "wise friendship" off limits to "strangers" and thus philosophy's pretension is in fact the result of an immanent *transference*. The conceit of philosophy is to treat such transference as *natural*: what is proper to a philosopher is to love truth; to love truth is the province of the philosopher. Thus Lacan will say that the psychoanalyst does not *love* truth, which is to say, does not privilege truth over the subject (who speaks), and this declaration, Badiou contends, prescribes the directions taken by anti-philosophy (C 129; TW 119). Badiou thus sets himself the task, as noted, of reversing this reversal – which is not to say "negating Lacan's negation" – by returning to truth under the condition of traversing the anti-philosophy of Lacan. Philosophy, in short, must be subject to truth, a truth that is not simply one of castration. Badiou, in other words, needs to construct a category of truth that avoids having the characteristics Lacan assigns to castration, yet that will be a truth that, in Lacan's words, "is always new" (Lacan 2008: 17).

But to be subject to truth, psychoanalysis teaches, is to affirm the void that separates truth from reality or from knowledge. In another register, it is precisely the conviction of the existence of the void that Lacanian psychoanalysis and Badiouean philosophy share, although their conceptions of the void differ in regard to its localization, as well as over the status of infinity – potential for the former, actual for the latter.[14]

Whereas the philosopher derives his wisdom and power from the love of truth, Lacan, invoking the clinical experience of truth coming to pass as slips, dream and comedy (to use several Freudian terms), argues that truth is effectively the impotence of power and wisdom – and not their substance. Truth is thus integrally affected by castration for Lacan. The love of truth is the love of castration and, further, love is the veil of truth as castration. Against the philosopher, truth is denied the power to say all.

Unlike Heidegger's pathos of forgetting, however, Lacan's contention is that truth is the name of what can only be "half-said" or "ill said", to borrow Beckett's term. As castration is structure itself, there can be no return for Lacan, as there must be for Heidegger, to the "primordially uncastrated" (TW 120; C 130). As Badiou puts it elsewhere in *Conditions* with regard to the formulas of sexuation, there is no angel or angelic order for Lacan, because "castration is effective for every speaking being, hence for every thinking being" (C 213). At the same time, truth as the name that disguises its "acute powerlessness" to say all contains for Badiou the essence of an ethics for philosophy. This is critical for Badiou precisely because – given his formal demonstration of a specific error in Lacan's use of the infinite with regard to the formulas of sexuation – it will allow contemporary philosophy to return to its Platonic foundations in such a way as to show the latter's formal break with the *linguistery* of the poets (of flux) to be one predicated on a *real*. That real is given in a mathematical "dream" of Plato's, as a rational disjunction rather than as an Ideal forgetting.

It might serve those who consider philosophy a sovereign discourse to recall that "philosophy" had no purchase in the city of its foundation, and Socrates, its exemplary figure, was excised from the body politic, of which he was a "citizen", precisely in so far as he presented his act under the guise of the love of the truth, which, being neither "substance or nature", and as such foreign to and subtracting from the city's self-representation, could not be tolerated. Badiou as a philosopher will therefore announce: "truth is bearable for thought, which is to say, philosophically loveable, only insofar as one attempts to grasp it in what drives its *subtractive* dimension, as opposed to seeking its plenitude or complete saying" (TW 120; C 130).[15]

In another essay, Badiou will note that the critical philosophical move is from "impotence" (i.e. castration) to impossibility (i.e. what an actual situation forecloses), a move that Plato accomplishes, and which Badiou seeks to re-found. The very condition of Lacan's anti-philosophy – that the philosopher under the name of "truth" presumes to know all – Badiou now invokes as the condition of philosophy itself. When this condition is incorporated with the discourse-specific inventions of art, politics and mathematics, philosophy once again becomes possible. But it becomes possible again not as a discourse of mastery, of knowledge *per se*, but as the love of truth in so far as the latter is no longer the knowledge of "all". Rather, in a subtractive and subjective sense, truth becomes that which is *for* all; or, to put it another way, *literally universal* in so far as it subtends an affirmative conception of the infinite, rather than one that makes use of an abusive, negative conception of the "inaccessible".

It is therefore possible to consider Lacan's work as an event *for* philosophy – just as Freud was an event for psychoanalysis – in so far as it breaks with predominating forms of philosophy, and with those discourses that announce the end of philosophy (C 236). On the one hand, the psychoanalytic charge against philosophy as pre-scientific is demonstrably true in so far as philosophy's constant referral to truth in transcendent and sovereign terms entails a refusal to think the truths of its times as they occur, instead finding within them mere repetitions whose concept is already captured by philosophical knowledge. On the other hand, Lacan's discourse refuses the sophistical discourse of the "end of philosophy" in so far as that signifies the end of a desire whose truth Lacan is nevertheless committed to unfolding within the desire of the subject, precisely as "anti-philosophy". Philosophy for Lacan is at once anachronistic and yet has not realized it has finished.

Lacan also maintains that philosophy in the contemporary world has fallen from being a discourse of the master to that of a university discourse, a discourse that prides itself on giving the "new master" the language appropriate to its ever more totalitarian mastery. One need only survey the policy documents of "our democracies", or often even the research output of the contemporary academy, to see the discourse of contemporary "non-philosophy" serving the interests of today's ruling classes and doing so often before the ruling class even knows *that this is its knowledge*.[16] In articulating the ruses of both the master and the university, Lacan opens an aporia, which is another way of saying "chance" – "the void of a suspended act" (C 202) – upon which philosophy, in Badiou's sense, can intervene or "return".

As noted in the chapter on "Conditions", Lacan's work proved crucial for Badiou in recognizing that post-Romantic "philosophy" was the outcome of various "sutures", of scientism, historicism, politicism and so forth. Precisely because Lacanian analysis explicitly theorizes its own backwardness and liminality *vis-à-vis* its own conditions of literature and science, and, above all, with respect to the utterances of its suffering analysands, this *modus operandi* becomes a kind of model for philosophy too. And precisely because Lacan only ever presented himself under the heading of a "return to Freud" in order to elaborate his own theory (i.e. a return to the origins, to the *problem* and to the *tumult* of the origin), one would have to say that Badiou's "return to Plato" is not only inspired by Lacan but is the result of "passing" Lacan's discourse in its entirety. The paradox is that it is at the very point of the impasse that Badiou passes through (C 222).

One dominant way in which contemporary philosophy is not modern accords with the discourse of ends, and that of the university is in its relation to mathematics. As Badiou notes in the *Pocket Pantheon*, Lacan, following the ruses of the signifier, turned to mathematics and to *topos* theory in order to provide a "geometry of the unconscious" in which its three agencies – the real, imaginary and symbolic, which knot the subject – could at last be rigorously formalized (PP 3). This operation recalls another, this time a primordial, philosophical gesture, one that Badiou constantly reminds us has been "registered, acclaimed, then reviled throughout the centuries" (C 129; TW 119), that of Plato's recourse to the matheme.

Once again, the twists and turns of Lacan's anti-philosophy return us to philosophy, and more specifically to non-Aristotelian variants of philosophy (LW 522). Badiou states that what ties him most closely to Lacan's teaching is the latter's "conviction that the ideal of any think-ing is that aspect of it which can be universally transmitted outside of sense. In other words, that senselessness [which should be understood as the absence of sense or ab-sense or even ab-sex-sens (see Badiou 2006d: 83–4; Lacan 2008: 18)], is the primordial attribute of the True." It is in this context that Badiou can align *within* philosophy the anti-philosopher and the "name of the father": "Platonism is the belief that in order to come close to this ideal, it is necessary to mathematise" (LW 522). Lacan famously states that "mathematics alone reaches the real" and that it is the science of the real.

In so far as we might treat Lacan as an event for philosophy, this notion of mathematics reaching a real should be considered a trace whose trajectory Badiou will follow and, in doing so, will re-formalize. In short, for Badiou mathematics is the discourse of ontol-ogy, of what can be said of being *qua* being. Being for Badiou is not the same as the real, even though, just as the real for Lacan, it will open in a space between sense and non-sense. Badiou notes that the real is this gap, also fundamental to Lacan's discourse, whether it is approached theoretically, anti-philosophically or clinically (Badiou 2006d: 86). It is precisely by following the Lacanian trace that Badiou arrives at Georg Cantor's infinities, and from there will deploy set theory and category theory – at once faithful to the ideal inscribed in Lacan's recourse to the matheme and yet breaking with the necessity for this discourse to formalize only the vicissitudes of subjectivity. In *Theory of the Subject* Badiou had already noted Lacan's "failure to oppose and conjoin explicitly algebra and topology" and, as such, that he "exposes himself to the risk of thinking of consistency only as an attribute of algebra. Consistency", Badiou continues, comes "danger-ously close to being a simple principle of existential interdependence" (TS 231–2).[17]

For Badiou, between the mathematics *of* being and the subject is the event, that which breaks with the impasse inscribed by ontology itself.[18] Badiou's conception of the subject, heavily indebted as it is to psychoanalysis, is therefore not situated in the same place as Lacan's. Badiou's subject does not occupy the void place between signifiers but depends on what takes place without a subject, at the site of this gap between that which is mathematically inscribable of being *qua* being and that which insists as the inconsistent mark of the former's consistency. Whereas the subject for Lacan is what one signifier represents to another, for Badiou the event comes to mark the non-relation between inscription and subjectivity.

For Lacan, the idea of the void is linked to that of the Other, and thus to the cause of the subject. This contrasts with philosophy, which, according to Lacan, founds itself on the presupposition that being thinks, on the presumption that, as with Parmenides, thought and being are the Same.[19] In a related point, Badiou notes that Lacan's "return to Freud" was also simultaneously a "return to Descartes": "The key to the matter resides in the statement that the subject of psychoanalysis is none other than the subject of science. This identity, however, can only be grasped by attempting to think the subject *in its place*" (BE 431). It is the necessity to think the *topos* of the subject that propels Lacan's double return to Freud and Descartes, which further requires that this subject is no longer self-present, but dislocated, split and void. For Badiou, moreover, it is this subject that *supports* the existence of truths and thus maintains as itself the ethical demand to continue. It is in no way coincident with Truth itself.[20]

Conclusion

For Lacan, the place of the subject is a lack, and it is a lack opposed to the fullness of thought he ascribes to philosophy. As Badiou puts it, Lacan conceives of philosophy as the "self-founding of thinking". The discourses of psychoanalysis and philosophy diverge over the most ancient philosophical problems, that of the infinite and the finite, and that of the same (Parmenides/Plato) and the other (Heraclitus and that which signifies). For the latter, the place of the other is that by which the subject is "dis-posed", and we can see why this subject can be thought as the subject of science in a Cartesian sense, born as it is out of the lack of "knowledge". For Lacan, however, philosophy's subject – "the same", the "thing itself" – is resolutely sovereign.

Badiou's response to this is highly nuanced. He notes that the Heraclitean ideal of being-as-signifying also gave rise within philosophy to hermeneutics, a discourse to which Lacanian psychoanalysis is constitutively hostile – all the more so because they were born of the same father. Badiou sides here with Lacan's enmity to hermeneutics, and affirms that it is better to sustain the disagreement than to "confuse philosophy with the interpretive custodianship of sacred texts" (C 204). Further:

We must recognize that we are indebted to Lacan – in the wake of Freud, but also of Descartes – for having paved the way for a formal theory of the subject whose basis is materialist; it was indeed by opposing himself to phenomenology, to Kant and to a certain structuralism, that Lacan could stay the course.   (LW 48)

In staying the course, however, Lacan was also inclined to impute to philosophy theses that the latter does not have to hold; indeed, it is, as we have been saying, precisely by confronting Lacan in an extraordinarily thoroughgoing way that has enabled Badiou to "purify" philosophy of these elements.

Badiou's is not the philosophy Lacan always targets, and this is so because of Lacan himself. The discourse of psychoanalysis – that which it thinks – is not appropriated *by* philosophy, but comes to function as one of its conditions. Without this thought, philosophy is nothing. It persists in name only under sway of a suture, as a "university discourse" that, as Lacan noted, is designed to "make sure that thought never has any repercussions" (2008: 26). Yet philosophy is the discourse that should make sure that what pertains to such a thought, that it happens, that it "has form" and that it convokes its subject, is retained in such a way that it *will have had* such repercussions. There is no doubt that it is via Lacan that Badiou returns philosophy to itself – as unlikely or rather, as *inexistent*, as such a thought might seem.

Notes

1. "The form. It is that of a seminar, a genre to which Lacan has given a definitive dignity" (TS xxxix). As the translator Bruno Bosteels remarks, "Badiou's fidelity to this model is actually quite extensive, ranging from the use of idiosyncratic wordplay, syntactic ambiguities, funny asides, and bold provocations of the audience, all the way to the disposition of the written text with numbered sections and a list of subtitles at the start of each chapter, as in Jacques-Alain Miller's edition of Lacan's original seminars" (TS xxvii). In "Truth, Forcing and the Unnameable", Badiou remarks that Lacan's seminar is itself a "strange appropriation of a real *Symposium*" (TW 119; C 129). We should note too that Badiou's constant varying of the form of his presentation to suit his content and place might be understood as a further development in this direction (see also Badiou's "Author's Preface" to TW, in which he remarks "that the philosophical corpus seems to encompass every conceivable style of presentation"; TW xiii).
2. It is perhaps for this reason that, despite the clear and overwhelming importance of Lacan for Badiou, there has been almost no published secondary research to date on the relationship between the two that is not either derisorily minimal or objectionably partisan (and sometimes simply wrong). The four exceptions to this rule are Hoens & Pluth (2004b); Grigg (2005); Chiesa (2006a,b); Feltham

(2007). These essays provide detailed critical accounts of one or another *particular* argument of Badiou's *vis-à-vis* Lacan; as such, they do not attempt to provide any overview of the relationship generally.

3. Note, too, that, in fine anti-philosophical style, Lacan speaks primarily of the *personage* of the anti-philosopher, while Badiou, in high philosophical mode, develops it into a trans-personal *concept*.

4. Badiou's doctrine of "sequences", itself under-developed and under-remarked to date in his own work, is nonetheless implicit in his own self-presentation as the "last" of the contemporary French philosophers; for example, "if there has been such a French philosophical moment, my position would be as perhaps its last representative" (2005a: 68). How can he say such a thing? Precisely because he considers his own doctrine to have taken into account all the problems raised by the French since Bergson (e.g. matheme versus animal, history versus eternity, virtual versus actual, etc.), and to have delivered a systematic philosophy on that basis that exhausts the possible current permutations of the field.

5. With regard to the distinction between Freud's unconscious and the unconscious prior to Freud, Lacan says "the unconscious is an unconscious that thinks hard" (2008: 7). On Badiou's notion of the "reverse" see *Logics of Worlds* 136–40. The reverse establishes negation as a result, Badiou says, thereby arguing that negation is not an ontological category. It is crucial to note that Badiou's intervention *into* Lacan in *Theory of the Subject* under the rubric of "Lack and Destruction" prefigures his intervention *with* Lacan into "Marxist Materialism", a section entitled "A Materialist reversal of Materialism".

6. "The reverse of the reverse of a degree of appearance is not necessarily identical to that degree". See *Logics of Worlds* 107 for a summation of Badiou's notion of the reverse; we might even suggest a redefinition of "return" ("to Freud", "to Lacan", "to Plato", etc.) here as a "reversal of the reverse".

7. See Badiou's further recent remarks on this thesis in Badiou with Truong (2009: 23–6).

8. Badiou also holds here that "There are, broadly speaking, two successive Lacans, the one of the lack of being and the one of the ontology of the hole, of the nodal topos, and, consequently, of the being of lack" (TS 133).

9. It is worth noting that Lacan lays claim to a "related" criminal heritage when he separates Socrates from Plato. In privileging the former he is not just analogizing the capture of the analyst's discourse by that of the master; he is also laying claim to the impiety and corruption of Socrates *vis-à-vis* the normal and knowing relations that pertain in the state of "the service of goods" (C 237). In *Conditions*, ch. 14, Badiou will underline the "sophistry" of this distinction and, relatedly, remark on the disturbing associations this false distinction conjures. Lacan himself admitted to being under the sway of Kojève's (for us) nonsensical thesis concerning Plato's esotericism, and this put him into company he was otherwise distant from – company, ironically, whose institutional home was the University of Chicago. One should be mindful of the fact that there are no greater nor more influential purveyors of the terroristic doctrine of the "double discourse" of the noble lie (esoteric/exoteric) than the economists trained under Milton Friedman, Arnold Harberger and the rest. For a thorough critique of this false distinction, see Bartlett (2009: esp. ch. 5). Let us just say that Plato may have concealed what *he* thought but he concealed nothing of the thought of philosophy. Cf. Badiou: "The individual, in truth, is nothing" (TC, 101, trans. mod.).

10. See Hallward (2003: esp. 185–91) and Bosteels (2008) for some of the Enlightenment thinkers who coined this term, as well as invaluable intra-Badiouean references to "anti-philosophy".
11. The question of Lacan's ontology was raised by Jacques-Alain Miller in 1964. See *Being and Event* (4). Badiou notes that it was the incompatibility of contemporary logic with Lacan's "doctrine according to which the real is the impasse of formalisation" that led him ultimately to "formulate a radical thesis concerning mathematics".
12. For the most condensed of Lacan's critiques regarding philosophy, see especially Lacan (2007).
13. The truth Lacan is talking about is the truth of the irrational or incommensurable. A. J. Bartlett has argued that Plato does not reject the incommensurable but indeed bases his own discursive operation, the construction of a body of thought, on the existence of such a thought. Lacan's discussion of reminiscence in Plato's *Meno* and *Phaedo* shows that he is entirely correct in his localization of the point at issue, but Plato's invocation of the diagonal – the mark of incommensurability – against the sophists' discourse shows that it pertains immediately to philosophy. Lacan is certainly correct in so far as the history of philosophy – that "patch-up job" as he calls it – has indeed covered this over. See Bartlett (2009).
14. See *Conditions* (201) for a poetic rendering of their distinction and *Conditions* (222–7) for a more formal explanation. In regard to some of the animosity that insists in certain Lacanian circles towards Badiou, we should note that in the essay cited – "Subject and Infinity" – Badiou has the temerity to correct Lacan. Badiou argues that Lacan understands infinity in terms of "inaccessibility" and this results in an inconsistency that seriously affects his formulas of sexuality. Badiou presumes to "save" Lacan by means of the "actual infinite" proposing a supplement to the "phallic function", which would entail a redistribution of the quantifiers "universal" and "existential" such that the formulas that result are irreducible to Lacan's original formulas of sexuation. This in turn demands a new conception of the Two, and the formalization of an access to this Two from what "precedes it". Badiou is keen to declare that in this advance he is faithful to the master and (albeit via Mallarmé), employing the language of Hilbert on Cantor, says that from "the Eden Lacan has opened up for us we shall not be banished" (C 227: cf. TS xl). For a contrary view concerning this, see Grigg (2005).
15. Lacan's attempt in *Seminar VIII* to invoke Socrates as exemplary analyst – apart from reminding us of Heidegger's not dissimilar efforts to enter Plato from behind – is a part of Lacan's strategy to subvert the discourse of the Platonic master by demonstrating that its origins are lacking, that its knowledge has a hole in it and that its rule is that of an illegitimate discursive "expropriation".
16. One should see Lacan's famous comment – "what you aspire to as revolutionaries is a master. You will get one" – in this context. "Look at them enjoying", indeed! See Lacan (2007: 207–8).
17. This same logical problem returns, Badiou forcefully demonstrates, in Lacan's discussion of Logical Time (TS 251).
18. Cf. "Lacan's formula, according to which that which is excluded from the symbolic reappears in the real, is here interpreted: under certain conditions, what's properly excluded from an *already produced* mathematical structure reappears as the establishing mark of the real (historical) process of *production* of a different structure" (Badiou 1968: 128).

19. In an elliptical point relevant to his conception of the subject, Badiou seems to suggest that the "effect of a cause" ≠ a "consequence" (C 244).
20. From Lacan's "ne pas céder sur son désir" Badiou will draw what he calls "the only ethical imperative": "continue!" That is to say: continue to be this "some-one", a human animal among others, which nevertheless finds itself seized and displaced by the eventy process of a truth" (E 91). What pertains to the subject of both is "courage" – which we must note in passing is, as Plato understood, distinct from bravery. Thus the heroism of the subject should not be confused with the tragico-romantic concept that prevails among our contemporary sophists and ethicists.

SIXTEEN

Deleuze

John Mullarkey

The *continuation* of philosophy is important for both Badiou and Deleuze. Unlike many of their generation, neither accepted that the end of philosophy was upon us. Indeed, as Badiou admits, both are classical in their approach, taking the perennial problems of metaphysics, such as the One and the Many, or the finite and the infinite, to be fundamental for their own projects. Further evidence of their classicism lies in Badiou and Deleuze equally disliking dialogue (or analytic "debate") as a model of philosophical procedure: theirs is the aristocratic style of *disputatio* (D 45). In addition, both of their enterprises are animated by modern thinkers – Spinoza for Deleuze and Descartes for Badiou. They are equally unique, for their time, in being avowedly pre-Kantian, albeit with a post-Kantian awareness of all the difficulties that follow from such a position.

But here is where some gaps between Deleuze and Badiou appear. Where Badiou still has faith in the project of modernity, and indeed in Cartesian rationalism, Deleuze's invocation of Spinoza (or Leibniz) is made only to conjoin them with a certain poststructuralist (rather than post-modernist) agenda that would be the ruin of various rationalist dogmas. For Deleuze, Descartes is a philosophical adversary, whose conceptual legacy must be overcome: the dualisms of mind and body, civilization and insanity, human and animal, representation and world, are all to be abandoned as enemies of any true philosophy of immanence (such as Spinoza's or Deleuze's). Badiou's work, by contrast, can be seen as the contemporary embodiment of mathematical Cartesianism (reconceived through set theory). The very last meditation in *Being and Event* (which, as a whole, can be read as the new Cartesian meditations

for our time) is entitled "Descartes/Lacan", encapsulating the philosophical lineage Badiou wants to continue.

Yet things are never so simple, in that Badiou's rationalism – despite
certain appearances – is not very faithful to Descartes at all, especially
given the fact that Badiou is certainly not a representationalist, and
his model of the rational is far more aleatory, being built upon the
contingency of event and choice rather than on the apodicity of simple intuitions. What really attracts Badiou to Descartes (and, behind
him, Plato) is his *mathematicism*. As he puts it himself, his heroes are
Lacan, Descartes, Galileo and Plato, because for each, their "vector ...
is none other than mathematicism". Even here, though, it is a radical
mathematics that interests Badiou, the new mathematics of set theory
that plays with unpredictable, unimaginable quantities, and new infinities that transform our previous modes of thinking (BE 124; TW 64).

Conversely, Deleuze is more modernist than Badiou on one essential
point: he sees philosophy having its own *exclusive* role as the creator
of concepts. In *What is Philosophy?* he makes a sustained case for "the
exclusive right of concept creation secur[ing] a function for philosophy"
(Deleuze & Guattari 1994: 8).[1] Philosophy generates its own content
through its own method. There is, then, such a thing as a philosophical
event wherein a concept is created by a philosopher. For Badiou, however, there are no philosophical events *per se*, but only the events (and
truths) created by the *conditions of philosophy*. Philosophy is constituted by an outside – its four conditions being in the non-philosophical
realms of science, politics, art and erotic love. Philosophy's condition
of possibility is not immanent to itself, but comes from these (to it)
transcending domains, one of which, moreover, takes over the mantle
of ontology from philosophy – mathematics. Philosophy no longer has
a direct relationship with what used to be called "first philosophy" or
ontological metaphysics: the study of being as such (ontology) is now
the proper object of mathematical set theory (IT 165).

This mathematicism on Badiou's part stems, of course, from his view
that truth is not relative to language (a claim he ascribes to the "sophists"). Mathematical inscription must always underscore the textual
letter. Set-theoretical inscriptions are impervious to being reduced to
culturally conventional language, and that is why Badiou believes that
they are *the* language of immanence – there is no "outside" beyond
them – and are the proper basis for understanding the universality of
truth. That said, Deleuze shares with Badiou his issues with linguistic
philosophies (Rorty and Wittgenstein, say, would be enemies for both).
Deleuze clearly rejects the power of language in theory, seeking a non-
linguistic semiotics of direct sensation instead (Sense as the Being of the

sensible). He wants to replace the linguistically dominated semiological approach with a "semiotics" – a "system of images and signs independent of language in general". Here, a language system only exists in its reaction to a *non-language-material* that it transforms. This is why, as one commentator put it, Deleuze is "rigorously antilinguistic" (Ropars-Wuilleumier 1994; see Deleuze 1989: 29).

Yet the logic of this Deleuzian sense (and sensation) is still too empiricist for Badiou, and he insists that only the matheme can penetrate the absolute and the infinite: the study of mathematics is the "obligation" of true philosophers (he is fond of citing the epigraph over the entrance to Plato's Academy, "Let none enter here who is not a geometer") (TW 14; MP 34). For Badiou, it is the rigour of mathematics (its certainty and universality) that appeals to him rather than its verification through other empirical knowledges. Indeed, mathematical formalism is ideal because it is empty: as soon as it is filled in (or applied), it is no longer mathematics but affect – the content that fleshes it out is always affective or intuitive.

In stark contrast to this, Deleuze's conflation of sense and sensation marks out his own non-Platonist tendencies, which, for Badiou, is precisely where he falls short of a sufficiently *Platonist* Platonism, that is, one that would exorcize the material (or rather a certain kind of naturalistic notion of matter) in favour of the abstract, quality in favour of quantity, animal vitality in favour of intellectual life. For Badiou, the perpetual "cross of metaphysics" has been the choice between the animal and number, the organic and the mathematical. Deleuze chooses "without hesitation" for the animal, according to Badiou (1994a: 55).

For Deleuze, the mathematical multiplicities that Badiou valorizes are always *only* "purely formal modalities", empty of value and abstract in the *wrong* way (TW 99). Indeed, another variance between Deleuze and Badiou here is in their respective notions of abstraction. Deleuze's constant complaint against philosophers is that their thought is not abstract enough, that it pitches its level of abstraction too low and consequently loses the virtues of proper abstraction. The notion of an "abstract machine" in *A Thousand Plateaus*, for example, is conceptual, yet without forfeiting the virtues of the concrete: it is a device by which to capture surface, large-scale entities as parts of even larger *material processes*. That which is more abstract is that which incorporates a larger, that is, *more multiple*, sample, considering not only human but also animal, inorganic and other inhuman processes.

According to Badiou, of course, this is not true abstraction. What Deleuze discounts as the mere formality of pure quantity is actually wherein its power rests for Badiou, and for two reasons: multiplicity must be pure quantity (no quality) if it is to generate the paradoxes that condition the possibility of an event; and it must be homogeneous and empty if it is to be the basis for a truly universalist politics. Conversely, according to Badiou, Deleuze's antipathy towards a wholly mathematicized ontology (Deleuze does, admittedly, embrace the differential calculus in his work, but more on account of its kinship with vital processes rather than its inherent formalism) is due in part to a poorly thought-out polemic against sets that erroneously reduces them to number (whereas number actually reduces to sets).

Before turning next to possibly the most important idea Badiou shares with Deleuze (the idea of the event), let me say a few words about two topics on which they appear to diverge most, the Subject and Truth. According to Badiou, truth and subjectivity are co-engendered through the "event", which must be understood conceptually, that is, through reason. A fundamental thesis of *Being and Event* is that "a subject is nothing other than an active fidelity to the event of truth" (BE xii–xiii). Where Deleuze gives the sensation (of) matter the transcendental function of constituting the subject, for Badiou, the event of truth and the subject come together so that neither supervenes on the other, as objectivism or subjectivism would respectively entail (BE xii–xiii). There is an identity of being and thinking, but only via events and the decisions immanent to them – they are co-engendered through one process. *Qua* a non-processual state, the subject is indeed transcended by truth – "every truth is transcendent to the subject" – but *qua* process, it is through subjectivization that a truth is possible (BE 392, 397).

In Badiou's eyes, this reverses the problematic of subjectivity: it is no longer the question of how an ineluctable subject is made to tally with Being (how does the Cartesian subject represent the world?), nor how Being generates subjectivity or some kind of naturalized self is produced by matter ("the brain becomes subject", "souls are everywhere in matter", says Deleuze; Deleuze & Guattari 1994: 209–11; Deleuze 1993: 11), but how subject and event (or truth) come into being *together* as precisely what ruptures being through a process of naming. This return to the subject, though clearly not reinstalling it as a "self-identical substance", nonetheless refuses to diffuse the subject (as Deleuze does) by immersion in a differential or libidinal ontology. The subject is immanently co-authored with the truth that it names and remains faithful to. The subject is now a "*fragment* of the process of truth"; a post-Cartesian *and* post-Lacanian thesis that distances the subject from any substance, but without either reducing or eliminating it.

Deleuze, by contrast, must be regarded as part of the poststructuralist paradigm that did its utmost to decentre the self, though in his case by looking to the differential forces of matter rather than language, as most others did (e.g. Barthes, Derrida *et al.*): "one does not ask how the subject gains its experience", Deleuze wrote, "but how experience gives us a subject" (1991: 87). That Badiou's notion of the subject is delineated into further types in *Logics of Worlds* (faithful, reactive and obscure) still brings it no nearer towards Deleuze's *naturally* fragmented self.

To speak more directly about truth – and against the litany of attacks on truth that constitutes most of twentieth-century philosophy according to Badiou – the central idea for him is, again, that truths and subjects *come together*: the truth of a multiple is produced *immanently* to this multiple, with a subject's intervention. That is why there is no need for a dogmatism of static correspondence (between a representing subject and "the" world) to reassert the claims of truth. For Badiou, then, truth is its own standard (it "is the proof of itself"), for as new, the true simply cannot *correspond* to anything (to any *previously* existing standard), but "depends on its own production" (E 117; IT 173).[2]

Badiou's notion of truth is not entirely alien to Deleuze. In *Cinema 2*, Deleuze links the problematic of truth to that of the event explicitly: "time has always put the notion of truth into crisis … it is the form or rather the pure force of time that puts truth into crisis" (1989: 130). Consequently, Deleuze prioritizes the "powers of the false"; but we should not let his terminology confuse us: it is the correspondence (or representational) theory of truth that Deleuze has it in his mind to attack here such that this power of the false has much in common with Badiou's evental truth (as Badiou must partly concede when he allows that "time *is* truth itself" for Deleuze, only what time essentially is being different for the two) (D 61). For, like Badiou, Deleuze does not see thought as an access to being – as representational – either, but as a quasi-being or event in itself. Truth itself is not entirely absent from Deleuze, then, but becomes its own, immanent standard (again, following Spinoza) (Zourabichvili 1994: 18). Where Deleuze and Badiou continue to differ on this immanent truth is in the fact that, for Badiou, such immanence must be entirely actual if it is to be its own standard. Hence Badiou thinks of Deleuze's dualism of virtual and actual as representational: actualities are ontical beings, or "simulacra of Being", that is, representations, and so in a relationship of inequality with Being (equivocal), rather than being both productive and genuinely univocal as Deleuze claims (D 26). Whether this is a fair assessment of the virtual–actual dyad is contentious, however, because Badiou ignores *what* is univocal in the Virtual, namely difference, the formula in *A Thousand Plateaus*, "monism = pluralism", conveying the fact that the only thing that is always the same is difference.

This returns us to the event (indeed, it is under this precise banner that Badiou rehearses his criticisms of Deleuze in *Logics of Worlds*). First, though, let us list the differences between them on this front. For a start, Badiou's events are rare and historical; Deleuze's are common and natural (they occur in both the human and inhuman realms). Badiou's events have to be thought; Deleuze's have to be felt. Going against the idea of a "pure empiricity of what happens" (and Badiou most likely has Deleuze in mind here), *Being and Event* opts for the *conceptual* construction of the event because "it can only be *thought* by anticipating its abstract form, and it can only be revealed in the retroaction of an interventional practice which is itself entirely thought through" (BE 178). Also, for Badiou the event is co-engendered with the subject – subject and event are tied together in the decision of the former to name the latter. The subject is not connected to the event as the one that pre-exists it, but as the one that comes into existence with that nomination. For Deleuze, alternatively, the event is a-subjective. The event comes before and generates the human subject out of "larval" selves. His events are ubiquitous in nature, following Cartier-Bresson's adage that there is nothing in this world that does not have a decisive moment. In Deleuze's *The Logic of Sense*, for instance, we get an image of the event as an incorporeal transformation that gathers up everyday objects and individuals for its own purpose. A genuine event does not happen *to* someone, but in and through someone (that makes him or her part of the event) (Deleuze 1990: 178). Again, as it so often does, *Logics of Worlds* ramifies the account in *Being and Event*, here rendering change in four types (modifications, facts, weak singularities and strong singularities); yet the most radical form of change remains the event (or strong singularity), one that still lies ill with Deleuze's conception of the event.

At one level at least, though, Badiou is close to Deleuze: for both, the event is about change. But it is an odd temporality for each of them. For Badiou, an event is what will *come to be*. The only temporality, therefore, is future anterior – purely intellectual and non-durational. An event is "decoupled" from temporality. The truth (of and in an event) for Badiou is neither temporal nor atemporal but, he claims, the "interruption" of "a time … of the situation". Likewise, for Deleuze, the event is understood in terms of multiplicity rather than process: be it the "original time" in his *Proust and Signs* or the "*eventum tantum*" in *The Logic of Sense* – in each case there is a de-temporalization of time (Deleuze 1995: 141). Why? Because, as with Badiou, time must be contained in eternity. But Deleuze's eternity is less futural and intellectual and more Proustian and affective, the event being what makes the present past because it is always what has been, a "past in general", the Virtual or *Aion*. Unlike Deleuze, Badiou says that he cannot "think that the new is a fold of the past … . This is why I conceptualise absolute beginnings (which require a theory of the void)…" (D 64; 91).[3] Here we see the real point of divergence between the two on this topic, Badiou partly echoing Deleuze's timeless theory of the Aionic event, but fundamentally rejecting the basis for that timelessness in the virtual (the fold of the past).

So where Deleuze argues that the new, change, is thinkable only through the Virtual, Badiou believes that it is thinkable only through the void. This is due to Badiou belonging to that philosophical tradition, starting in Plato, that gives nothingness a direct ontological bearing. Deleuze, however, and following Bergson once more, equates nothingness with a derivative act of negation, with desire as productive rather than as inherent lack. For him, desire gives rise to (the illusion of) lack. Nothingness is not ontological (Deleuze & Guattari 1984: 25). For Badiou and the "Platonic" tradition, the void is the ontological atom, for if the "first" presented multiplicity was not a multiple of nothing – if it was a multiple of something – then that something would be a One. But the One is not.

All the same, Badiou is careful, at least in *Being and Event*, to distinguish the void from nothingness *per se* (BE 56).[4] The void is always particular; it is not a universal null or *nihilo*: it is a localized voiding of a situation made possible on account of the void immanent to every situation. Every situation, every multiple, is built on a void that will, if given a chance, wipe it out. The void is operational, but it is not the gift of an ulterior subject, of a *pour-soi*; nor is it the derivative of desire: it is rather this voiding that allows for the possibility of a subject at all.

With this difference concerning the void and negation, we come to the final, crucial "difference within sameness" shared between Deleuze and Badiou – the theory of the multiple. In Badiou's eyes, as we saw, far from reducing difference to one hypostatic pole of a dualist ontology (as Deleuze would charge), the void actually supports multiplicity. Badiou concedes that Deleuze was on the right track to think in terms of multiplicities, but adds that he was not successful in this endeavour because he missed the correct starting point for thinking the multiple. For Badiou, the science of the multiple *qua* multiple must be set theory, because it is the theory of the multiple in the purest sense, which, through its axioms and theorems, articulates all that can be said about the pure multiple. Its discourse is the least constrained by the need to articulate the qualities of particular beings, a mathematical writing marked by "dis-qualification and unpresentation" (IT 14,19; BE 9–10). Anything less dis-qualified – resting on the virtual, on life, on the animal, on affect, on intuition – will remain a philosophy of the One, a Platonism of the One (Deleuze's Platonism). Only mathematics supports pluralism, absolutely.

Badiou's attraction to set theory, we should finally note again, is on account of its wholly abstract, pure and empty formalism, involving no particular qualities. This emptiness, or void, is what allows no particular thing to be privileged, and so, for every particular thing to be affirmed equally, universally. The "politics" of set theory (against privilege, for universality) is consequently as important as its mathematical abstractness. And this reminds us that Badiou's ontology is also a politicized one.

Yet the same can be said of Deleuze's vitalist ontology, that life, too, "is the fundamental political category" for him (May 1991; see also Zourabichvili 1994: 335–57). Again, however, although this objective is laudable for Badiou – to think political change – he would add that starting with the concept of life is the wrong way of going about it: "Life makes the multiplicity of evaluations possible, but is itself impossible to evaluate" (D 97). Deleuze's principle that "politics precedes being" requires a more abstracted starting point (Deleuze & Guattari 1987: 203; Deleuze 1990: 149). Oddly enough, then, the charge against Deleuze (formulated most clearly by Peter Hallward's recent Badiouean critique) is that political change requires abstraction from any particular world, whereas Deleuze's vitalism – seemingly more concrete and engaged in its micropolitical analyses – can only be descriptive and thereby quietist, lacking the means to think how change can be evaluated. To think change, one cannot begin *with* change, but only outside of it; one must commence with Parmenides, not Heraclitus. As *Logics of Worlds* puts it: "Plato treats Heraclitus as an adversary and Parmenides as a 'father'" (LW 542). And we might add that Badiou, having the same parentage as Plato, must also treat Deleuze as an adversary, yet not because of the "differends" that alone separate them (of the event, of the multiple), but despite them.

Notes

1. Deleuze (and Guattari) will delineate the scope of creation in a threefold manner – in philosophy (creation of concepts), art (creation of affects) and science (creation of functions).
2. Badiou says that he has the same conception of truth as Spinoza in his later work.
3. See also Badiou (1994a: 56).
4. See IT 176: "In *Théorie du sujet* I thought that negativity was creative in itself and I don't think that now. I think that creativity is a sort of affirmation and not a sort of negation."

SEVENTEEN

New Directions

Z. L. Fraser

And when I speak of the other division of the intelligible, you will understand me to speak of that other sort of knowledge which reason herself attains by the power of the dialectic, using the hypotheses not as first principles, but only as hypotheses – that is to say, as steps and points of departure into a world which is above hypotheses ...   (Plato, *Republic* VI, 511)

Prove all things; hold fast that which is good.
                    (Paul, First letter to the Thessalonians, 5:21)[1]

Let a hundred flowers blossom – I think we should go on doing that.   (Mao Tsetung, "Talks at a Conference of
                    Secretaries of Provincial, Municipal and
                    Autonomous Region Party Committees,"
                    in *Selected Works*, vol. 5)

What does Badiou's philosophy offer the philosopher? He has developed a compelling array of concepts that militants, whether political or scientific, amorous or artistic, can apply to their disciplines in order to see them in new light. Crucially, the utility of Badiou's philosophy for each of these practices, scholarly and militant, owes much to its foundation on a series of *axiomatic decisions*. The abruptness of its axiomatic base grants the scholar a freedom to examine it as self-contained system, logically isolated from its exterior, yet also gives it its remarkable mobility, letting it be transported and applied to domains quite foreign to those of its initial construction.

This coupling of autonomy and mobility is precisely what the pioneers of the axiomatic method sought through the axiomatization and formalization of mathematics. By means of this method, the arch-formalist David Hilbert once said, a theory can be grasped as:

> a scaffolding or schema of concepts together with their necessary relations to one another, and that the basic elements can be thought of in any way one likes. If in speaking of my points I think of some system of things, e.g. the system: love, law, chimney-sweeps… and then assume all my axioms as relations between these things, then my propositions, e.g. Pythagoras' theorem, are also valid for these things. (Frege 1980: 40, letter from Hilbert to Frege, 29 December 1899)

If we can legitimately address Badiou's philosophy on these terms, what can the philosopher *qua* philosopher *do* with Badiou's remarkable constructions? Especially if it is neither application nor explication that a philosopher desires of a thought, but its *continuation*. If this continuation is to deliver anything that is both new (and so exceeds the trailing out of already-implicit consequences) and yet significant to the philosophy interrogated, it must take its mark from those points of the philosophy that are most fundamental: to seek continuation of the thought *in the direction of its foundations*. In Badiou's case, the appearance of a series of *axiomatic decisions* at its foundations – decisions that claim no extrinsic justification for themselves – seems to foil the philosopher's desire. What traction can thought find in the opacity of a decision that makes no claim to evidence? How can it get "behind" a decision that subtracts itself from any background?

If Badiou's thought indicates "new directions" for philosophy, we might look for something like *proofs of his axioms*. Yet this demand may seem wrong-headed, to spring from a complete misunderstanding of the *very idea* of an "axiom". Is it still possible to extract from the idea of *proof*, something other, or something more than the fixing of *certainty* with respect to first principles? If proof was *nothing but* a tool for fixing certainty, it could be substituted by other forms of evidence. We do not attempt proof in order to fix certainty any more than a desire seeks its object in order to erase itself; certainty, similarly, is not the *ideal* of proof but a terminus of its movement. Imre Lakatos has given the best description of the isolation of the operations of proof. He proposes that we:

> retain the time-honoured technical term "proof" for a thought-experiment – or quasi-experiment – which suggests a decompo-

sition of the original conjecture into subconjectures or lemmas, thus embedding it in a possibly quite distant body of knowledge. ... This decomposition of the conjecture suggested by the proof opens new vistas for testing. The decomposition deploys the conjecture on a wider front, so that our criticism has more targets.

(Lakatos 1976: 9–10)

The movement of decomposing, embedding and possibly transforming a conjecture can proceed even in the absence of principles that would anchor its certainty. Indeed, this conception of "proof" will even "allow for a *false* conjecture to be 'proved'" (*ibid.*: 23) – not shown to be true, but *rendered intelligible*. Nothing prevents us from putting the same operations to work on the *axioms* of a system, to illuminate what would otherwise go unnoticed.

Such decompositions and embeddings of a proof can have effects on the conjecture in question. They have the power to *force a transformation of the conjecture*, bearing not only on its epistemic status, but on its content as well. By *decomposing*, proof aims to expose points at which the conjecture opens onto something other than what is *explicitly* contained in it, and the *embedding* of these points in "possibly distant bodies of knowledge" seeks something like a *condition*, in Badiou's sense of the term. The difference between an example and a condition, in general terms, can perhaps be expressed by saying that while an example serves to reflect, illustrate and perhaps corroborate its concept, a condition subjects a concept to rational demands that might otherwise remain foreign to it, exigencies that "put the concept to work", that enrich and transform it.[2]

But is Badiou's philosophy not a *philosophy of decision, a decisional philosophy*, and the axiomaticity of his thought a performative necessity? There is no reason to abandon Badiou's insight that any project of thought, philosophical or not, is punctuated by a series of axiomatic decisions (explicit or obscure). The project of seeking "proof" for any such axioms could not proceed otherwise. But to treat these as hermetically sealed dogmata, which can be accepted or rejected but never dismantled or tampered with, is to indulge in an anti-philosophical fetishization of axioms. This is an indulgence Badiou himself resists. "The principal thing for me", he remarks to Tzuchien Tho,

is that there are always axiomatic decisions. I do not believe at all that it is necessary to posit an opposition between the decision, on the one hand, and, on the other hand, intuition or experimentation, since the decision is always the formation or concentration of a series of experimentations or intuitions in the process of the perception of a situation. It is rather the notion of a common point between them that renders a network. (CM 101)

If I echo here Plato's injunction to "destroy hypotheses", it is not in order to arrive at a revelation of principles that would make decisions unnecessary, but to activate experiments informing those decisions, and extend them into new series, leading (perhaps) to the crystallization of new axioms. This is what I mean by the *continuation* of a philosophy.

Let us apply this thought to a particular decision of Badiou: the axiomatic identification of mathematics and ontology. When it surfaces for the first time in Badiou's writings, in a 1984 review of Lyotard's *Le Différend*, this thesis takes the form of a conjecture to be proven.[3] Against Lyotard's reduction of mathematics to an ensemble of "free and regulated word games", Badiou opposes the conjecture that: "mathematics, throughout its history, is the science of being *qua* being, that is, of being insofar as it is not, the science of impresentable presentation. I will prove it one day" (1984: 861).

By the time of *Being and Event*, the project of *proving* this identity has been all but forgotten. How could we resume this project today? We can begin by unfolding this crucial thesis, "mathematics" = ontology and marking out a series of "lemmas" to be proved. As a first approximation, the following seems reasonable: throughout its history, mathematics has constituted itself, in truth, as ontology: the discourse in which being *qua* being is articulated according to the pure forms of its presentation – forms that, in light of the non-being of the One, can only be thought as pure multiplicities. The being, or rather the presentational form, of anything that is can be thought only in and through mathematics. Today, the ontological vocation of mathematics is best approached by way of set theory, and its Zermelo–Fraenkel axiomatization (ZF) in particular. This discourse makes explicit the ontological univocity of mathematics, as the science of multiplicity *qua* multiplicity, and its suture to "being in so far as it is not" by way of its nomination of the void, whose ontological name is Ø. Without exhausting its complexity, at least six threads can be pulled from the skein of the identity thesis. In order of exposition, these can be called: *History, The one is not, Presentation, Void, Truth, Description*. Each thread, in some way or another, loops around a blind spot in Badiou's apparatus, and helps to localize a site at which the apparatus can be opened to experimentation and, it is hoped, productive critique. Unfortunately, there is room here to give an explication only of the first of these: this should, however, be sufficient in this context to give a sense of how ongoing and future philosophical interventions into Badiou's work might proceed.

Badiou's identification of mathematics and ontology is frequently addressed as if it concerned set theory alone, but we are repeatedly reminded that this is not the case:

- [M]athematics, *throughout its history*, is the science of being *qua* being ... (Badiou 1984: 861, emphasis added)
- [M]athematics, *throughout the entirety of its historical becoming*, pronounces what is expressible of being qua being (BE 8, emphasis added).
- Ontology: Science of being-*qua*-being. Presentation of presentation. Realized as thought of the pure multiple, thus as Cantorian mathematics or set theory. *It is and was already effective, despite being unthematized, throughout the entire history of mathematics* (BE 517, emphasis added).
- The effective history of ontology coincides exactly with the history of mathematics (TO 159).
- [Ontology] is *historically identical* to mathematics (LW 590, emphasis added).

Nothing deploys the conjecture identifying mathematics and ontology on a wider front than the implication, in this conjecture, of mathematics' entire and incompletable history. The recognition of this fact immediately opens the terrain to experiments, for which Quentin Meillassoux, in "Nouveauté et événement" (2002), has suggested an ingenious protocol: while adhering as closely as possible to the spirit of Badiou's thought, try to construct a "spectral Badiouism", a system that proceeds, as Badiou's does, from an identification of mathematics and ontology, but which either:

(a) pursues the corollary that ontology has a history independent of philosophy, and so attempts to construct a theory of ontological novelty that is not tethered to any *particular* theory of ontology proper, a theory of ontological novelty that pivots on neither events nor truth (see Meillassoux 2008) (both being tethered, somewhat exorbitantly, to ZF in *Being and Event*); or else
(b) selects a mathematical scaffolding differing radically from ZF – perhaps one that satisfies as many of Badiou's meta-ontological preferences as possible, such as univocity and generality: the lambda calculus and non-commutative operator algebra spring

to mind – around which to construct an otherwise "Badiousian" meta-ontology.

If these variants ultimately prove to be *less* compelling than "actual Badiouism", then the latter appears all the more robust. If they prove *equally* or *more* compelling than their model, then the identity thesis shows itself to be more fruitful than we initially expected. It would be interesting, as well, to isolate the elements of "Badiouism" that survive this division, as invariants across these spectral mutations. The axioms that crystallize *actual Badiouism*, and distinguish it from "lambda Badiouism" and other spectral variants, would also be thrown into sharp relief by this protocol, as "a hundred schools of thought contend".

Logics of Worlds makes undeniable advances over *Being and Event* by introducing a mediating apparatus built up from *topos* theory and an accompanying "minimal phenomenology". The method of analogical decoration is no doubt more sophisticated in this text, but nevertheless remains rather indeterminate (the order relation on a Heyting algebra, for instance, is interpreted according to the fundamental "phenomenological" notion of "order of intensity", but this is so underdetermined that, depending on the occasion, it is applied to phenomena as diverse as causal ordering, pictorial emphasis and military strength, to name just a few examples). The reader is left to wonder: if it is the role of "minimal phenomenology" to systematically correlate mathematical structures and observable phenomena, what is it that the empirical sciences have been doing?

To escape this blind alley, in which "all that mediates between ontological presentation *stricto sensu* … is Badiou's own metaontological discourse" (Brassier 2004: 114), we must insist on the importance of the empirical sciences as *conditions* of philosophy – an office Badiou extends to them in principle, but rarely invites them to execute. It is to the sciences that we owe those moments in which formal thought latches onto its outside – an outside thoroughly mediated by experimental and observational practices – with any degree of rigour whatsoever. If the relation between mathematical ontology and "concrete situations" is to be made philosophically intelligible, then we need a general theory of empirical-scientific objects, one that would allow us to grasp them as *models* (or parts of models) of a mathematical ontology.

It is in this light that the metaphysical investigations currently taking place under the rubric of *Ontic Structural Realism* (OSR) might take on a profound significance for Badiouean philosophy. A manifesto for this project is to be found in James Ladyman and Don Ross's recent text, *Every Thing Must Go*. The problem that their work seeks to solve is one that has troubled metaphysicians of science at least since Kuhn's groundbreaking *Structure of Scientific Revolutions*: how can we maintain that the empirical sciences disclose the very nature of reality in the face of a history littered with "scientific revolutions", each incessantly sweeping into the dustbin everything we took to make up "the furniture of the world"? At what point do our most rigorous enquiries into the nature of reality touch on the real itself, enquiries that, in virtue and not in spite of their critical rigour, are in a perpetual state of self-effacing flux? OSR's gambit is to shift our attention from the ephemeral furniture of these revolutionary sequences to their "pivots" – the *invariant structures* that approximately endure the waves of revolution. It is in these structures, captured by mathematical formalization, that the reality tracked by science is seized, and not in the inventory of posited objects by means of which we might, at a given historical conjuncture, keep tabs on structural reality.

It is this insight that must inform our attempt to develop a theory of *any empirical-scientific object whatever*. To this end, Ladyman and Ross introduce the concept of *real pattern*. A real pattern, more or less, is an *algorithm* anticipating the unfolding of phenomena, from the standpoint of some physically possible position, by means of computations whose only constraints are those imposed by the mathematical theory of computation itself, on the one hand, and by the laws of physics, on the other.[4]

Is this concept capable of fastening mathematical ontology onto the real precisely where the Badiouean notions of "situation" and "world" flounder in fogs of analogy? The greatest challenge that Badiouean philosophy, or perhaps one of its spectral variants, would face on this path concerns the *genericity* Badiou requires of truth procedures. OSR adheres strictly to what Badiou terms the "constructivist orientation of thought", an orientation that denies reality to the generic. In so far as the generic, by definition, exceeds algorithmic projectibility, there can be no generic "real patterns", and so no "real" "truths" ("real" in OSR's sense, "truths" in Badiou's). Philosophical naturalism finds its zenith in the radical conformity that OSR enforces between being and knowledge, and in doing so finds the greatest point of discord between its project and Badiou's – a discord that, perhaps, does much to explain the distance Badiou has maintained from naturalisms of every stripe. The Badiouean's task would be to carve a path for an unnaturalizable, but non-supernatural, subjectivity in the mathematics of real-patternhood.[5] This task exposes the Badiouean to a host of problems that, from the high towers of set theory, were scarcely even legible, but that, once seen, cannot fail to enrich the philosophical project.

There is nothing conclusive in this sketch for proofs and variations on a theme, and I offer them here only as notes and suggestions for further investigation. I hope that they might be of some use to readers who find themselves searching for paths by which the Badiouean project can be continued.

Notes

1. Quoted in Lakatos (1976: 23).
2. *Les Cahiers pour l'analyse*, the Lacano-Althusserian epistemological journal that Badiou helped to edit between 1967 and 1969, and in which he published two of his most important early texts, opened every issue with a slogan from Georg Canguilhem, which gives us a good sense of what it means to put a concept to work: "To work on a concept, to put a concept to work, is to vary its extension and comprehension, to generalize it by incorporating exceptional traits, exporting it beyond its region of origin, taking it for a model or, conversely, seeing a model for it, in short, to progressively confer upon it the function of a form by regulated transformations." The difference between example and condition, in Badiou's work, has been examined in Clemens (2006: 102–43). Clemens argues that while the non-philosophical is encountered in *Being and Event* primarily in the form of *conditions*, in *Logics of Worlds* it appears primarily in the guise of *examples*.

   An echo of this distinction between example and condition, in the context of logical semantics, can be read in Jean-Yves Girard's introductory remarks to "Linear Logic", where he writes: "Some people think that the purpose of semantics is to interpret sets of equations in a complete way; in some sense, the semantic comes like an *official blessing* on our language, rules, etc.: they are perfect and cannot be improved. The success of this viewpoint lies in Gödel's completeness theorem which guarantees, for any consistent system, a complete semantics. A more controversial view consists in looking for *disturbing* semantics, which shed unexpected lights on the systems we know. Of course, this viewpoint is highly criticisable since there is no absolute certainty that anything will result from such attempts. But the stakes are clearly higher than in the hagiographic viewpoint and a change of syntax (as the one coming with linear logic) may occur from *disturbing semantics*" (Girard 1987: 14–15).
3. There is no doubt rewarding philological work to be done in exhuming some of *Being and Event*'s conceptual roots from Badiou's reading of *Le Différend* – not least of all because it is from there that Badiou extracts the fundamental "meta-ontological" category of "presentation". What Gorgias was for Plato, Lyotard no doubt is for Badiou. As Feltham has already pointed out, in his contribution to this volume (Chapter 2), "One can detect thousands of tiny post-structuralist influences in every one of [Badiou's] texts", and no small number of these are distinctly "Lyotardian".
4. For a more detailed account of the concept of *real pattern*, see Ladyman & Ross (2008: ch. 4).
5. The following remarks of Ladyman and Ross's give us a sense of the resistance that the Badiousian conception of subjectivity would be up against on this terrain: "Now, physics also constrains the domain of the computable. Computation

is a kind of flow of information, in at least the most general sense of the latter idea: any computation takes as input some distribution of possibilities in a state space and determines, by physical processes, some other distribution consistent with that input. Physics can tell us about lower bounds on the energy required to effect a given computation, and since it also sets limits on where, when and how physical work can be done, it can show us that various hypothetical computations are (physically) impossible. … If one shows that no physically possible machine could perform a given inference, then one thereby shows that brains cannot perform it (nor quantum computers nor supercomputers nor enculturated people either). … This does not imply that thinking *reduces* to computation, but only the weaker claim that what cannot be computed cannot be thought" (Ladyman & Ross 2008: 208–9).

Badiou's futures

A. J. Bartlett and Justin Clemens

In keeping with the tenor of this collection, we shall conclude by summarizing the aetiology and import of some of Badiou's key concepts in order to ask: where to from here? Above all, we need to reiterate that Badiou is continuing to practise philosophy in "the fullness of its ambition". For Badiou, this has meant returning to the "origin" of Western philosophy in order to show that: "Plato" exceeds the critiques of "Platonism" that dominated the twentieth century; that this "excessive" Plato offers a mode of thinking that entails an attention to the "conditions" of science, art, love and politics; that this further involves the construction of philosophy against its intimate others, such as "sophistry"; finally, this enables the reconstruction of a Platonism for today, one that runs diagonally to the received divisions in the existing situation (such as the distinction between "analytic" and "continental" philosophy), while maintaining such classical philosophemes as "truth", "ontology" and the "subject".

Yet we also have to emphasize that Badiou, as a philosopher, can never be entirely happy with his own philosophy. As we have seen, Badiou's own work has shifted markedly from his early work up to *Theory of the Subject*, before creating the most significant rupture in his own *oeuvre* with *Being and Event*. Since then, he has reaffirmed, refined and extended fundamental aspects of his BE project (including mathematics = ontology, the priority of the conditions), but radically reconfigured others (especially the scope and status of logic and the theory of the subject) – as is evident from *Logics of Worlds*, the sequel to *Being and Event*.

There are both immanent and external reasons for such shifts. As Badiou points out in justifying his release of a *Second Manifesto for*

Philosophy in 2009, things have radically changed in the twenty years since the first *Manifesto*. At the time of the first, a post-Heideggerean animus held sway in philosophy, which held that metaphysics had entered the regime of its inexorable closure, and that what remained of thought had the literary as its destiny; the political context in France was Mitterandism, and all that implied. Today, however, everybody has become a "philosopher", in the world of Sarkozy and US global militarism.

In his reconstruction of a contemporary Platonism, then, Badiou's philosophy has clearly already had significant effects – on himself, as on philosophy more generally. Yet he is in turn affected by the effects of these effects, and he has not ceased interrogating his own philosophy on that basis too (see his accounts of his relations to contemporary thinkers in LW). Given that Badiou is highly productive – a film, *The Life of Plato*, is allegedly in the works, as well as a translation of the *Republic* into French, plus other writings – it is not possible to say where he himself will now go (he hints at another work on the Subject), beyond the extension of his established concepts, and according to his own principles of justice, novelty, risk and commitment. From *Theory of the Subject*, it would have been impossible to anticipate *Being and Event*; even knowing *Being and Event* intimately, it would have been impossible to anticipate a great deal of *Logics of Worlds*. The key problem here is: *how to remain contemporary?*

From commentators, at least, one should expect more of the following:

(i) immanent philosophical critique of Badiou's work, regarding the consistency of its concepts and the structures of its arguments (such as is suggested by Luke Fraser's contribution in the current volume – Chapter 17);

(ii) the use of Badiou's component concepts or specific arguments in new contexts (e.g. Brassier's work on scientific realism, which uses Badiou's arguments regarding the relation between the void and the one);

(iii) explorations of the sense of the conditions (e.g. the use of Badiou's categories to think further about, say, education in Plato, Beckett's writings or the theory of cinema);

(iv) the further academicization of "Badiou studies" (e.g. more introductory works such as the current volume, "compare and contrast" studies such as "Badiou and Deleuze on mathematics", and contextualizing monographs);

(v) para-philosophical works "inspired by" Badiou (e.g. those by Quentin Meillassoux or Mehdi Belhaj Kacem).

It is also worth mentioning some of the ongoing contemporary influences upon Badiou that we were unable to trace in this volume. The first among the contemporaries are those whose positive propositions are integral to Badiou's own work. Like Lacan, they have also made it possible for Badiou to think through the singularity of philosophy's conditions. Primary are Natacha Michel (novelist and political activist), Sylvain Lazarus (political thinker and activist), Judith Balso (critic of Fernando Pessoa), as well as Barbara Cassin, whose L'effet sophistique has proven highly provocative for Badiou.[1] We should also mention Badiou's respectful yet antagonistic relation to the "unconditioned" revolutionary "philosophy of the One" of Guy Laudreau and Christian Jambet (LW 544; BE 484), as well as the extended "Notes, Commentaries and Digressions" section of Logics of Worlds where readers will find Badiou's own account of his complicated relationships to his immediate precursors and contemporaries (among the most notable being Jacques Derrida, Jacques Rancière, Jean-François Lyotard, Giorgio Agamben and Slavoj Žižek).[2]

Taking all the above into account, we have to remember that Badiou's central and overarching question concerns how the new appears in being. Translated into the terms of Logics of Worlds, this concerns the creation of a present. As this collection attests, the "new" is not to be thought in the same manner that we look for a new soap powder, a new running shoe, new software or a new school. These, no matter how they supposedly exemplify the "freedom of choice", conform to an established logic; while the truly new, in its apparent impossibility, as in its difficult and proscribed manifestation, is that which is subtracted from any such predication. In other words, a present is lacking – and therefore what has to be produced.

It is the true, then, that is always new. The present will be the step-by-step, point-by-point, subjective realization of that which truly is, of that which will have been "thought through". What truly is, is, ontologically speaking, presented under the sign of belonging. Belonging, axiomatically indiscerning one element from another, which is to say, knowing nothing of identity, nothing of difference or the logic of placements, denotes, then, a pure collective – a situated in-difference. Such a collective, that it exists, engenders an idea that politics thinks as equality, art reveals as series of works, love denotes in the form of a Two and philosophy, Badiou says, thinks in turn as justice. Justice, Badiou declares, affirms that people think, that they are capable of thought. The philosophical axiom par excellence is that "people are capable of truth". This is why Badiou says that philosophy, in its invention, is consecrated to communism.

Let us not be confused or seduced into the all-too-simplistic conflation that belonging = justice, or as is commonly touted in certain circles, mathematics equals totalitarianism. Belonging ≠ justice; it is the ontological real of any situation. As such, thought approaches the real through its Idea. This Idea marks the passage of this real into thought, into philosophy. Plato called this participation. Philosophy is called upon to think *through* participation, to compose a discourse on the basis of the real and of its Ideal manifestation through various conditions of its possibility. There is no seamless passage here – it is not the ontological real that appears but its Idea that is made manifest. The latter, as we have seen, is the difficult, contingent and patient work of the subject, the militant. It is "rare work", courageous, opposed by all the resources of the situation's state, the logic of the "atonic" world, for whom this militant "must not be", for whom there is no Idea precisely because there is no *lack* of interest. Yet we know that, albeit minimally, *there is* – that which is not.

To think the new in situations whose impossibility is always existent and whose chance is given in the event – that it will have happened (there is no need to wait, waiters!) – is the demand that falls to philosophy. This in turn is its animating desire. Philosophy, under these conditions, *is not ever* that which gives way – to "our democracies", parliamentary "debates", the predations of capital, totalization, the linguistic turn, the logic of ends or the pathos of the animal – all of which can be summed up in a single ancient term whose recent rehabilitation speaks the temper and timidity of our times, "sophistry".

As Badiou points out, there were, are and will be great sophists, but, as Plato found, there is no great sophistry: like even and odd, these *forms* do not mix. Nevertheless, determined by the fact that all thought is situated, that all singularity is multiple, philosophy, via and through its conditions, has no option but to truck with this "false conceit of wisdom". In other words, just as three is intimately related to four, sophistry is intimately related to philosophy. Yet it remains that, as odd is not ever even, sophistry is not ever philosophy. Philosophy, committed to thinking that which is new in situations, that which is generic to them, is the guardian of this thought, which is to say, the guardian of an Idea both anticipated and retrospective. Philosophy, for Badiou, is the desire to continue in thought that which from time to time manifests itself without predicate and against all *odds*: if we are in earnest, if we are attentive to our times then, yes, "we shall have our human life turned upside down". To continue to do philosophy before, with and after Badiou means: to have our human life turned upside down in essaying to live as contemporaries of an Idea.

Notes

1. In the dedication for *The Century* Badiou remarks that "The very idea for these texts could only have arisen thanks to Natacha Michel, who one day – against the current of all the anathemas launched at revolutions and militants, and flouting their obliteration by today's 'democrats' – pronounced the verdict: 'The 20th century has taken place'". See also *The Century* (90), *Polemics* (239), *Logics of Worlds* (554–5). On Lazarus, see *Metapolitics* (ch. 2), *Being and Event* (483), *Logics of Worlds* (519–22), where Badiou says that attempts (by others) to oppose his "philosophy to [his] organised commitment, or to the political and anthropological creation of Sylvain Lazarus, have no more chance of success today than they did in the past". In a note Badiou says, "Regarding the theoretical function of heteronyms in Pessoa's poetry, and in particular the intellectual set-up that such a 'technique' authorises with respect to the relations between poetry and metaphysics, one should refer to the only genuine 'specialist' in these questions, Judith Balso" (TC 212 n.41). See Cassin (1995, 2000).
2. For J.-P. Sartre's "formative" influence, for example, see *Logics of Worlds* (535–6), *Pocket Pantheon* (14–35).

Bibliography

Works by Badiou

Badiou, A. 1967. "Le (re)commencement du matérialisme dialectique". *Critique* **240**: 438–67.

Badiou, A. 1968. "La Subversion Infinitésimale". *Cahiers pour l'analyse* 9 (Summer): 118–37.

Badiou, A. 1969a. *Le Concept de modèle*. Paris: Maspero.

Badiou, A. 1969b. "Marque et Manque: à propos du zero" (Mark and Lack: On Zero). *Cahiers pour l'analyse* **10**: 150–73. Written in 1967.

Badiou, A. 1975a. "Édification du parti et question syndicale". *Théorie et politique* 3/4: 114–18.

Badiou, A. 1975b. "Syndicalisme et révisionnisme moderne. *Théorie et politique* 5: 58–87.

Badiou, A. 1975c. *Théorie de la contradiction*. Paris: Maspero.

Badiou, A. 1977. "Le Flux et le parti: dans les marges de L'Anti-Oedipe". In *La Situation actuelle sur le front philosophique, Cahiers Yenan* no. 4, 24–41. Paris: Maspero.

Badiou, A. 1978a. *La contestation dans le P.C.F.* Paris: Potemkine.

Badiou, A. 1978b. *Le Noyau rationnel de la dialectique hégélienne. Traduction, introductions et commentaires autour d'un texte de Zhang Shiying, Pékin, 1972.* Paris: Maspero.

Badiou, A. 1982. *Théorie du sujet*. Paris: Seuil.

Badiou, A. 1984. "Custos, quid noctis?" *Critique* **450**: 851–63.

Badiou, A. 1985. *Peut-on penser la politique?* Paris: Seuil.

Badiou, A. 1987a. "À bas la société existante!" *Le Perroquet* **69**: 1–3.

Badiou, A. 1987b. "L'usine comme site événementiel". *Le Perroquet* **62–3**: 1–6. Available in English in *Prelom* 8, www.prelomkolektiv.org/eng/08.htm (accessed April 2010).

Badiou, A. 1988. *L'Être et l'événement*. Paris: Seuil.

Badiou, A. 1989. *Manifeste pour la philosophie*. Paris: Seuil.

Badiou, A. 1990. *Rhapsodie pour le théâtre*. Paris: Le Spectateur français.

Badiou, A. 1991a. "On a Finally Objectless Subject". In *Who Comes After the Subject*, E. Cadava, P. Connor & J.-L. Nancy (eds), B. Fink (trans.), 24–32. New York: Routledge.

Badiou, A. 1991b. "Objectivité et objectalité". Review of Monique David-Ménard, *La Folie dans la raison pure: Kant lecteur de Swedenborg* (Paris: Vrin, 1990). Unpublished typescript.

Badiou, A. 1992a. *Conditions*. Paris: Seuil. Reprinted 1998.

Badiou, A. 1992b. "Qu'est-ce que Louis Althusser entend par 'philosophie'?". In *Politique et philosophie dans l'oeuvre de Louis Althusser*, S. Lazarus (ed.), 29–45. Paris: Presses Universitaires de France.

Badiou, A. 1994a. "Gilles Deleuze, The Fold: Leibniz and the Baroque". In *Deleuze and Theatre of Philosophy*, C. Boundas & D. Olkowski (ed.), T. Sowley (trans.), 51–69. New York: Columbia University Press.

Badiou, A. 1994b. "Silence, solipsisme, saintété: L'antiphilosophie de Wittgenstein". *Barca*! 3: 13–53.

Badiou, A. 1995. "L'Impératif de la négation". Review of Guy Lardreau, *La Véracité* (Paris: Verdie, 1993). Unpublished typescript.

Badiou, A. 1996a. "Descartes/Lacan", S. Jöttkandt & D. Collins (trans.). *UMBR(a)* 1: 13–17.

Badiou, A. 1996b. "Hegel", M.Coelen & S. Gillespie (trans.). *UMBR(a)* 1: 27–35.

Badiou, A. 1996c. "Psychoanalysis and Philosophy", R. Comprone & M. Coelen (trans.). *UMBR(a)* 1: 19–26.

Badiou, A. 1996d. "What is Love?", J. Clemens (trans.). *UMBR(a)* 1: 37–53.

Badiou, A. 1998a. "Is There a Theory of the Subject in Georges Canguilhem?", Graham Burchell (trans.). *Economy and Society* 27(2/3): 225–33.

Badiou, A. 1998b. *Petit manuel d'inesthétique*. Paris: Seuil.

Badiou, A. 1998c. "Politics and Philosophy: An Interview with Alain Badiou". *Angelaki* 3(3): 113–33.

Badiou, A. 1998d. *Court traité d'ontologie transitoire*. Paris: Seuil.

Badiou, A. 1999a. *Manifesto for Philosophy*, N. Maderasz (trans.). Albany, NY: SUNY Press.

Badiou, A. 1999b. "Philosophy and Politics", T. Sowley (trans.). *Radical Philosophy* 96: 29–32.

Badiou, A. 1999c. "La scène du Deux". In *De l'amour*, L'Ecole de la Cause Freudienne (ed.), 177–90. Paris: Flammarion.

Badiou, A. 2000a. "On a Contemporary Usage of Frege", J. Clemens & S. Gillespe (trans.). *UMBR(a)* 1: 99–115.

Badiou, A. 2000b. *Deleuze: The Clamor of Being*, L. Burchill (trans.). Minneapolis, MN: University of Minnesota Press.

Badiou, A. 2000c. "Of Life as a Name of Being, or, Deleuze's Vitalist Ontology", A. Toscano (trans.). *Pli: The Warwick Journal of Philosophy* 10: 191–9.

Badiou, A. 2000d. Metaphysics and the Critique of Metaphysics", A. Toscano (trans.). *Pli: The Warwick Journal of Philosophy* 10: 174–90.

Badiou, A. 2001a. "The Ethic of Truths: Construction and Potency", S. Sowley (trans.). *Pli: The Warwick Journal of Philosophy* 12: 245–55.

Badiou, A. 2001b. *Ethics: An Essay on the Understanding of Evil*, P. Hallward (trans.). London: Continuum.

Badiou, A. 2001c. "On Evil: An Interview with Alain Badiou". *Cabinet* 5, www.cabinetmagazine.org/issues/5/alainbadiou.php (accessed April 2010).

Badiou, A. 2001d. "The Political as a Procedure of Truth", B. P. Faulks (trans.). *Lacanian Ink* 19: 71–81.

Badiou, A. 2001e. "Who is Nietzsche?", A. Toscano (trans.). *Pli: The Warwick Journal of Philosophy* 11: 1–10.

Badiou, A. 2002. "Existence and Death", N. Power & A. Toscano (trans.). *Discourse* 24(1): 63–73.

Badiou, A. 2002. "One Divides into Two", A. Toscano (trans.). *Culture Machine* 4: http://www.culturemachine.net/index.php/cm/article/viewarticle/270/255.

Badiou, A. 2003a. *On Beckett*, A. Toscano & N. Power (eds & trans.). Manchester: Clinamen.

Badiou, A. 2003b. "Beyond Formalisation: An Interview", B. Bosteels & A. Toscano (trans.). *Angelaki: Journal of the Theoretical Humanities* 8(2): 111–36.

Badiou, A. 2003c. *Infinite Thought: Truth and the Return to Philosophy*, J. Clemens & O. Feltham (ed. & trans.). London: Continuum.

Badiou, A. 2003d. "Logic of the Site", S. Corcoran & B. Bosteels (trans.). *Diacritics* 33(3–4): 141–50.

Badiou, A. 2003e. *Saint Paul: The Foundation of Universalism*, Ray Brassier (trans.). Stanford, CA: Stanford University Press.

Badiou, A. 2004a. "Afterword: Some Replies to a Demanding Friend". In *Think Again: Alain Badiou and the Future of Philosophy*, P. Hallward (ed.), 232–7. London: Continuum.

Badiou, A. 2004b. "Fifteen Theses on Contemporary Art". *Lacanian Ink* 23: 103–19.

Badiou, A. 2004c. "The Flux and the Party: In the Margins of Anti-Oedipus", L. Balladur & S. Krysl (trans.). *Polygraph* 15/16: 75–92.

Badiou, A. 2004d. "Of an Obscure Disaster", B. P. Faulks (trans.). *Lacanian Ink* 22: 58–99.

Badiou, A. 2004e. *Theoretical Writings*, A. Toscano & R. Brassier (eds & trans.). London: Continuum.

Badiou, A. 2005a. "The Adventure of French Philosophy". *New Left Review* 35: 67–77.

Badiou, A. 2005b. "Democratic Materialism and the Materialist Dialectic", A. Toscano (trans.). *Radical Philosophy* 130 (March/April): 20–24.

Badiou, A. 2005c. *Handbook of Inaesthetics*, A. Toscano (trans.). Stanford, CA: Stanford University Press.

Badiou, A. 2005d. "Manifesto of Affirmationism", B. P. Faulks (trans.). *Lacanian Ink* 24/25: 92–109.

Badiou, A. 2005e. *Metapolitics*, J. Barker (trans.). London, Verso.

Badiou, A. 2005f. "The Subject of Art". *The Symptom* 6 www.lacan.com/symptom6_articles/badiou.html (accessed April 2010).

Badiou, A. 2005g. *Le Siècle*. Paris: Seuil.

Badiou, A. 2006a. "Anxiety", B. P. Faulks (trans.). *Lacanian Ink* 26: 70–71.

Badiou, A. 2006b. *Being and Event*, O. Feltham (trans.). London: Continuum.

Badiou, A. 2006c. *Briefings on Existence: A Short Treatise on Transitory Ontology*, N. Maderasz (trans.). New York: SUNY Press.

Badiou, A. 2006d. "The Formulas of *L'Étourdit*", S. Saviano (trans.). *Lacanian Ink* 27: 80–95.

Badiou, A. 2006e. "The Formulas of the Real (Being, Number, Analytic Cure, Artistic Creation)". *Lacanian Ink* 28: 50–53.

Badiou, A. 2006f. "An Interview with Alain Badiou: After the Event: Rationality and the Politics of Invention", conducted by "Radical Politics". *Prelom* 8 (Fall): 180–84.

Badiou, A. 2006g. "Lacan and the pre-Socratics". In *Lacan: The Silent Partners*, S. Žižek (ed.), 7–16. London: Verso.

Badiou, A. 2006h. *Logiques des mondes: l'être et l'événement, 2*. Paris: Seuil.
Badiou, A. 2006i. "Philosophy, Sciences, Mathematics: Interview with Alain Badiou". *Collapse* 1: 11–26.
Badiou, A. 2006j. "Plato, Our Dear Plato!", A. Toscano (trans.). *Angelaki* 2(3): 39–41.
Badiou, A. 2006k. *Polemics*, S. Corcoran (ed. & trans.). London: Verso.
Badiou, A. 2006l. "The Question of Democracy: Analía Hounie Interviews Alain Badiou". *Lacanian Ink* 28: 54–9.
Badiou, A. 2007a. *The Concept of Model: An Introduction to the Materialist Epistemology of Mathematics*, Z. L. Fraser & T. Tho (ed. & trans.). Melbourne: re.press.
Badiou, A. 2007b. "The Event in Deleuze", J. Roffe (trans.). *Parrhesia* 2: 37–44.
Badiou, A. 2007c. "The Factory as Event Site", A. Toscano (trans.). *Prelom* 8: 172–6.
Badiou, A. 2007d. "Marcel Duchamp". Paper presented at the Philosophie & Art Contemporain seminar, 9 March, École Normale Supérieure, Paris.
Badiou, A. 2007e. "A Musical Variant of the Metaphysics of the Subject", J. Clemens (trans.). *Parrhesia* 2: 29–36.
Badiou, A. 2007f. "Towards a New Concept of Existence". *Lacanian Ink* 29: 63–72.
Badiou, A. 2007g. "What is a Philosophical Institution? Or: Address, Transmission, Inscription", A. J. Bartlett (trans.). In *The Praxis of Alain Badiou*, P. Ashton, A. J. Bartlett & J. Clemens (eds), 13–19. Melbourne: re.press.
Badiou, A. 2007h. "Art and Politics". Paper presented at the Centre International d'Étude de la Philosophie Française Contemporaine Seminar, 25 April 2007, École Normale Supérieure, Paris.
Badiou, A. 2007i. *The Century*, A. Toscano (trans.). Cambridge: Polity.
Badiou, A. 2007j. "Jullien l'apostat". In *Oser construire: Pour François Jullien*. Paris: Les Empêcheurs de penser en rond.
Badiou, A. 2007–8. "Pour aujourd'hui: Platon!". Séminaire d'Alain Badiou, www.entretemps.asso.fr/Badiou/07-08.htm (accessed April 2010).
Badiou, A. 2008a. "The Communist Hypothesis". *New Left Review* 49 (Jan./Feb.): 29–42.
Badiou, A. 2008b. *Conditions*, S. Corcoron (trans.). London: Continuum.
Badiou, A. 2008c. "Figures of Subjective Destiny: On Samuel Beckett". *Lacan.com*, www.lacan.com/article/?page_id=21 (accessed April 2010).
Badiou, A. 2008d. *The Meaning of Sarkozy*, D. Fernbach (trans.). London: Verso.
Badiou, A. 2008e. *Number and Numbers*, R. Mackay (trans.). Cambridge: Polity.
Badiou, A. 2008f. *Petit panthéon portatif*. Paris: La fabrique éditions.
Badiou, A. 2008g. "Philosophy as Biography". *The Symptom* 9, www.lacan.com/symptom9_articles/badiou19.html (accessed April 2010).
Badiou, A. 2008h. "L'aveu du philosophe". Centre International d'Étude de la Philosophie Française Contemporaine. www.ciepfc.fr/spip.php?article70 (accessed April 2010).
Badiou, A. 2009a. "Cinema as a Democratic Emblem", A. Ling & A. Mondon (trans.). *Parrhesia* 6 1–6.
Badiou, A. 2009b.
Badiou, A. 2009c. *L'hypothèse communiste (Circonstances, 5)*. Paris: Lignes.
Badiou, A. 2009d. *Logics of Worlds*, A. Toscano (trans.). London: Continuum.
Badiou, A. 2009e. *Pocket Pantheon*, D. Macey (trans.). London: Verso.
Badiou, A. 2009f. "The Scene of Two", B. P. Fulks (trans.). *Lacanian Ink* 21, www.lacan.com/frameXXI3.htm (accessed April 2010).
Badiou, A. 2009g. *Seconde Manifeste de Philosophie*. Paris: Fayard.
Badiou, A. 2009h. *Theory of the Subject*, Bruno Bosteels (trans.). London: Continuum.

Badiou, A. & F. Balmès 1976. *De l'idéologie*. Paris: Maspero.
Badiou, A. & B. Bosteels 2005. "Can Change Be Thought?: A Dialogue with Alain Badiou". In *Alain Badiou: Philosophy and its Conditions*, G. Riera (ed.), 237–61. New York: SUNY Press.
Badiou, A. & E. During 2007. "A Theatre of Operations: A Discussion between Alain Badiou and Elie During". In *A Theatre without Theatre*, B. Blistène *et al.* (eds), 22–7. Barcelona: Macba (Museu d'Art Contemporani de Barcelona).
Badiou, A. & S. Lazarus (eds) 1977. *La Situation actuelle sur le front de la philosophie*. Cahiers Yenan no. 4, 24–41. Paris: Maspero.
Badiou, A. & L. Sedofsky 1994. "Being by Numbers". *Artforum* (October 1994), www.highbeam.com/doc/1G1-16315394.html (accessed April 2010).
Badiou, A. & L. Sedofsky 2006. "Matters of Appearance: An interview with Alain Badiou". *Artforum* 45(3): 246–253/322.
Badiou, A., with N. Truong. 2009. *Éloge de l'amour*. Paris: Flammarion.
Badiou, A., T. Benatouil, E. During 2003. *Matrix: machine philosophique*. Paris: Ellipses.
Badiou, A., Z. L. Fraser & T. Tho 2007. "An Interview with Alain Badiou: The Concept of Model Forty Years Later". In *The Concept of Model*, Z. L.Fraser & T. Tho (trans.), 79–106. Melbourne: re.press.

Other works

Agamben, G. 1993. *The Coming Community*, M. Hardt (trans.). Minneapolis, MN: University of Minnesota Press.
Althusser, L. 1967. *Pour Marx*. Paris: Maspero.
Althusser, L. 1974. *Philosophie et philosophie spontanée des savants*. Paris: Maspero.
Althusser, L. 1990. *Philosophy and the Spontaneous Philosophy of the Scientists & Other Essays*, G. Elliott (ed. & intro.), B. Brewster *et al.* (trans.). London: Verso.
Althusser, L. 1996. *Lire le Capital*, rev. edn. Paris: Presses Universitaires de France.
Althusser, L. 2001. *Lenin and Philosophy and Other Essays*, B. Brewster (trans.). New York: Monthly Review Press.
Althusser, L. 2005a. *Pour Marx*. Paris: La Découverte.
Althusser, L. 2005b. *For Marx*, B. Brewster (trans.). London: Verso.
Althusser, L. 2006. *Philosophy of the Encounter: Later Writings, 1978–87*, F. Matheron & O. Corpet (eds), G. M. Goshgarian (trans.). London, Verso.
Ashton, P., A. J. Bartlett & J. Clemens (eds) 2006. *The Praxis of Alain Badiou*. Melbourne: re.press.
Balibar, E. 2002. "The History of Truth: Alain Badiou in French Philosophy". *Radical Philosophy* 115: 16–28.
Barker, J. 2002. *Alain Badiou: A Critical Introduction*. London: Pluto Press.
Barker, J. 2003. "The Topology of Revolution". *Communication and Cognition* 36(1–2): 61–72.
Barker, J. 2005. "Topography and Structure". *Polygraph* 17: 93–104.
Bartlett, A. J. 2006. "Conditional Notes on a New *Republic*". See Ashton *et al.* (2006), 210–42.
Bartlett, A. J. 2006. "The Pedagogical Theme: Alain Badiou and an Eventless Education". *anti-Thesis* 16, "The Event": 129–47.
Bartlett, A. J. 2009. "The One Drachma Course: Plato, Badiou and 'An Education by Truths'". Unpublished PhD thesis, University of Melbourne.

Baumbach, N. 2005. "Something Else Is Possible: Thinking Badiou on Philosophy and Art". *Polygraph* 17: 157–73.

Beistegui, M. de 2005. "The Ontological Dispute: Badiou, Heidegger, and Deleuze", R. Brassier (trans.). See Riera (2005), 45–58.

Bensaid, D. 2004. "Alain Badiou and the Miracle of the Event". See Hallward (2004b), 94–105.

Besana, B. 2005. "One or Several Events? The Knot Between Event and Subject in the Work of Alain Badiou and Gilles Deleuze". *Polygraph* 17: 245–66.

Bosteels, B. 2001. "Alain Badiou's Theory of the Subject: The Recommencement of Dialectical Materialism? (Part I)". *Pli: The Warwick Journal of Philosophy* 12: 200–229.

Bosteels, B. 2002. "Alain Badiou's Theory of the Subject: The Recommencement of Dialectical Materialism? (Part II)". *Pli: The Warwick Journal of Philosophy* 13: 173–208.

Bosteels, B. 2004a. "Logics of Antagonism: In the Margins of Alain Badiou's 'The Flux and the Party'". *Polygraph* 15–16: 93–107.

Bosteels, B. 2004b. "On the Subject of the Dialectic". See Hallward (2004b), 150–64.

Bosteels, B. 2005a. "Badiou without Žižek". *Polygraph* 17: 221–44.

Bosteels, B. 2005b. "Can Change Be Thought? A Dialogue with Alain Badiou". See Riera (2005), 237–61.

Bosteels, B. 2005c. "Post-Maoism: Badiou and Politics". *positions: east asia cultures critique* 13(3): 575–634.

Bosteels, B. 2005d. "The Speculative Left". *South Atlantic Quarterly* 104(4): 751–67.

Bosteels, B. 2008. "Radical Antiphilosophy". *Filosovski Vestnik* 29(2): 155–87.

Bosteels, B. 2009. "The Jargon of Finitude. Or, Materialism Today". *Radical Philosophy* 155: 41–7.

Brassier R. 2000. "Stellar Void or Cosmic Animal? Badiou and Deleuze. *Pli: The Warwick Journal of Philosophy* 10: 200–216.

Brassier R. 2004. "Nihil Unbound: Remarks on Subtractive Ontology and Thinking Capitalism". See Hallward (2004b), 50–58.

Brassier R. 2005. "Badiou's Materialist Epistemology of Mathematics". *Angelaki: Journal of Theoretical Humanities* 10(2): 135–50.

Brassier R. 2006. "Presentation as Anti-phenomenon in Alain Badiou's *Being and Event*". *Continental Philosophy Review* 39(1) (March): 59–77.

Brassier R. 2007. "Enigma of Realism". *Collapse* 2 (March): 15–24.

Brassier R. 2008. *Nihil Unbound*. London: Continuum.

Brassier R. & A. Toscano 2004. "Aleatory Rationalism, Post-Face to Alain Badiou's *Theoretical Writings*". Unpublished manuscript.

Canguilhem, G. 1970. "Dialectique et philosophie du non chez Gaston Bachelard". In *Études d'historie et de philosophie des sciences*, 196–210. Paris: Vrin.

Cassin, B. 1995. *L'effet sophistique*. Paris: Gallimard.

Cassin, B. 2000. "Who's Afraid of the Sophists? Against Ethical Correctness", C. T. Wolfe (trans.). *Hypatia* 15(4) (Fall): 102–20.

Cassin, B. 2006. "From Organism to Picnic: Which Consensus for Which City?" *Angelaki* 11(3) (December): 21–38.

Chiesa, L. 2006a. "Count-as-one, Forming-into-one, Unary Trait, S1". *Cosmos and History* 1(1–2): 68–93. Reprinted in Ashton *et al.* (2006), 147–76.

Chiesa, L. 2006b. "Le Resort de l'amour: Lacan's Theory of Love in his Reading of Plato's Symposium". *Angelaki* 2(3) (December): 61–80.

Clemens, J. 2001. "Platonic Meditations". *Pli: The Warwick Journal of Philosophy* 11: 200–229.

Clemens, J. 2003a. "Letters as the Condition of Conditions for Alain Badiou". *Communication and Cognition* 36(1–2): 73–102.

Clemens, J. 2003b. *The Romanticism of Contemporary Theory: Institution, Aesthetics, Nihilism*. Aldershot: Ashgate.

Clemens, J. 2005. "Doubles of Nothing: The Problem of Binding Truth to Being in the Work of Alain Badiou". *Filozofski Vestnik* 26(2): 21–35.

Clemens, J. 2006. "Had We But Worlds Enough, and Time, this Absolute, Philosopher …". *Cosmos and History* 1(1–2): 277–310. Reprinted in Ashton (2006), 102–43.

Clemens, J. 2007. "To Rupture the Matheme with a Poem: A Remark on Psychoanalysis as Anti-Philosophy". In *Trauma, History, Philosophy*, J. Freddi *et al.* (eds), 308–12. Newcastle: Cambridge Scholars.

Clemens, J. & J. Roffe 2008. "Philosophy as Anti-Religion in the Work of Alain Badiou". *Sophia* 47(3) (November): 345–58.

Dauben, J. W. 2004. "Georg Cantor and the Battle for Transfinite Set Theory". In *Proceedings of the 9th ACMS Conference*, 1–22. Santa Barbara, CA: Westmont College.

Deleuze, G. 2004. *Difference and Repetition*, P. Patton (trans.). London: Continuum.

Deleuze, G. 1989. *Cinema 2: The Time-Image*, H. Tomlinson & R. Galeta (trans.). London: Athlone.

Deleuze, G. 1990. *The Logic of Sense*, M. Lester & C. Stivale (trans.). New York: Columbia University Press.

Deleuze, G. 1991. *Empiricism and Subjectivity: An Essay on Hume's Theory of Nature*, C. V. Boundas (trans.). New York: Columbia University Press.

Deleuze, G. 1993. *The Fold: Leibniz and the Baroque*, T. Conley (trans. & foreword). London: Athlone.

Deleuze, G. 1995. *Negotiations, 1972–1990*, M. Joughin (trans.). New York: Columbia University Press.

Deleuze, G. & F. Guattari 1984. *The Anti-Oedipus*, R. Hurley, M. Seem & H. R. Lane (trans.). London: Athlone.

Deleuze, G. & F. Guattari 1987. *A Thousand Plateaus*, B. Massumi (trans.). London: Athlone.

Deleuze, G. & F. Guattari 1994. *What is Philosophy?*, H. Tomlinson & G. Burchill (trans.). New York: Columbia University Press.

Desanti, J. T. 2004. "Some Remarks on the Intrinsic Ontology of Alain Badiou". See Hallward (2004a), 59–66.

Dolar, M. 2006. *A Voice and Nothing More*. Cambridge, MA: MIT Press.

During, E. 2005. "How Much Truth Can Art Bear? On Badiou's 'Inaesthetics'". *Polygraph* 17: 143–55.

Feltham, O. 2000. "As Fire Burns". Uunpublished PhD thesis, Deakin University, Melbourne.

Feltham, O. 2004. "Singularity Happening in Politics: The Aboriginal Tent Embassy, Canberra 1972". *Communication and Cognition* 37(3–4): 225–45.

Feltham, O. 2005. "And Being and Event and …: Philosophy and Its Nominations". *Polygraph* 17: 27–40.

Feltham, O. 2006a. "Translator's Preface to *Being and Event*". In A. Badiou, *Being and Event*, O. Feltham (trans.), xvii–xxxiii. London: Continuum.

Feltham, O. 2006b. "On Changing Appearances in Lacan and Badiou". *UMBR(a)* 1: 115–28.

Feltham, O. 2008. *Live Theory*. London: Continuum.

Fraser, Z. 2006. "The Law of the Subject: Alain Badiou, Luitzen Brouwer and the Kripkean Analyses of Forcing and the Heyting Calculus". See Ashton *et al.* (2006), 23–70.

Fraser, Z. 2008. "This Infinite, Unanimous Dissonance: A Study in Mathematical Existentialism, through the Works of Jean-Paul Sartre and Alain Badiou". Unpublished Masters thesis, Brock University, St Catharines, Ontario.

Frege, G. 1980. *Philosophical and Mathematical Correspondence*, G. Gabriel (ed.). Chicago, IL: University of Chicago Press.

Garrett, A. 2003. *Meaning in Spinoza's Method.* Cambridge: Cambridge University Press.

Gibson, A. 2001. "Badiou, Beckett, Watt and the Event". *Journal of Beckett Studies* **12**(1–2): 40–52.

Gibson, A. 2004. "Repetition and Event: Badiou and Beckett". *Communication and Cognition* **37**(3–4): 263–78.

Gibson, A. 2005. "Badiou and Beckett: Actual Infinity, Event, Remainder". *Polygraph* **17**: 175–203.

Gibson, A. 2007. *Beckett and Badiou: The Pathos of Intermittency.* Oxford: Oxford University Press.

Gillespie, S. 1996a. "Hegel Unsutured (an Addendum to Badiou)". *UMBR(a)* **1**: 57–69.

Gillespie, S. 1996b. "Subtractive". *UMBR(a)* **1**: 7–10.

Gillespie, S. 2001a. "Neighborhood of Infinity: On Badiou's Deleuze: The Clamor of Being". *UMBR(a)* **1**: 91–106.

Gillespie, S. 2001b. "Placing the Void – Badiou on Spinoza". *Angelaki* **6**(3): 63–77.

Gillespie, S. 2003. "Beyond Being: Badiou's Doctrine of Truth". *Communication and Cognition* **36**(1–2): 5–30.

Gillespie, S. 2006. "Giving Form to Its Own Existence: Anxiety and the Subject of Truth". *Cosmos and History* **1**(1–2): 161–85.

Gillespie, S. 2008. *The Mathematics of Novelty: Badiou's Minimalist Metaphysics.* Melbourne: re.press.

Girard, J.-Y. 1987. "Linear Logic". *Theoretical Computer Science* **50**: 1–102.

Grigg, R. 2005. "Lacan and Badiou: Logic of the pas-tout". *Filozofski Vestnik* **26**(2): 53–66.

Hallward, P. 2000a. "Ethics Without Others: A Reply to Critchley on Badiou's Ethics". *Radical Philosophy* **102**: 27–30.

Hallward, P. 2000b. "The Singular and the Specific: Recent French Philosophy". *Radical Philosophy* **99**: 6–18.

Hallward, P. 2001. "Translator's Introduction". In *Ethics: An Essay on the Understanding of Evil*, P. Hallward (ed.), vii–xlvii. London: Verso.

Hallward, P. 2002. "Badiou's Politics Equality and Justice". *Culture Machine: Generating Research in Culture and Theory* **4**: http://www.culturemachine.net/index.php/cm/article/viewarticle/270/255.

Hallward, P. 2003. *Badiou: A Subject to Truth.* Minneapolis, MN: University of Minnesota Press.

Hallward, P. 2004a. "Introduction: Consequences of Abstraction". See Hallward (2004b), 1–20.

Hallward, P. (ed.) 2004b. *Think Again: Alain Badiou and the Future of Philosophy.* London: Continuum.

Hallward, P. 2005a. "Depending on Inconsistency: Badiou's Answer to the 'Guiding Question of All Contemporary Philosophy'". *Polygraph* **17**: 7–21.

Hallward, P. 2005b. "The Politics of Prescription". *South Atlantic Quarterly* **104**(4): 769–89.

Hallward, P. 2006. *Out of This World: Deleuze and the Philosophy of Creation*. London: Verso.

Hallward, P. 2008. "Order and Event: On Badiou's *Logics of Worlds*". *New Left Review* 53 (October): 97–122.

Hallward, P. forthcoming. *Concept and Form: The Cahiers pour l'analyse and Contemporary French Thought*: http://www.web.mdx.ac.uk/cahiers/.

Hausdorff, F. 1962. *Set Theory*. New York: Chelsea Publishing.

Hegel, G. W. F. 1974. *Lectures on the History of Philosophy*, vol. 3, E. S. Haldane & F. H. Simson (eds & trans.). London: Routledge & Kegan Paul.

Hegel, G. W. F. 1977. *Phenomenology of Spirit*, A. V. Miller (trans.). Oxford: Oxford University Press.

Hegel, G. W. F. 1995. *Lectures on the History of Philosophy*, vol. 2, E. S. Haldane & F. H. Simson (trans.). Lincoln, NE: University of Nebraska Press.

Heidegger, M. 1998. *Pathmarks*, W. McNeill (ed. & trans.). Cambridge: Cambridge University Press.

Heidegger, M. 1993. *The Birth to Presence*, B. Holmes *et al.* (trans.). Stanford, CA: Stanford University Press.

Heidegger, M. 2000. *Introduction to Metaphysics*. G. Fried & R. Polt (trans.). New Haven, CT: Yale University Press.

Henry, M. 2001. *La Barbarie*. Paris: Presses Universitaires de France.

Hewlett, N. 2004. "Engagement and Transcendence: The Militant Philosophy of Alain Badiou". *Modern and Contemporary France* 12(3): 335–52.

Hoens, D. 2004. "Miracles Do Happen: Essays on Alain Badiou". *Communication and Cognition* 37(3–4): 165–6.

Hoens, D. & E. Pluth 2004a. "Working Through as a Truth Procedure". *Communication and Cognition* 37(3–4): 279–92.

Hoens, D. & E. Pluth 2004b. "What if the Other is Stupid? Badiou and Lacan on 'Logical Time'". See Hallward (2004a), 182–90.

Johnston, A. 2008. "What Matters in Ontology: Alain Badiou, the Hebb-Event, and Materialism Split from Within". *Angelaki* 13(1): 27–49.

Kant, I. 1997a. *Critique of Practical Reason*, M. Gregor (trans.). Cambridge: Cambridge University Press.

Kant, I. 1997b. *Critique of Pure Reason*, P. Guyer & A. Wood (trans.). Cambridge: Cambridge University Press.

Kant, I. 1997c. *Groundwork of the Metaphysics of Morals*, M. Gregor (trans.). Cambridge: Cambridge University Press.

Lacan, J. 1965–6. "Le seminaire, Livre XIII: L'objet de la psychanalyse". Unpublished seminar.

Lacan, J. 1966–7. "Le seminaire, Livre XIV: La logique du fantasme". Unpublished seminar.

Lacan, J. 1976–7. *Seminar XXIII, 1975–6*, J.-A. Miller (ed.), L. Thurston (trans. from *texte établi*). *Ornicar?*: 6–11.

Lacan, J. 1988. *Seminar VII: The Ethics of Psychoanalysis*, D. Porter (trans.). London: Routledge.

Lacan, J. 1991. *The Seminar of Jacques Lacan, Book I: Freud's Papers on Technique 1953–1954*, J.-A. Miller (ed.), J. Forrester (trans.). New York: Norton.

Lacan, J. 1992. *The Seminar of Jacques Lacan, Book VII: The Ethics of Psychoanalysis, 1959–1960*, J.-A. Miller (ed.), D. Porter (trans.). New York: Norton.

Lacan, J. 1998. *The Seminar of Jacques Lacan, Book XX: On Feminine Sexuality, The Limits of Love and Knowledge, 1972–1973*, J.-A. Miller (ed.), B. Fink (trans.). New York: Norton.

Lacan, J. 2006. *Ecrits: The First Complete Edition in English*, B. Fink with H. Fink & R. Grigg (trans.). New York: Norton.

Lacan, J. 2007. *The Seminar of Jacques Lacan, Book XVII: The Other Side of Psychoanalysis*, J.-A. Miller (ed.), R. Grigg (trans.). New York: Norton.

Lacan, J. 2008. *My Teaching*, D. Macey (trans.). London: Verso.

Lacan, J. & E. Granzotto. 2004. "Il ne peut pas y avoir de crise de la psychoanalyse". *Magazine Littéraire* **428** (February): 26–8.

Lacoue-Labarthe, P. 2007. *Heidegger and the Politics of Poetry*, J. Fort (trans.). Champaign, IL: University of Illinois Press.

Ladyman, J. & D. Ross, with D. Spurrett & J. Collier 2008. *Every Thing Must Go*. Oxford: Oxford University Press.

Lakatos, I. 1976. *Proofs and Refutations*. Cambridge: Cambridge University Press.

Lazarus, S. (ed.) 1992. *Politique et philosophie dans l'oeuvre de Louis Althusser*. Paris: Presses Universitaires de France.

Lazarus, S. 1996. *L'Anthropologie du nom*. Paris: Seuil.

Lecercle, J.-J. 1999. "Cantor, Lacan, Mao, Beckett, *même combat*: The Philosophy of Alain Badiou". *Radical Philosophy* 93: 6–13.

Lecercle, J.-J. 2004. "An Ethics of Militant Engagement". See Hallward (2004b), 120–37.

Ling, A. 2010. *Badiou and Cinema*. Edinburgh: Edinburgh University Press.

Ling, A. 2006. "Can Cinema Be Thought?: Alain Badiou and the Artistic Condition". See Ashton *et al.* (2006), 291–305.

May, T. 1991. "The Politics of Life in the Thought of Gilles Deleuze". *SubStance* **66**: 24–35.

Meillassoux, Q. 2002. "Nouveauté et événement". In *Alain Badiou: Penser le multiple – Actes de Colloque de Bordeaux, 21–23 October 1999*, C. Ramond (ed.), 36–94. Paris: L'Harmattan.

Meillassoux, Q. 2008. *After Finitude: An Essay on the Necessity of Contingency*, R. Brassier (trans.). London: Continuum.

Mullarkey, J. 2006. *Post-Continental Philosophy: An Outline*. London: Continuum.

Nails, D. 1995. *Agora, Academy, and the Conduct of Philosophy*. Dordrecht: Kluwer.

Nails, D. 2002. *The People of Plato: A Prosopography of Plato and other Socratics*. Indianapolis, IN: Hackett.

Nancy, J.-L. 1993. *The Birth to Presence*, B. Holmes *et al.* (trans.). Stanford, CA: California University Press.

Nancy, J.-L. 2004. "Philosophy without Conditions". See Hallward (2004b), 39–49.

Nancy, J.-L. & P. Lacoue-Labarthe (eds) 1983. *Le Retrait du politique*. Paris: Galilée.

Noys, B. 2003a. "Badiou's Fidelities: Reading the Ethics". *Communication and Cognition* 36(1–2): 31–44.

Noys, B. 2003b. "The Provocations of Alain Badiou". *Theory, Culture and Society* **20**(1): 123–32.

Osborne, P. 2007. "Neo-Classic: Alain Badiou's *Being and Event*". *Radical Philosophy* **142** (March/April): 19–29.

Plato 1997. *Complete Works*, J. M. Cooper & D. S. Hutchinson (eds). Indianapolis, IN: Hackett.

Power, N. 2006. "Towards an Anthropology of Infinitude: Badiou and the Political Subject". *Cosmos and History* **1**(1–2): 186–209.

Power, N. & A. Toscano 2003. "Think Pig!' An Introduction to Badiou's Beckett". In *On Beckett*, A. Toscano & N. Power (eds & trans.), xi–xxxiv. Manchester: Clinamen.

Power, N. & A. Toscano 2009. "The Philosophy of Restoration: Alain Badiou and the Enemies of May". *boundary 2* 36(1): 27–46.

Rancière, J. 1989. *The Nights of Labour: The Workers' Dream in Nineteenth-Century France*, J. Dury (trans.). Philadelphia, PA: Temple University Press.

Rancière, J. 1991. *The Ignorant Schoolmaster: Five Lessons in Intellectual Emancipation*, K. Ross (trans.). Stanford, CA: Stanford University Press.

Rancière, J. 1999. *Disagreement: Politics and Philosophy*, J. Rose (trans.). Minneapolis, MN: University of Minnesota Press.

Rancière, J. 2004a. "Aesthetics, Inaesthetics, Anti-Aesthetics". See Hallward (2004b), 218–31.

Rancière, J. 2004b. *The Politics of Aesthetics: The Distribution of the Sensible*, G. Rockhill (trans.). London: Continuum.

Rancière, J. 2007a. "The Emancipated Spectator". *Artforum* (March): 271–80.

Rancière, J. 2007b. *On the Shores of Politics*, L. Heron (trans.). London: Verso.

Rancière, J. & P. Hallward 2003. "Politics and Aesthetics: An Interview", F. Morlock (trans.). *Angelaki* 8(2): 191–211.

Riera, G. (ed.) 2005. *Alain Badiou: Philosophy and its Conditions*. New York: SUNY Press.

Roffe, J. 2007. "The Errant Name: Badiou and Deleuze on Individuation, Limitation and Infinite Modes in Spinoza". *Continental Philosophy Review* 40(4): 389–406.

Ropars-Wuilleumier, M.-C. 1994. "The Cinema, Reader of Gilles Deleuze", D. Polan (trans.). In *Gilles Deleuze and the Theatre of Philosophy*, D. Olkowski & C. V. Boundas (eds), 255–60. London: Routledge.

Ross, K. 1988. *The Emergence of Social Space: Rimbaud and the Paris Commune*. Minneapolis, MN: University of Minnesota Press.

Ross, K. 2002. *May '68 and its Afterlives*. Chicago, IL: University of Chicago Press.

Scolnicov, S. 1988. *Plato's Metaphysics of Education*. London: Routledge.

Spinoza 1985. *The Collected Works of Spinoza*, vol. 1, E. Curley (ed. & trans.). Princeton, NJ: Princeton University Press.

Toscano, A. 2004a. "Communism as Separation". See Hallward (2004b), 138–49.

Toscano, A. 2004b. "From the State to the World? Badiou and Anti-Capitalism". *Communication and Cognition* 37(3–4): 199–223.

Toscano, A. 2006. "The Bourgeois and the Islamist, or, The Other Subjects of Politics". *Cosmos and History* 1(1-2): 15–38.

Toscano, A. 2008. "Marxism Expatriated: Alain Badiou's Turn". In *Critical Companion to Contemporary Marxism*, J. Bidet & S. Kouvelakis (eds), 529–48. Leiden: Brill.

Wahl, F. 1992. "Le Soustractif". In A. Badiou, *Conditions*, 10–54. Paris: Seuil.

Žižek, S. 1991. *Looking Awry: An Introduction to Jacques Lacan Through Popular Culture*. Cambridge, MA: MIT Press.

Žižek, S. 1997. *The Plague of Fantasies*. London: Verso.

Žižek, S. 1999. *The Ticklish Subject: The Absent Centre of Political Ontology*. Cambridge: Polity.

Žižek, S. 2001. *Enjoy Your Symptom: Jacques Lacan in Hollywood and Out*. New York: Routledge.

Žižek, S. 2002. *For They Know Not What They Do*. London: Verso.

Žižek, S. 2003. *Organs Without Bodies: On Deleuze and Consequences*. London: Routledge.

Žižek, S. 2004. "From Purification to Subtraction: Badiou and the Real". See Hallward (2004b), 165–81.

Žižek, S. (ed.) 2006a. *Lacan: The Silent Partners*. London: Verso.

Žižek, S. 2006b. *The Parallax View*. Cambridge, MA: MIT Press.
Žižek, S. 2007. "Badiou: Notes from an Ongoing Debate". *International Journal of Žižek Studies* 1(2), http://zizekstudies.org/index.php/ijzs/issue/view/4 (accessed April 2010).
Žižek, S. 2008. *In Defense of Lost Causes*. London: Verso.
Žižek, S. 1998. "Psychoanalysis and Post-Marxism: The Case of Alain Badiou". *South Atlantic Quarterly* 97(2): 235–61.
Zourabichvili, F. 1994. *Deleuze: Une philosophie de l'événement*. Paris: Presses Universitaires de France.
Zupančič, A. 2003. *The Shortest Shadow: Nietzsche's Philosophy of the Two*. Cambridge, MA: MIT Press.
Zupančič, A. 2004. "The Fifth Condition". See Hallward (2004b), 196–7.
Zupančič, A. 2005. "Enthusiasm, Anxiety and the Event". *Parallax* 11(4): 31–45.

Index